Political Thought and German Reunification

Anglo-German Foundation for the Study of Industrial Society

The Anglo-German Foundation for the Study of Industrial Society was established by an agreement between the British and German governments after a state visit to Britain by the late President Heinemann, and incorporated by Royal Charter in 1973. Funds were initially provided by the German government; since 1979 both governments have been contributing.

The Foundation aims to contribute to the knowledge and understanding of industrial society in the two countries and to promote contacts between them. It funds selected research projects and conferences in the industrial, economic and social policy areas designed to be of practical use to policymakers.

Titles include:

Bernhard Blanke and Randall Smith (*editors*)
CITIES IN TRANSITION
New Challenges, New Responsibilities

John Bynner and Rainer K. Silbereisen (*editors*)
ADVERSITY AND CHALLENGE IN LIFE IN THE NEW GERMANY AND IN ENGLAND

Maurie J. Cohen (*editor*)
RISK IN THE MODERN AGE
Social Theory, Science and Environmental Decision-Making

Stephen Frowen and Jens Hölscher (*editors*)
THE GERMAN CURRENCY UNION OF 1990
A Critical Assessment

Eva Kolinsky (*editor*)
SOCIAL TRANSFORMATION AND THE FAMILY IN POST-COMMUNIST GERMANY

Howard Williams, Colin Wight and Norbert Kapferer (*editors*)
POLITICAL THOUGHT AND GERMAN REUNIFICATION
The New German Ideology?

Anglo-German Foundation
Series Standing Order ISBN 0–333–71459–8
(*outside North America only*)

You can receive future titles in this series as they are published by placing a standing order. Please contact your bookseller or, in case of difficulty, write to us at the address below with your name and address, the title of the series and the ISBN quoted above.

Customer Services Department, Macmillan Distribution Ltd, Houndmills, Basingstoke, Hampshire RG21 6XS, England

Political Thought and German Reunification

The New German Ideology?

Edited by

Howard Williams
Professor of International Politics
University of Wales
Aberystwyth

Colin Wight
Lecturer
Department of International Politics
University of Wales
Aberystwyth

and

Norbert Kapferer
Visiting Professor
University of Wroclaw
Poland

palgrave

in association with
ANGLO-GERMAN FOUNDATION
FOR THE STUDY OF INDUSTRIAL SOCIETY

Published by PALGRAVE
Houndmills, Basingstoke, Hampshire RG21 6XS and
175 Fifth Avenue, New York, N. Y. 10010
Companies and representatives throughout the world

PALGRAVE is the new global academic imprint of
St. Martin's Press LLC Scholarly and Reference Division and
Palgrave Publishers Ltd (formerly Macmillan Press Ltd).

Outside North America
ISBN 0–333–74977–4

In North America
ISBN 0–312–22924–0

This book is printed on paper suitable for recycling and
made from fully managed and sustained forest sources.

A catalogue record for this book is available from the British Library.

Library of Congress Cataloging-in-Publication Data
Political thought and German reunification : the new German ideology?
/ edited by Howard Williams, Colin Wight, and Norbert Kapferer.
    p.   cm.
Includes bibliographical references and index.
ISBN 0–312–22924–0 (cloth)
1. Germany—Politics and government—1945–1990.   2. German
reunification question (1949–1990)   3. Ideology—Germany.
I. Williams, Howard (Howard L.)   II. Wight, Colin, 1954–
III. Kapferer, Norbert 1948–   .
JN3971.A58P59   1999
320.943'09'049—dc21   99–43352
                                                               CIP

10   9   8   7   6   5   4   3   2
08   07   06   05   04   03   02   01

Printed and bound in Great Britain by
Antony Rowe Ltd, Chippenham, Wiltshire

Contents

Notes on the Contributors

Catherine Bishop was formerly Research Assistant in the Department of International Politics, University of Wales, Aberystwyth. She is now completing a PhD at Reading University.

Georg Cavallar is the author of *Pax Kantiana* (Vienna, 1992). He is currently a visiting Research Fellow at the Department of Political Science, University of California, Riverside. He is the author of *Kant and the Critique of International Law* (Cardiff, 1999).

Tuomas Forsberg is currently Director of the Finnish Institute of International Affairs. His research has focused on German foreign policy, security in northern Europe and IR theory. He received his PhD from University of Wales, Aberystwyth in 1997. The thesis dealt with German–Soviet relations and the resolution of the German question at the end of the Cold War.

Norbert Kapferer is a former Assistant Professor at the Free University, Berlin. At present he is Visiting Professor at the University of Wroclaw, Poland. He is the author of *Das Feinbild der marxistisch-leninistischen Philosophie der DDR* 1945–89 (Darmstad 1990).

Jan Mueller is a fellow of All Souls College, Oxford. His research interests include German intellectual history, collective memory and liberal political theory.

Nicola Piper is a researcher at the Nordic Institute of Asian Studies in Copenhagen, Denmark. She has written on international labour migration and ethnic minority issues in Germany, Britain and Japan as well as on forced migration and trafficking in the Asian context. She is currently working on a new project comparing the different ways of coming to terms with the past in the context of the issue of war crimes and responsibility in postwar Japan and Germany.

Manfred Riedel is Professor of Philosophy at Halle University, Sachsen-Anhalt. He is one of Germany's most distinguished political philosophers. His publications include *Hegel und die antike Dialektik*

(1990); *Metaphysik und Metapolitik* (1975); and *Freilichtgedanken. Nietzsches dichterische Welterfahrung* (1998).

Ralf Rytlewski is Professor of Political Science at the Free University, Berlin. He is directing a project with Werner Süß on Berlin as the new capital city. They have recently co-published: *Berlin. Die Hauptstadt. Geschichte, Fakten, Reflexionen* (1999).

Werner Süß is a Privat-Dozent at the Department of Political Science at the Free University, Berlin. He has written extensively on contemporary German politics. His publications include *Die Bundesrepublik Deutschland in den achtziger Jahren* (1991) and *Hauptstadt Berlin I. Nationale Hauptstadt, Europäische Metropole* (1995).

Mark R. Thompson is professor of political science at the University of Erlangen-Nuernberg and honorary research fellow at the University of Glasgow. He has written on regime types, opposition movements and democratization in Asia and Eastern Europe. He is currently working on a project comparing 'democratic revolutions' cross-nationally, as well as writing about the current crisis of authoritarianism in the Asia-Pacific.

Colin Wight is a lecturer in the Department of International Relations at the University of Wales, Aberystwyth. His main research interests are in the philosophy of social science, social theory, international relations theory and political theory. He is currently working on the Idea of Science in International Relations Theory, and Processes of Reunification in Divided Countries.

Howard Williams is the author of *Kant's Political Philosophy* (1983) and *Concepts of Ideology* (1988). His most recent books are: *International Relations and the Limits of Political Theory* (1996) and (with D. Sullivan and G. Matthews) *Francis Fukuyama and the End of History* (1997). He is at present professor in political theory at the University of Wales, Aberystwyth.

Maria Zens is a former editor of *Blätter für deutsche und internationale Politik* in which she has published several articles. She is completing research at Bonn University on German intellectuals and the foundation of national culture in the nineteenth and twentieth centuries.

Acknowledgements

We should like to thank Ray Cunningham of the Anglo-German Foundation; Professor K.O. Morgan, former Vice-Chancellor of the University of Wales, Aberystwyth; and the present Vice-Chancellor Professor D.L1. Morgan for providing financial support to sustain the project on which this book is based. Our thanks go also to our co-editor, Norbert Kapferer, for help with the organisation of the German side of the work.

The Department of International Politics at Aberystwyth and its Head of Department, Professor Steve Smith, have provided a good working environment within which to complete the book. Maja Zefuß provided the first draft of the translation of Manfred Riedel's essay and Georg Cavallar helped with the final draft. Daniela Kroslak provided the final translation of Maria Zens's chapter. Hannah Munibari and Daniela Kroslak helped standardize the footnotes. We are grateful to them all.

Colin Wight undertook the difficult task of collating the manuscripts and generally keeping in touch with all the various authors. The two other editors are in his debt.

We would like to thank Frank Cass for permission to reprint Howard Williams, Colin Wight and Catherine Bishop's chapter 'German (Re)Unification: Habermas and his Critics', first published in *German Politics* 25:2 (1996), Telos Press for permission to reprint Jan Mueller's chapter 'Preparing for the Political: German Intellectuals Confront the Berlin Republic', first published in *New German Critique* (Fall 1997); and *Allgemeine Zeitschrift für Philosophie* for Manfred Riedel's 'Menschenrechtsuniversalismus und Patriotismus', 18/1 (1993), pp. 1–22.

Introduction

Howard Williams and Colin Wight

The unification of Germany, which took place in 1989–90, was an occurrence not only of extreme local (national) importance but also of global significance. Unification was of world-wide significance because it marked the end of a 40-year confrontation between two rival political, economic, social and – critically – military systems. Although the border between East Germany and West Germany stretched hundreds of miles, from eastern Bavaria in the south to near Hamburg in the north, the point of most startling contrast between the two systems was to be found in Berlin. Divided into four sectors by the victorious occupying powers after the Second World War – the United States, the Soviet Union, Britain and France – it remained a starkly divided city throughout the Cold War. The three western sectors occupied by the United States, Britain and France were formed into one unit very early on, but the Soviet zone in east Berlin sealed itself from the rest of Berlin to form the capital of the new East German communist state. Berlin stood not only at the crossroads between two halves of an historic natural community, but also at the crossroads between an authoritarian socialism and a liberal-democratic capitalism.

The unification of Germany provided some symbolic events of lasting impact. The images of the hated Wall finally coming down; of the East German people streaming over the checkpoints and bridges dividing east and west Berlin and, finally, of the bit-by-bit deconstruction – often with the puniest of tools – of the Berlin Wall at the Brandenburg Gate have imprinted themselves in an unforgettable way on the minds of those who witnessed the events. The ending of the division of Berlin came at the highpoint of the collapse of Soviet and Eastern European communism. This was seemingly the conclusive evidence of the complete bankruptcy of authoritarian, centralized socialism. Above all it appeared to demonstrate that the East had conceded supremacy to the West. As Fukuyama, prematurely and perhaps rashly put it, we were at 'the end of history'.

If the unification of Germany did not represent the end of history it did at least inaugurate a new historical epoch, one where no one precisely could find his or her bearings. This uncertainty and apparent confusion is reflected in the essays gathered here. Suddenly the German people, in both East and West, were faced with a further crisis of identity, and at a wider level the people of Europe and the Western world as a whole had to come to terms with a newly united Germany. Attention switched from the apparently irreconcilable difference between East and West, communism and mass capitalism, to less easily defined issues and problems of adjustment and reconstruction. But it would be wrong to see this as a complete hiatus in the postwar development of Germany. As Edinger and Nacos put it, 'if the Federal Republic has arrived at a crossroads, as conventional wisdom has it, a fundamental change of direction is just as unlikely as the notion that the Berlin Republic will simply be a carbon copy of the Bonn Republic.'[1]

Although the present unification is an intensely German experience it is at the same time part of a universal experience. The breakdown of centralized, authoritarian socialism in Eastern Europe and the Soviet Union, and the apparent outright victory of consumer capitalism, meant that political leaders and the politically conscious everywhere had to rethink some of their fundamental presuppositions.

During the Cold War, ideologies had clustered around the differentiation between communism and capitalism – the centrally planned economy and the market economy – it seemed that political commentators could discern quite easily where an individual stood on the left or the right in politics. This anchor point disappeared suddenly with the collapse of Soviet communism, not only particularly dramatically for the German people, but for everyone who was politically aware. Political movements, political activists and ideologists needed to redefine themselves throughout the world. This was so not only for socialists of the democratic variety who had always disdained the Soviet model, but also for liberals and conservatives who were critical of socialism in all its forms.

Conservatives had to rethink since in the Cold War their conservatism defined itself fundamentally by its rejection of the ideas of the radical left and the dogmas of the Communist East. Similarly, liberalism had sought to steer a course between the perceived dogmatism of socialist thought and the apparent lack of innovatory spirit in Western conservatism. After the unification of Germany liberals were to find that everyone was now a liberal. All sides claimed their traditional ground. Liberals ceased, apparently, to have a distinctive home of their own.

The German experience is, then, at the heart of a universal experience. The apparent exhaustion of one central ideology of the twentieth century has left everyone in the Western world with a problem of political reorientation. But the German experience is particularly acute. In the twentieth century Germany has sequentially moved from a monarchy to a constitutional democracy; from a constitutional democracy to a brutal, right-wing dictatorship; from this totalitarian regime to a divided nation; from division and defeat to federal democracy and unprecedented economic prosperity in the West and a further bout of totalitarian dictatorship in the East – this time with a socialist façade; to a united federal republic offering stable democracy but, thus far, a faltering economy. This is a bewildering array of political conditions. The German people have experienced without doubt the worst extremes of twentieth-century politics. How they emerge from this experience is a matter of extraordinary interest.

The new Germany will take shape in Berlin. As Edinger and Nacos note:

> In the late 1990s when an array of giant structures arose in the heart of Berlin on what was Europe's and perhaps the world's largest construction site, officials in Germany wondered if they could meet the timetable for relocating the federal government. Whether completed by the year 2002, as planned, or a later date, chances were that the physical move from Bonn to Berlin would not end the period of transition in German politics that began with the reunification of the two Germanys.[2]

Within this building site the old Reichstag is being revamped under the direction of a British architect to form the centre of the new constitutional democracy.

In the same neighbourhood former government offices (some reaching back into the Nazi period) of the German Democratic Republic are being converted for the transfer of the Bonn bureaucracy, members of the Bundestag and their office staff to Berlin. At the same time, major international concerns are capitalizing on the new development, creating new headquarters in the heart of the new capital.

On the one hand, this represents a tremendous adventure – a new frontier where a new Germany will be built – but, on the other hand, this development is fraught with difficulties. Germans want to put their past behind them, to become its master rather than its victim, but in boldly rebuilding Berlin they are confronted daily with the graveyard of many of their previous hopes and aspirations. The recolonization of Berlin by the Federal German government brings out starkly the dilemmas that have to be resolved in creating a new German identity.

For those who have visited Berlin since 1990 what is overwhelming is how much historical change is concentrated into a very small physical space. Space and time seem almost in contradiction with themselves. Although a great deal of time separates the Hohenzollern monarchy, the Weimar Republic, the Nazi period, the German Democratic Republic and the new (predominantly west German) liberal democratic state, in the centre of Berlin the symbols of these regimes and the buildings they made their own are shrunk into the smallest of spaces. In the square mile around the Brandenburg Gate the architectural remains of these five regimes jostle together for space – and no amount of favouring one set of remains (such as those of the imperial Hohenzollern era) at the expense of others – can obscure the tragic mélange which is Germany's past.

But, as we have said, we should not isolate this past as a solely German experience. The German people underwent in the twentieth century in the most dramatic and destructive form the contradictions that affected the whole of Western society. The Germans saw the end of the monarchy and its imperial pretensions, they saw the rise of a militant mass working-class movement, the powerful and equally militant right-wing reaction, the apparent collapse of capitalism with runaway inflation, two world wars, the manic and genocidal persecution of the Jews, fascism, Stalinist communism and, finally, the resurgence of capitalism in a social welfare form. Germans suffered most acutely and in an extreme manner the difficulties encountered by modern society everywhere. Some countries may have been less subject to these difficulties than others, and may only have experienced one or two indirectly, but all experienced catastrophic wars, economic depression and the rise of militant socialism and its reaction in the Cold War. As the German people come to terms with their past and seek to shape a new future for themselves, they are coming to terms with a common European heritage. How they fare cannot be treated as a matter for them alone. Their success in dealing with their inherited problems will affect us all.

To walk down Unter den Linden, the street which leads from East Berlin to the Brandenburg Gate, is to encounter directly the forces that have shaped contemporary Germany. If we begin at the river Spree by the former parliament building of the German Democratic Republic, the Palast der Republik, we can sense from the austere modernist lines of this glass-plated building the air of self-righteousness the communist functionaries attached to themselves as they rebuilt a Berlin shattered by war in the spirit of anti-fascism. The building appears to exude a small-mindedness and bureaucratic correctness which contrasts starkly with the Museum Insel of Imperial Germany, which stands on the opposite side of Unter den Linden. The imperial grandeur is perhaps less forbidding than the modernist correctness of the parliament building, but possibly only because the resurrection of the former is even less likely than the resurrection of the latter. The memory of the Palast der Republik in full swing is a good deal less distant than the memory of the last Kaiser's military parades.

The Brandenburg Gate comes into view from the Opera House and the Humboldt University, a stone's throw from the Palast. It may be that, symbolically, the Gate will always now be associated with the destruction of the Berlin Wall and the night when the people of Berlin streamed over the unguarded borders for the first time, but we need not forget that the Gate itself is a symbol of Imperial grandeur constructed by Kaiser Frederick Wilhelm II to demonstrate the strength and military prowess of Prussia.

As the visitor approaches the Brandenburg Gate, past, on the left, the former Soviet Embassy to East Germany, the Reichstag finally comes to view (on the right). There is a great boldness in retaining this as the parliament building of the new republic, even in a restructured form. For the Reichstag is still, in some respects, a symbol of the tragedy Germany suffered in the twentieth century. Set to the torch by a Nazi agent in 1933, and the conflagration duplicitously blamed on a communist, the building is set to recommence its working life in the twenty-first century as the political centre of German democracy. Will the occupation of the Reichstag by the members of parliament of the federal republic extinguish its tragic past? This scarcely seems possible for those who were born in the twentieth century. Will the tragic events that led to the emasculation of the Reichstag in the 1930s be forgotten as the successful constitutional democracy of West Germany transfers from Bonn to Berlin? Democracy flourished respectably in West Germany from 1945 to 1990 on the back of economic prosperity. The continuance of this unprecedented prosperity now seems in doubt. Here is a stark test for the will and conscience of the citizens of the new Germany. The challenge is immense. As Edinger and Nacos put it: 'three unique features ... distinguish politics in Germany from politics in America and similar democracies, namely the consequences of reunification, the geographical location in the heart of post-Cold War Europe, and the legacy of the Weimar and Nazi past.'[3] Germany seems set to continue for some time with all the complex problems of modern society pressing upon it but in a unique and occasionally oppressive way.

The outcome of the Federal elections of 27 September 1998 does not fundamentally alter this picture. New leaders and new parties will now, however, feel the pressures. For the first time the Greens will have to share the burden of federal government, and for the first time in 16 years the SPD will have to put policies into practice. It has to be said that large sections of the SPD, including its chairman, Oskar Lafontaine, did not share the enthusiasm for unification shown by Chancellor Helmut Kohl. The SPD did not oppose it, but they did, like Jürgen Habermas, question Kohl's motivation, the method of unification and the rapid timetable. Possibly this more circumspect attitude will lead to a greater sensitivity towards Eastern perspectives. The presence of the reformed Communist Party, the PDS in the Bundestag, based this time on crossing the 5 per cent hurdle, may provide an added dimension of sensitivity to the law-making of the new republic. In many dimensions the new government will be able to explore approaches that were ruled out by the ideological predispositions of the Christian Democratic parties. These contributions map out the terrain on which this debate will take place.

What should not be overlooked is the European dimension of the 1998 German general election. The outcome brought Germany into the European mainstream. Schroeder's victory confirmed the predominantly social democratic direction that European politics has taken. Within the European Union centre-left governments are now in the overwhelming majority. This promises a greater meeting of minds on pressing economic issues such as unemployment, regional regeneration and welfare programmes. Schroeder has already called for the greater co-ordination of economic programmes with greater commonality in the raising of taxes taking priority. There remains the danger that without such co-ordination a damaging spiral of competitive tax and welfare reductions might take place. All European states compete strongly with one another in seeking to attract inward flows of capital. Without some European-wide agreement on what tax-breaks it is fair to offer, this remains a potential destabilizing factor in relations within the Union.

The emphasis that the new Red-Green government has placed upon continuity in foreign policy means that Germany will retain its position as the prime mover behind European integration.[4] But this is not a mantle that the Greens and the Social Democrats will take on from without; both parties have powerful pro-European tendencies. These tendencies may, especially with the Greens, derive from security concerns and less from business concerns. But for both parties the drive towards European integration is symbolic of the effort to overcome Germany's past.

The European dimension is a unifying feature in German political culture. Aside from one or two lone voices in the Bavarian Christian Socialist Union (the former partners of the CDU in Bonn), and the occasional ambiguous comment by Schroeder himself, the only total opposition to the European Union comes from the extreme right. Although there are popular doubts about the wisdom the new European currency and fears amongst the politically aware that the former prosperity of the old West Germany might never be restored, there is almost universal agreement on the importance of European unification. As the left critic Habermas says of Kohl, 'his historical merit was to embed German unification in a wider enterprise of European unity'.[5] The constitutional left and the constitutional right agree that a post-national Germany embedded in a European political community represents the best way forward.

Perhaps the other remarkable feature of the German election of 1998 was the entry of the reformed Communist Party of the former East Germany into the Bundestag on the basis of the popular vote throughout Germany. Although still primarily a party of the East, there seems to be some general acceptance that the party has gone through a process of radical change ridding itself partly of its Stalinist past. For a large number of Germans – East and West – the PDS has attained a level of democratic acceptability. As the party of many intellectuals of the former East this is an encouraging sign, and may suggest that the PDS can contribute not only to the democratic enrichment of the former East Germany, but to the wider federal republic as a whole. There is scarcely any chance that the PDS will play any formal role in the new Red-Green government, but it is widely understood that the new government represents the PDS's preferred outcome and can count on the PDS's indirect support.

For better or worse, the German people have moved into the era of the new Berlin Republic. They enter the new capital aware of the burdens of the past and conscious of the challenges of the future. That the politically conscious in Germany see the need to take the step within the context of the Europeanization of Germany brings out the universal dimension of German unification. This is poignantly expressed by Habermas when asked about his hopes for the new republic:

> I believe we would all like to live in a civil country that is cosmopolitan in outlook and ready to play a thoughtful, co-operative role amongst other nations. We would all like to live amongst fellow citizens who are accustomed to respecting the particularity of strangers, the autonomy of individuals, and the plurality of regional, ethnic and religious identities. The new republic would do well to remember the role of Germany in the catastrophic history of the twentieth century, but equally those rare moments of emancipation and achievement of which we can be proud.[6]

Yet the spectacular rebuilding of Berlin both illuminates and obscures a multitude of dilemmas, paradoxes and antinomies that confront the new Germany. In chapter 1, Mark Thompson addresses a paradox confronting the population of the former GDR in the new Germany; communist rule in the former GDR was the least legitimate in Eastern Europe, but the regime faced only a self-limiting official opposition. Thompson argues that the oppositionists in the GDR did not want to overturn the regime, but merely wished to enter into a dialogue with it in order to convince it to live up to its own ideals. According to Thompson, the strength of anti-fascism and the weakness of a distinct East German national identity are the keys to understanding this paradox. The conflicting feelings towards unification of the former GDR population are the subject of Norbert Kapferer's chapter on 'GDR nostalgia'. Kapferer explains this 'GDR nostalgia' as a political and a cultural phenomenon, and analyses the extent to which it will have consequences for the continuing process of unification in Germany. The existence of GDR nostalgia demonstrates, of course, part of the gulf that still separates the people of the former GDR from West Germans. GDR nostalgia, argues Kapferer, constitutes a part of the transformation process itself and is a result of the unprepared and rapid reunification after a period of more than 40 years of separation.

Chapter 3, by Howard Williams, Colin Wight and Catherine Bishop, is concerned with the attitude towards unification of one Germany's greatest living philosophers, social theorist and critic – Jürgen Habermas. Habermas has been a vocal and highly critical voice in the rush towards unification which followed the fall of the Wall. In particular he objects to right-wing historians, who see unification as an opportunity to develop revisionist accounts of history, which are then utilized as devices in the 'normalization' process. Normality, for the new German state, argues Habermas, can only be based on the notion of constitutional patriotism, a commitment to liberal democracy and a confronting of the past, not a return to an older type of German consciousness.

Maria Zens's chapter links into these issues through an examination of Germany's post-unification 'historical culture'. Through an examination of the reception of Daniel Jonah Goldhagen's *Hitler's Willing Executioners*, Zens shows how the controversial reception of the book makes clear not only how closely connected aspects of morals, politics and history in Germany are, but also how deeply any discussion of the Holocaust affects today's politics; a point which substantially supports Habermas's argument. Regardless of all programmatic efforts to consider the Nazi past as a closed matter, the subject still is a minefield.

The chapter by Nicola Piper brings the issue of minorities into a contemporary setting and focuses its attention on a particular ethnic group in the new Germany – the Turkish minority. German attitudes towards the treatment of minorities and foreigners are clearly tied up with debates on the past, but also with constitutional issues of the present which surfaced in the 'asylum debate'. Piper explores the definitions of citizenship and national identity held by the majority population and the implications these have for 'foreigners', with particular reference to the period following reunification. Settled immigrants, she argues, do not enjoy full and equal status as citizens, despite their long periods of residence and the emergence of subsequent generations raised and/or born in German society. This, she argues, is due to the fact that there is a conceptual or ideological link between the processes of racialization and nationalism, concretized by the intermingling of nationality and citizenship and aggravated in times of 'crisis'.

In Chapter 6 Werner Süß considers the Berlin/Bonn controversy. Süß believes that opposition between the 'Berlin Republic' and the

'Bonn Republic' goes deeper than might first appear and argues that it marks not simply a physical change but an historical and symbolic space of capital location change. The political symbolism of the change serves an analysis of the tasks of political power and function assignment to the new German capital. This symbolism operates within the classical understanding of capital functions, in which the political structure and the nation's destiny are evident in the capital. Speaking about the 'Berlin Republic' is not possible without characterizing the capital or the future-oriented parameters of Berlin's role. The debate about the 'Berlin Republic' bears witness to how little the Germans' capital quest has been completed, despite the capital debate. In this respect, much of the most important rebuilding of Berlin is taking place far beyond the immediately visible physical construction sites of the Berlin skyline.

This importance of symbolism is carried over into Tuomas Forsberg's chapter on German foreign policy. According to Forsberg, there is no other state in which the prevailing ideas seem to have changed so profoundly during the course of history. The debate revolves around the question whether Germany will remain a state conducting a low-profile foreign policy or will become a great power with wider national interests. In the literature on foreign policy two distinct positions emerge. First there are those who incline towards liberalism, or a more Habermasian position, and argue that Germany's postwar commitment to institutionalism and multilateralism will continue. These views are opposed by those voices that expect that, as a result of unification and its regained full sovereignty, Germany will pursue a more proactive foreign policy. Again, the debate has centred on the notion of normality with the argument for a more assertive role in world politics expressed as a need to normalize Germany's foreign policy.

Chapter 8 is Manfred Riedel's important interpretation of Kantian patriotism which can be seen as an implicit criticism of Habermas's position on constitutional patriotism. The main theses of Riedel's essay are that Kantian universalism does not exclude patriotism; Kantian patriotism goes beyond mere allegiance to the constitution; Kant is critical of cosmopolitan dreamings of a universal republic. Riedel wants to convince us that Kantian cosmopolitanism is more down-to-earth than that of the 'vulgar' Enlightenment. The Enlightenment idea of the world as a fatherland is, according to Riedel's Kant, uncritical ideology. Riedel advocates a new Germany that straddles the two extremes of a utopian cosmopolitanism and an exclusive nationalism.

In Chapter 9 Georg Cavallar takes issue with Reidel's attempt to relocate Kant. Against the relativist tide that is sweeping through the academy Cavaller bravely advocates a cosmopolitan world outlook. Cavallar's point of entry here is the implicit debate between Habermas's and Riedel's version of Kant. He concludes that Riedel has got both Kant and Habermas wrong. Cavallar begins with an analysis and evaluation of Habermas's theory, follows this with an engagement with Riedel's understanding of Kant, and concludes by arguing that Habermas's constitutional patriotism is, in fact, a form of procedural patriotism and that Riedel has simply got Kant wrong. Whatever the problems with Habermas's position it is clearly Habermas rather than Riedel who builds on the Kantian tradition. Cavallar vigorously defends the idea of cosmopolitanism over what he sees as the more dangerous particularlism and relativism of nationalism.

The issue of the peaceful revolution in Germany in 1989 forms the basis for the chapter by Ralf Rytlewski. Through an analysis of the peaceful revolution of 1989 Rytlewski reaches three main conclusions. First, the Germans in East and West were both, and still are, committed to the socio-political conviction that equality shall be considered an indispensable prerequisite of peace. As such, both are committed to a belief that the prosperity and well-being of the population shall be managed through the instruments of the state. Second, the unification and integration of Germany was principally stimulated and managed by the political strategy of Bonn, not to put national interest and everyday 'political realism' in the political centre of attention. Third, favourable personal, normative and institutional conditions were to be created which would permit the successful management of the peaceful change of system. Only the existence of these normative commitments could account for the fact of peaceful change.

The final chapter is Jan Mueller's perceptive look at public interventions of German intellectuals who have attempted to give a grounding or rationale for the Berlin Republic in the sense of laying down normative foundations for the future polity. Intellectuals have had ample opportunity to formulate normative frameworks for the new republic and to provide what German political scientists like to call a legitimation narrative. Since unification German intellectuals have been afforded the opportunity to draw lessons from 1989 and its aftermath and project them onto 1999 and beyond. Of central concern for Mueller is the attempt to reconsider what it means to talk of the 'political'. And of course, in any such discussion in Germany the figure of Carl Schmitt plays a fundamental role. According to a

Schmittian view of politics, the German future is one in which the regaining of sovereignty in 1990 constitutes the possibility of a more active Berlin Republic in the sense of a sovereign pursuit of national interests outside of the state and a state confronting a more active civil society within. The alternative vision is a republican one, in which the memories of 1989 are kept alive, civil society valorized and foreign policy is increasingly dealt with through European federal structures, such as those favoured by Hannah Arendt. Rejecting these two polar opposites Mueller argues for a third possibility, one which continues to be as generally stable, consensus-oriented and, plainly speaking, boring, as it has in fact been since 1989. According to Mueller, unexciting as it may be, politics can and should do without the political.

Notes

1 Edinger, Lewis J., and Nacos, Brigitte L., *From Bonn to Berlin: German Politics in Transition* (New York: Columbia University Press, 1998), p. 252.
2 *Ibid.*
3 *Ibid.*, p. 253.
4 See Michelmann, H. J., 'Germany and European Integration', in *Germany – Phoeniz in Trouble*, ed. Zimmer, M. (Edmonton: University of Alberta Press, 1997).
5 Habermas, J., 'There are Alternatives', *New Left Review* No. 231 (1998), p. 4.
6 *Ibid.*, p. 12.

1
A Hostile People but a Loyal Opposition: National Identity and anti-Fascism in the GDR

Mark R. Thompson

Understanding the East German revolution has been hampered by an apparent paradox: communist rule there was the least legitimate in Eastern Europe, but the regime faced only a self-limiting opposition. Surveys show that the East Germans were much more critical of their country's economic performance and politics than were citizens of other Eastern European socialist states.[1] Yet 'oppositionists' in the German Democratic Republic (GDR) saw themselves as part of a citizens' movement which merely wished to enter into a dialogue with the regime in order to persuade it to live up to its own ideals. How can this paradox of a hostile people but a loyal opposition be explained?

Despite socialist ideology, Soviet economies were always seen as competing with the capitalist West. Ironically, the wealthiest communist countries suffered most from such comparisons because their populations were well aware of the gap between their living standards and those of their immediate capitalist neighbours. For example, the Balts compared themselves unfavourably with the Scandinavians as the Hungarians did with the Austrians. But the problem confronting the East German Sozialistische Einheitspartei Deutschlands (SED) was particularly taxing, despite their country enjoying the 'highest' living standard in Eastern Europe. The GDR not only shared a border, but also a common language, history and national identity with the most economically robust major West European country, the Federal Republic of Germany (FRG). Jeffrey Kopstein argues that 'no country in the communist world faced this dilemma more squarely than the GDR ... [P]opular perceptions of the SED's inability to raise living standards' contributed greatly to 'the fragility of the regime'.[2] The SED had been terrified of its own people ever since the uprising of 17 June 1953.[3] The regime only survived by 'walling in' its population to

1

prevent their flight to West Germany. With the rejection of Gorbachev's *glasnost* and the continuance of hard-line rule despite reforms in other Eastern European countries, the East German regime found its popularity plummeting even in its own closely controlled polls.[4] Thus, despite being relatively wealthy and stable compared to its Eastern Europe neighbours, the GDR faced an invidious comparison with the richer and freer Federal Republic. The vast majority of the people not not only disliked the regime, but also disapproved of East Germany as a *state*.

Yet East German dissidents remained loyal to the idea of socialism as a form of rule and to the continued existence of the GDR. They never became openly anti-communist – as did their counterparts in Poland, Hungary and Czechoslovakia in the 1970s – and resisted German unification in 1989–90. Despite their criticism of the repressive policies of the SED, East German dissidents remained committed to reforming what they considered 'the better German state'. In the GDR, the idea of 'socialism with a human face' survived the brutal suppression of the Prague Spring and the persistence of anti-reformist communist leadership in East Germany. An opposition favouring socialism and the continued existence of East Germany faced a general population wanting to get rid of the GDR itself through unification.

In this chapter I shall argue that the strength of anti-fascism and the weakness of a distinct East German national identity are the keys to understanding these seemingly contradictory phenomena. Anti-fascism was particularly appealing to many East German intellectuals after the horrors of Nazism had made all forms of German nationalism taboo. It also provided a justification for a socialist alternative to the capitalist Federal Republic. Most cultural elites never opposed the regime. Even the citizens' movement only criticized it within the constraints of anti-fascist discourse. Yet most East Germans continued to compare the GDR with the Federal Republic and to identify themselves more with the latter than with the former. In the 1950s, this strong identification with West Germany weakened the SED's economic policies (not least through massive emigration) and made political consolidation difficult to achieve. Only by building the Berlin Wall could the SED achieve political stability and modest economic prosperity. Yet subsequent efforts by the ruling party to introduce economic reforms or political liberalization literally ran into the Wall. Such changes risked raising the issue of the population's containment. But further economic decline and political illiberality increased the regime's unpopularity. In Poland and Hungary, by contrast, reform efforts could be legitimated by means of national appeals. These nationally legitimated communist regimes claimed to be doing the most they could for their populations given their countries' forcible integration in the Soviet bloc. By contrast, the East German regime lost its last residue of credibility when it resisted Gorbachev's reforms.

Strong anti-fascism and a weak East German identity also enable us to understand the distinctive character of the GDR revolution. It explains why a revolution was necessary, why it was sparked off by mass *emigration* and why the citizen movement leaders *refused to seize power* as the regime began to collapse. While Polish and Hungarian communists negotiated a democratic transition with the opposition, the East German regime refused to budge from its anti-reformist stance, even in the face of Gorbachev's reforms. Thus, hard-line SED rule had to be brought down because it refused to step down. 'Public' demonstrations only became important after emigration had weakened the regime. Instead of demanding that the SED cede office to the opposition, dissidents co-operated with the newly installed communist reformers in a combined effort to save the GDR.

The SED's legitimacy crisis

East Germany was long considered Eastern Europe's best economic performer. In 1980 the World Bank reported that it had the world's tenth highest per capita income; greater than Britain's.[5] In the GDR itself, popular prejudices about the 'Polish [economic] mess' and, to a lesser extent, about lower living standards in Czechoslovakia and Hungary, tended to put the more 'orderly' GDR in a favourable light.[6] But material comparisons with the Federal Republic of Germany were, beginning in the 1950s, extremely unfavourable to the GDR. Even more important than West Germany's financial strength was its political freedom. The lack of freedom of speech and other political liberties were the chief reasons East German refugees gave for leaving the GDR for the Federal Republic.[7] In what has been called a 'nightly emigration' almost all East Germans could watch West German television, which was much more popular than local programmes.

In the best study of popular discontent in the GDR, Karl-Dieter Opp, Peter Voss and Christiane Gern went to great lengths to measure regime legitimacy.[8] They conducted the first representative survey in the former GDR. Although done retrospectively (in 1990), data checks show a high degree of reliability.[9] They also correspond roughly to the non-representative surveys conducted by East German social scientists among young people in the GDR before the revolution, which had revealed the regime's growing unpopularity.[10] A serious problem with the Opp *et al.* survey, however, is that it was confined to the city of Leipzig. But the authors reasonably hypothesized that while levels of discontent may have been higher in Leipzig than elsewhere because of the city's neglect by the Berlin-dominated GDR leadership, the nature of this dissatisfaction was similar to that in other parts of the country. At a minimum, their poll provides important information about what they claim was the birthplace of the uprising.

Opp and his co-authors distinguish between social, economic and political dissatisfaction.[11] Social dissatisfaction – about inequality, pre-school nurseries and educational opportunities – was relatively low. (This suggests that German unity and its discontents had much to do with the abrupt transformation of the social system of the former GDR.) Economic dissatisfaction, by contrast, was widespread and increased throughout 1989. Measured in terms of goods available in the shops, dissatisfaction stood at 4.3 on a scale of 1 (very satisfied) to 5 (very dissatisfied). The key to understanding this high level of dissatisfaction was that while Opp and his co-authors found that most GDR citizens felt their economic situation to be better than elsewhere in Eastern Europe, their survey showed that two-thirds of East Germans actually compared their economic situation with that of the FRG.[12] Political dissatisfaction reached the same high levels as economic dissatisfaction. This was measured in terms of the quality of the environment (where dissatisfaction was highest), the relationship to the SED, the opportunities for free speech, surveillance by the secret police ('popularly' known as the *Stasi*) and the fairness of the legal system. Less than half of those surveyed claimed that they had ever identified themselves strongly with the political system of the GDR; the majority said they felt a stronger identification with the Federal Republic of Germany.[13]

Opp *et al.* are careful to point out that discontent cannot in itself explain the East Germans' revolt against their regime. This requires a belief that protest will be effective; in other words, that it has a good chance of success. In the East German case, reforms in the Soviet Union and other Eastern European countries as well as the exodus of hundreds of thousands of East Germans through suddenly porous socialist borders (discussed below) were the key reasons for a sudden – and widespread – sense of revolutionary efficacy. Also, problems of revolutionary 'free-riding' had to be overcome by what Opp and his co-authors call the 'communitarian principle' and which I have argued elsewhere can best be understood as moral 'value rational' appeals which override individual instrumental rationality.[14] But the point to be made here is that the SED regime experienced a severe crisis of legitimation, and that this was a necessary, though not a sufficient, cause for the protests of 1989.

But how did the legitimacy crisis that the SED faced compare with the situation in other Eastern European regimes? Survey data suggest that East Germans were more dissatisfied than their socialist neighbours were. In a poll conducted by Richard Rose, Wolfgang Zapf, Wolfgand Seifert and Edward Page, only 32 per cent of East Germans approved of the SED's economic performance and only 36 per cent approved of its politics. By contrast, the mean of answers taken in representative polls at the same time (1993) of Bulgarians, Czechs, Slovaks, Hungarians, Poles, Romanians and Slovenians showed satisfaction with their respective communist regimes was much higher: 44 per cent for economic performance and 57 per cent for political performance.[15] Identifying more strongly with the Federal Republic than their own country, East Germans were more dissatisfied than East Europeans, despite enjoying higher living standards.

Division over the 'national question'

Claus Offe has put this point about the identification of East Germans with the Federal Republic and their sense of the economic and political inferiority of the GDR well:

> Despite all political-pedagogical attempts of the regime to extinguish the orientation towards a single German history, polls after the Wende [turnaround, change: a word commonly used to describe the East German revolution] allow the conclusion that GDR citizens more closely identified with the German nation than did West Germans. Even the sovereignty of the GDR was precarious and its integration into the international community came late. The Federal Republic's commitment to unity put the existence of a separate GDR state in question from the very beginning. The special role the Federal Republic gave to every GDR citizen as a virtual citizen of the Federal Republic and the identification over the borders of the GDR with a common history, culture, and language doomed every attempt by East German society to consti-

tute a repressively-backed, economically legitimated order to failure.[16]

He suggests that while the 'common' people in the GDR had an instinctive understanding of the national character of their revolt against the SED leadership, East German dissidents refused to think in national terms.[17] As in the rest of Eastern Europe, most people in the GDR longed for the freedoms of the West. As Jeffrey Kopstein suggests, this was conceived in terms of a 'lifestyle' which included consumer choice, foreign travel and political rights.[18] But elsewhere in the Soviet bloc, dissidents used a national discourse against Soviet domination while affirming capitalism and democracy as practised in the West. But as one of the most thoughtful dissidents of the GDR period has observed, the 'national question' was 'taboo' for the citizens' movement in East Germany because of the Nazi past.[19]

How do we explain this gap between the average East German and the dissidents? Why did the critical attitude of most East Germans towards the economic policy and politics of the SED leadership not rub off on the most outspoken opponents of the regime? My argument is that despite its courageous criticisms of an unbending dictatorship, the East German opposition shared the SED regime's commitment to anti-fascism. In the end, anti-fascism tied the SED and its opponents closer together in their defence of the continued existence of East Germany than it did the opposition to the angry population they claimed to represent during the 1989 revolution. To understand the opposition's political views, we must briefly explore the character of official anti-fascism in the GDR.

The character of official anti-fascism in the GDR

In no other Eastern bloc country did anti-fascism play such an important role in legitimating communist rule than in East Germany. Of course, anti-fascism had been a key *Kampfbegriff* of communism since the 1920s. After the Second World War, anti-fascism recalled the enormously costly but successful struggle against Nazi Germany. Across Europe, but in Eastern Europe in particular, communist parties found an 'anti-fascist' platform the best way to win support in non-communist and even non-socialist circles. The communists' fascism theory placed the ultimate blame for the horrors of the Second World War on capitalism in general, rather than on particular conditions in Italy or Germany. Viewing fascism as the most reactionary, chauvinistic and imperialistic form of finance capitalism – as the Bulgarian communist Gyorgi Dimitrov defined it in 1935 – reinforced widespread scepticism about capitalism in Eastern (and parts of Western) Europe after the Second World War. For Eastern European communist leaders, anti-fascism also helped them to identify Western Europe and North America – capitalist and integrated into an anti-communist military alliance – as the enemy of the Soviet bloc in the emerging Cold War.

But nowhere was the polarization between communism and capitalism more evident than in the divided Germany. While the American, British and French Zones were gradually merged into a capitalist, democratic and pro-Western Federal Republic, the Soviet Occupation Zone (Sowjetische Besatzungszone, SBZ) and, as of 1949, the GDR, became its socialist, anti-fascist and anti-Western counterpart. Anti-fascism allowed a rump state that was smaller, less free and soon to be poorer than West Germany none the less to present itself in a heroic light. It justified the GDR's existence despite the lack of a distinct national identity, a claim canonized in the 1974 amendments to the GDR's Constitution, which dropped all references to German unification.[20] After all, East Germany claimed to have solved the problem of Germany's fascist past through the adoption of state socialism. The Federal Republic, on the other hand, could be portrayed as an unredeemed German capitalist state in which many Nazis had found refuge and which was vulnerable to a resurgence of full-fledged fascism.

Whereas elsewhere in Eastern Europe it was, at most, the spectre of collaboration with fascists that haunted those liberated from Nazism by the Soviets (although in puppet states such as Croatia and Slovakia collaboration with the Nazis had been very 'enthusiastic'), Germany was the 'land of the perpetrators' ('Das Land der Täter'). The thesis that fascism was the inevitable result of the capitalist economic system was thus of crucial importance to the Germans because it generalized the blame for the Nazi past and helped lift the burden of guilt. This claim allowed the GDR to provide a legal basis for the reintegration of the 'little Nazis' (local and mid-level functionaries during the Nazi period) as well as the millions of *Mitläufer* (fellow travellers) into East German society while still highlighting the involvement of ex-Nazis in the Federal Republic for propaganda purposes. While the Federal Republic was portrayed as a proto-fascist, capitalist state, which felt no compunction about sheltering ex-Nazis, the GDR leadership felt it could safely enlist all who were loyal to the state in the anti-fascist project of socialism. Jürgen Danyel has described this 'symbiosis of anti-fascist legitimation and integrative policy' as a *'Schlußstrich-Mentalität'* in which a line is drawn at the end of the Nazi period allowing all those willing to follow the 'guidance' of the Communist Party the opportunity to participate in a socialist future.[21] Theories that blamed German history generally for the rise of Nazism were rejected as a 'bourgeois' myth. Instead, the SED advocated a two-track view of Germany's past in which 'progressives' continually fought reactionaries, until the former finally triumphed with the creation of the German Democratic Republic.[22] This policy of absolution was taken so far as to make those East Germans who had demonstrated loyalty to the new socialist state – good anti-fascists they – into *victims* not perpetrators of the Nazi period. This view was codified by Stalin in October 1949 when he congratulated East Germans on the founding of their new state with a reminder that it was the German and Soviet peoples who had 'suffered the most' in the Second World War.[23]

Official anti-fascism justified extreme 'vigilance' against the threat supposedly posed by the proto-fascist Federal Republic. The 1953 uprising was portrayed by the SED as a 'fascist provocation against the GDR'. The SED reinterpreted the massive, and largely peaceful, rebellion led by workers against a repressive state as 'Day X': the supposedly long-planned attempt by the Federal Republic and the US to incite the few remaining fascists in East Germany to rebel in order to roll back the gains of communism in Eastern Europe. In reaction to the 1953 revolt, as well as the 1956 uprising in Hungary, the SED leadership built an extraordinary housing project in Wandlitz, a wooded area near Berlin, designed to isolate and protect Politburo members. Shortly before his death, Horst Sindermann told an interviewer that the Politburo practised the *Verteidigungsfall* (military defence in the event of attack) at least once a year in order to be prepared for a fascist invasion.[24] Claiming that the emigration of millions of East Germans to the Federal Republic had been a deliberate strategy to 'bleed' the GDR to death and that another 'Day X' (supposedly led by then West German Defence Minister, Franz Josef Strauß) was imminent, the SED ordered a cement-block wall topped with barbed wire to be built around West Berlin on 13 August 1961. The Wall, built to close the chief escape route of East Germans, was called the *anti-faschistischer Schutzwall* (the anti-fascist protective wall). The 1968 invasion of Czechoslovakia by Warsaw Pact forces – in which the SED took an active part, despite the parallel with the German invasion of the country in 1939 – was also justified in the name of anti-fascism, as were loud calls by the SED for the crushing of the Solidarity Movement in Poland in 1981. The grotesque grip of the East German Stasi (twice the size of the Gestapo, though controlling a population less than one fifth that of Nazi Germany) and the military which – in per capita terms – was probably the largest in the world, showed that Big Brother was both well armed and watchful in the face of a continual fascist threat.[25] As late as March 1990 former Politburo member Horst Sindermann continued to justify the construction of the Wall by claiming: 'We did not want to bleed to death, we wanted to maintain the anti-fascist-democratic system that existed in the GDR. This, it seems to me, is still the right position today.'[26]

The limits of opposition in the GDR

East German oppositionists have rightly insisted on a distinction between the prescribed (*verordneter*) anti-fascism of the SED to justify its hold on power and an anti-fascism which is 'not manipulated and instrumentalized'.[27] In their *samizdat* publications, for example, leading dissidents criticized the theory and practice of official anti-fascism.[28] But their critique had less to do with the substance of anti-fascism – particularly the belief that fascism and capitalism are closely connected – than with the arbitrary and Machiavellian manner with which the SED deployed it. My argument is *not* that this criticism of the regime was insincere – it took considerable courage to confront the regime on such a sensitive issue – rather, I wish to suggest that however heretical the opposition's anti-fascism, *it still placed certain limits on dissent*. Anti-fascism included a belief in the GDR's 'good beginning'. Commitment to anti-fascism tied the cultural elite of the GDR so closely to the regime that even major literary figures banned from publishing in the GDR exercised no more than 'semi-opposition' to the regime. This meant that major artists were 'absent' from the opposition, making dissident circles more a counter-cultural movement than a counter-elite. Not only were the personnel of the opposition distinctive in comparative Eastern European perspective, but also in their ideological orientation. I will argue that anti-fascism underpinned the opposition's continued commitment to 'revisionism' (calling for a more humane socialism) and its unwillingness to turn to Eastern European-style 'dissent' (anti-communism and the advocacy of Western-style capitalist democracy). Finally, anti-fascism led oppositionists to remain loyal to the GDR as the 'better German state', no matter how critical they were of the SED regime. The opposition distanced itself from would-be emigrés and the human rights issues associated with their cause.

Christian Joppke argues that the GDR's 'myth of the good beginning ... proved indestructible'. He suggests that the opposition's commitment to the 'Utopia' of anti-fascism was due to the fact that they considered it 'the more adequate response to the German catastrophe'.[29] This can be illustrated through the views of Robert Havemann, the GDR's leading oppositionist in the 1960s and 1970s. Until his death in 1982, Havemann claimed that the GDR was the 'better German state' because of its anti-fascist origins. Although GDR leader Erich Honecker placed him under house arrest and maltreated him in covert ways that have recently been revealed in a public trial, Havemann continued to consider him a 'comrade of the anti-fascist resistance movement' as he and Honecker had sat together in a Nazi prison.[30]

Because of their commitment to anti-fascism, few members of the GDR's cultural elite ever joined the opposition. While they criticized the regime occasionally on matters relating particularly to artistic freedom, they never made a complete break with the opposition. They offered a largely 'in-house' criticism which is typical of what Juan J. Linz has termed 'semi-opposition'.[31] The cultural elite would abstain from undertaking active opposition throughout the Soviet occupation and the GDR's 40-year lifespan. An impressive number of exiled German intellectuals and artists had chosen to return to East Germany, rather than remain in the West.[32] But although increasingly disillusioned by the events of 1953 and subsequently, they never completely severed their ties to the state founded on the myth of East Germany's anti-fascism.

The case of Stefan Heym is one of the most interesting, as he went further than most other major figures in criticizing the regime in the 1970s and 1980s, yet never denounced it openly, nor did he leave the country. His novel *Schwarzenberg*, published in West Germany in 1984, is an anti-fascist fantasy about a village in Germany close to the Czechoslovak border which was, inadvertently, left briefly unoccupied by the Soviets and the Americans.[33] During this short respite, a 'genuine' anti-fascist government takes power there. As one of Heym's characters says at the end of the novel, the dream of anti-fascism remains, no matter how unpleasant reality becomes.

Why was there no Václav Havel in the GDR?

Heym, along with Christa Wolf, Heiner Müller, Volker Braun, Jurek Becker, Stefan Hermlin and other leading literary and intellectual figures sharply criticized the expulsion of Wolf Biermann the critical singer and close friend of Havemann from the GDR in 1976. Yet none of them followed this initiative with bolder opposition measures. No East German Václav Havel came forward.

Lacking major figures from the intelligentsia in its ranks, the GDR opposition of the 1970s and 1980s was more a counter-cultural movement than a counter-elite. The small size of the opposition distinguished the GDR from Poland and to a lesser extent Hungary, but not from Czechoslovakia. In Czechoslovakia, hard-line rule after the crushing of the Prague Spring in 1968 had reduced the opposition to a size comparable to East Germany's. The Ministry of State Security (*Stasi*) estimated that 2,500 people in the GDR were involved in opposition activities as of June 1989, with 60 belonging to the 'hard core' (*'harter Kern'*). The Czechoslovak secret service put the number of active oppositionists in Czechoslovakia as late as 1989 at only 500, with a leadership of about 60 individuals. (The figure is somewhat higher if we include the 1,883 people who had signed 'Charter 77', the opposition human rights appeal.[34]) But the Czechoslovak opposition enjoyed the support of some of the best known figures in society – both former reform communists and intellectuals/artists. The East German opposition, by contrast, consisted of little known artists (such as Bärbel Bohley), pastors and church-goers (hardly representative in a largely atheistic society) and other outsiders.[35]

The answer to the question 'Why no Havel in the GDR?' is a complicated counterfactual. One answer, as we have seen, is that leading cultural figures in East Germany distanced themselves from the opposition, in large part because of their continued loyalty to the GDR as an anti-fascist state. Another is that the *Stasi* had penetrated and destabilized (*zersetzt*) most of the small opposition groups, setting them against each other and undermining their cause.[36] But ultimately, the *Stasi* was powerless against the spontaneous popular revolt in autumn 1989. This suggests that, as in Czechoslovakia, an opposition leader or leaders could have emerged from relative isolation to lead the revolution once repression had eased. A third answer is that Havemann – who came closest to assuming a commanding moral authority over the opposition – died before the revolution occurred. But would Havemann have been willing to lead a revolution that began to move towards unification and thus against his anti-fascist principles?[37] This raises the issue of the GDR opposition's ideological orientation.

The crushing of the Prague Spring by Soviet tanks in 1968 convinced many leading East European oppositionists – including Adam Michnik, Václav Havel and Gyorgi Konrad – that they had to move from revisionism to dissidence. Instead of striving for a better socialism, they came to the conclusion that communism could not be reformed. This view contrasts with Havemann's after the failure of the Prague Spring in 1968 that the experiment of reform communism should be tried again and again until it finally succeeded.[38] In fact, far from discrediting revisionism, the Prague Spring became the model for further opposition activity in the GDR.[39] Turning away from the socialism/capitalism dichotomy thesis, Havel and other East European dissidents saw the battle as that between totalitarianism and democracy. With their commitment to anti-fascism, by contrast, East German oppositionists called for socialism with a human face but remained sceptical about capitalism and representative democracy. While their criticisms of the regime were harsher and their actions bolder than the 'semi-opposition' of key members of the cultural elite, the East German opposition still clung to socialism largely thanks to their anti-fascist ideals.

Why did anti-fascism prove so powerful among the intellegentsia but so powerless among the 'ordinary' East Germans? To answer this one must look first at the relativization of the dichotomy. As Antonia Grunenberg and others have shown, anti-fascism had great appeal to most East Germans, in part because of their genuine revulsion at Nazism, but also because it provided a kind of absolution for those who had lived through the Nazi period.[40] This leads to the modified question: 'Why were opposition intellectuals *more* committed to the doctrine of anti-fascism than the average East German?' Cultural elites and citizen movement activists believed the SED's anti-fascist credentials had earned them respect and precluded a strong sense of German national identity, which encompassed capitalist West Germany. As Christa Wolf has written:

> Because we, as young people, who grew up under fascism were filled with guilt, [we were] thankful to those who had saved us from it. It was the anti-fascists and communists who emerged from the concentration camps and the prisons, or returned from emigration to direct the political life of the GDR more than was the case in the

Federal Republic. We felt strongly inhibited in opposing people who had sat in concentration camps during the Nazi period.[41]

The average East German, on the other hand, continued to identify with West Germany, ignoring, or at least untroubled by, the way in which this contradicted the anti-fascist creed. They may also have been less willing to forgive the blantant instrumentalization of official anti-fascism by the GDR leadership than were intellectuals, who continued to cling to the pure idea despite the messy reality.[42] For most East Germans, then, it seems that in the end national identity trumped official anti-fascism. For citizen movement oppositionists, the reverse was true.

The East German peace movement and human rights issues

The East German peace movement, the major motor for opposition in the early 1980s, retained an implicit loyalty to the GDR despite its activities critical of the regime. The movement aimed to force the regime to live up to its self-description as a 'peace state' by protesting against military training in schools and a government campaign of 'vigilance' against its Western enemies. Although outspoken, the anti-regime activists maintained what the oppositionist Wolfgang Rüddenklau has called a 'misplaced [*verfehlte*] loyalty' to the East German state about which 'at best a few Stasi officers may have giggled'.[43] This was demonstrated when the Initiative for Freedom and Human Rights (IFM) – the most important opposition group emerging from the peace movement and the source of much of the leadership of the largest organization during the 1989 revolution, the Neues Forum – rejected West German criticism of the GDR's human rights policies. One IFM spokesman, Gerd Poppe, suggested that the West German critics instead 'concentrate on improving the human rights situation in the Federal Republic'.[44]

The opposition's ambivalence concerning human rights was most apparent when it came to contact with would-be emigrants. Because they were commited to reforming East German communism, most oppositionists rejected co-operation with 'exit' groups who wanted to abandon it. The anti-regime but pro-GDR groups went so far as to cancel demonstrations when the 'wrong' kind of activists (i.e. would-be emigrants) attended. This conflict reached its peak when the IFM refused to co-operate with 'exiters' in a January 1988 protest.[45] By opposing emigration, the opposition was siding, however unwillingly, with a regime whose authority was based in large part on the 'imprisonment' of an entire country.

Why the SED regime failed to reform

Dissidents in the GDR had long hoped for a dialogue with the regime that would lead to political reforms whilst preserving the socialist economy and East Germany as a separate state. But this goal was only realized through round-table talks *after* the regime was in an advanced state of collapse. In Poland and Hungary, by contrast, negotiations began *before* the major protests. Polish and Hungarian communists initated democratization through talks with opposition leaders and these led to a successful political transition. In the GDR, the regime long resisted liberalization even of the kind Gorbachev practised in the Soviet Union. Of course, opposition pressure and the latent strength of *Solidarnosc* helped bring the Polish regime to the negotiating table. But in Hungary, where the opposition was much smaller, the regime nevertheless initiated negotiations with the dissidents. Why did the SED leadership in East Germany so adamantly resist political change? A brief survey of GDR history shows that the weakness of the country's national identity was the major reason.

The GDR failed in what theorists of Third World politics have called 'nation-building'. The SED began (and ended) as an organization traumatized both by Soviet attempts to 'trade off' the GDR for concessions from the Federal Republic (the so-called Stalin Note of 1952) and then popular calls for unification in the course of the 1953 revolt. Along with demands for lowering worker productivity, demonstrators in the nationwide June 1953 protests also called for democratization and national unification.[46] The East German regime's greatest successes – political consolidation, economic growth and diplomatic recognition – came after the 'national question' appeared to have been closed off by the Wall. However, the large crowds and spontaneous ovations West German Chancellor Willy Brandt received when he visited East Germany in 1970, despite efforts by the SED regime to keep him away from the general population, showed the persistence of such identification even after the building of the Wall. West Germany's *Ostpolitik* – which raised the danger of increased contacts and identification with West Germany – led to a full-blown attempt to create a separate GDR identity. (One of the most absurd aspects of this policy was a ban on singing the GDR national anthem – it was to be listened to wordlessly because the text made mention of German unification.) A policy of *Abgrenzung* (delimitation) from the Federal Republic was practised, which included a massive expansion of the Stasi.

The failure of economic reform (the 'New Economic System') in the 1960s was due to many factors, including fear of raising productivity after the 1953 uprising, resistance by SED bureaucrats to new, unfamiliar procedures, and Walter Ulbricht's impatience to catch up economically with the West Germany as soon as possible.[47] The attempt to introduce an unsubsidized pricing system and give enterprises more autonomy, begun in the early 1960s, had been abandoned by the middle of that decade. The chief economic reformer committed suicide in 1965. One of Ulbricht's most important allies, Anton Ackermann, wrote to the SED leader in 1968 arguing against the assumptions of the (failed) reforms. His argument is worth quoting:

> In the present situation, where the class enemy concentrates from the outside on discrediting the socialist planned economy, on stimulating 'convergence theory' and the change from a socialist economy to a so-called 'socialist market economy', must we not wage a struggle, not only against the open but also against the hidden forms of this ideological diversion?[48]

Ulbricht had tried – and failed – to make the GDR economically competitive with the FRG through reforms. Ackermann was suggesting that such efforts were not only fruitless, but even dangerous, because they underlined the comparisons with West Germany and East Germany could only come second. In this light, it is interesting to see that the lesson drawn by most GDR Politburo members from the Prague Spring was that economic reform can lead liberalizers to seek allies in the cultural field which can eventually lead to unforeseen political consequences. In Hungary, by contrast, economic reformers continued to push ahead even after the crushing of the Prague Spring. In the late 1980s, the Hungarian reformers were even willing to allow political liberalization, including negotiation with the opposition. In the GDR, by contrast, such political liberalization was viewed as particularly dangerous because it threatened not only the regime, but also the existence of the GDR as a state. In fact, the first official act by the GDR leadership in rejecting Gorbachev-style reforms in the GDR in the late 1980s was the banning of the German-language version of the Soviet magazine *Sputnik*, after an article appeared which claimed that there was no GDR identity, 'only a German one'.[49]

Shortly before the collapse of the GDR, Otto Reinhold, the Rector of the Central Committee's Academy of Sciences and one of the country's chief ideologists, warned that East Germany was 'conceivable only as an anti-fascist, as a socialist alternative to the Federal Republic'. He predicted that reforms would undercut this *raison d'état* and lead to the GDR's absorption in the Federal Republic.[50] In short, the SED believed the only possible GDR was a hard-line, 'anti-fascist' one. Reform communism, with its emphasis on national identity as practised by Wladyslaw Gomulka in Poland or Janos Kadar in Hungary, was impossible in the GDR. These Eastern European reformers had carried out major economic and political liberalization in an effort to demonstrate that they were doing their utmost to serve their countries' national interests within the parameters of Soviet control. In the GDR, the state's self-preservation did not correspond with the national interest as it was interpreted by most East Germans. Ulrich Beck has encapsulated this difference in the following way: 'Poland minus communism is Poland: but the German Democratic Republic minus communism is – the Federal Republic.'[51]

'Exit' drives 'voice'

In what is perhaps the most influential analysis of the East German revolution, Albert Hirschman has applied his theory of 'exit, voice, and loyalty' to the uprising.[52] Hirschman contends that emigration from the GDR to the Federal Republic initially undermined opposition protest – 'exit as an antagonist of voice', as he phrases it. Particularly after the Wall was built, the ruling SED was able to 'behead' opposition groups by exiling troublesome leaders to West Germany. But when the East German leadership lost control of 'exit' as Hungary began lifting its border controls in mid-1989, emigration threatened the regime's survival. The opposition was then able to launch demonstrations – 'voice' – to demand political reforms in East Germany for those who refused to leave because of their loyalty to the GDR as a state. Hirschman argues that 'exit' and 'voice' had then become 'confederates'.

This formulation is not strong enough, however. In fact, 'exit' *drove* 'voice'. Oppositionists, 'voice', had scored points with revelations of SED manipulation of the May 1989 'elections', but they were still unable to mobilize crowds for planned demonstrations in June. Only after the flight of tens of thousands of East Germans in the summer did anti-fascist regime critics move to form an opposition coalition organization, the Neues Forum.[53] The demonstrations did not begin in Berlin, where most oppositionists were based, but in Dresden and Leipzig, where groups of organized *Ausreisewillige* (those who want to leave) were strongest. In Dresden, where negotiations with the authorities for non-violent protest were first successfully conducted, opposition 'voice' was a direct reaction to the 'battle for the railway station' in the city during the night of 3–4 October 1989. Thousands of would-be 'exiters', who had congregated at the station hoping to board the special trains full of East German refugees passing through from Prague, clashed with the police. In September and October in Leipzig it was actually 'exit' groups who held the first demonstrations. In Hirschman's terminology, they also used 'voice'.[54] The demands of the *Ausreisewillige* ('We want out!') in demonstrations after the Monday prayers for peace were answered by cries of 'We're staying here!' by oppositionists calling for reforms in the GDR. Reports in the West German media of the two antagonistic groups missed the point that the *Bleibers* (stayers) were reacting to an initiative taken by the *Ausreisewillige*.[55]

This illustrates Hirschman's argument about the consequences of 'loyalty' (in this case to the GDR as a state): pro-GDR 'voice' was attempting to rescue a deteriorating organization (country) from complete collapse. Professionals, such as Jens Reich who had previously been only critical of the regime in private now began to speak out publicly.[56] Leading GDR artists Christa Wolf and Stefan Heym were inspired by the exodus to call a major rally on 4 November 1989 and then began a campaign for reforms, called 'For Our Country', to save the GDR.[57] They stressed the importance of preserving East Germany as an anti-fascist, socialist alternative to the Federal Republic. They were joined in their efforts by several Berlin-based oppositionists as well as self-proclaimed reformers in the SED and affiliated 'bloc' parties. Concentrated in Berlin, critical but pro-GDR artists, oppositionists and SED reformers were trying to catch up with a dynamic begun by mass emigration and centred in the state of Saxony where 'exit' groups and 'exit' chances were concentrated.

From the very start, the opposition lagged behind the dynamics of the revolution. Not only did large anti-regime demonstrations only take place after mass emigration had begun, but even the millions of East Germans who took to the streets soon demanded a collective 'exit' into the Federal Republic of Germany. The slogan chanted at rallies changed from 'We are the people!' to 'We are one people!' showing that opposition leaders' calls for regime reform were being overwhelmed by the demonstrators' desire for German unification. Oppositionists – now at last supported by the cultural elite and SED reformers – rejected this popular demand with initiatives to preserve the GDR. But the opinions of 'exiters' revealed overwhelming support for unification. John Torpey reports: 'a resounding 83.9% of all emigrants from the GDR hoped for the accession of East German to the Federal Republic, as provided for in Article 23 of the Basic Law [the Federal Republic's constitution]: here was a clear harbinger of things to come.'[58] This was similar to the survey finding of Karl-Dieter Opp and his collaborators in Leipzig, which showed support for unification even before the events of autumn 1989.[59]

Leipzig and Dresden

The opposition's most significant contribution came during the demonstrations leading up to the decisive 9 October protest in Leipzig. Up to that point, the regime had used force against protesters and seemed prepared to crush the rally planned in Saxony's largest city. One of the few remaining puzzles about the East German revolution is why this demonstration was, in fact, peaceful.[60] Claims by General Secretary Egon Krenz that he countermanded orders for soldiers to shoot have been contradicted by all other major participants.[61] The explanation of this non-violent outcome involves the following factors: (a) the precedent of the opening of a peaceful dialogue between demonstrators and local party officials in Dresden the day before; (b) the size, discipline and non-violent tactics of the estimated 70,000 Leipzig demonstrators; (c) a group of three artists and intellectuals, most prominently the conductor Kurt Masur, and three lower-level party officials who together drafted a statement calling for peaceful dialogue in Leipzig; and (d) indecision in the East Berlin Politburo whom the hard-line Leipzig party leaders consulted on the evening of 9 October. Instead of mass detentions and the possible use of live ammunition against protestors as planned and publicly threatened by the regime, only ten demonstrators were detained, while a few demonstrators and policemen suffered minor injuries on that *Schicksalstag* (fateful day) in Leipzig.[62]

Daniel Friedheim argues that the general decline in elite legitimacy and, in particular, its sharp drop in Saxony and at lower levels of the SED, contributed to the peaceful breakthrough in Dresden and Leipzig.[63] But there is no doubt that leading oppositionists too played a major role in setting a tone conducive to avoiding conflict with the police. Their commitment to active non-violence and their repeated efforts to seek dialogue with regime officials contributed to the peaceful character of the demonstrations in Saxony. Most importantly, it was protest leaders and Protestant Church officials who devised strategies which, in co-operation with lower-level party officials, defused a potentially violent confrontation with the regime at the last minute in Dresden and Leipzig.[64] Without the leadership of key oppositionists, a bloody outcome in Saxony, which might have endangered the course of the entire East German democratic revolution, would have been much more likely.

Reluctant revolutionaries

Once the danger of violent conflict had passed, opposition leaders in East Germany continued to spurn calls for the regime's resignation. It is at this point that the character of opposition in the GDR differed profoundly from that in Czechoslovakia. Rather than calling a general strike to force a transfer of power, the opposition began co-operating closely with communist reformists, first informally and then in round-table talks. With hundreds of thousands of GDR citizens leaving the country for West Germany, the opposition were concerned about the survival of the East German state. They even took up positions that can be considered anti-democratic. Bärbel Bohley, a Neues Forum co-founder, publicly criticized the Krenz regime's ineptness in 'prematurely' opening the Wall.[65] Friedrich Schorlemmer, from the opposition group Democracy Now, insisted, 'the Wall should stay for a while'.[66] The official statement of the Neues Forum was more measured, but it shared the fear that the 'masses', if not provided with an anti-fascist, socialist alternative, might abandon the GDR and become 'rent slaves' in West Germany.[67] The Vereinigte Linke (United Left), another opposition group, was quite explicit. After listing its socialist goals, they proclaimed: 'We favour a controlled opening of the Wall, but are against tearing it down.'[68] It was at this point that the opposition, contrary to reports suggesting the initiative lay with Hans Modrow, proposed round-table talks with the government.[69] The opposition and the reformist regime represented together, in the words of Gert-Joachim Glaeßner, 'a GDR identity'. During the talks they were, however, 'isolated from the majority of the population who wanted to put an end to the GDR as quickly as possible'.[70] Although critical of East German communism, oppositionists had believed in its anti-fascist ideals. But they soon discovered that democratic transition would condemn their state and leave them on the political sidelines during the unification process. Many oppositionists reacted angrily to this turn of events, speaking of a revolution 'stolen' by East German emigrants and West German politicians. The isolation of the opposition was evident when a political party formed by several 'citizen movement' groups polled under 4 per cent of the popular vote in the March 1990 legislative elections. As Henry Ashby Turner, Jr. comments:

> In their first free election the people of East Germany had voted decisively against preservation of a reformed German Democratic Republic, against a gradual amalgamation of the two Germanies, and for the earliest possible union with the Federal Republic.[71]

Conclusion

Most members of the East German citizens' movement did not consider themselves oppositionists because they saw their role as reforming the SED regime, not dismantling it.[72] Despite their critical stance, they believed in 'their' state's anti-fascist ideals. For this same reason, prominent artists and intellectuals refused to join dissident circles. The absence of the cultural elite from the opposition and the power of the GDR's anti-fascist ideology help explain why no Havel-like opposition leader ever emerged in the GDR. When the revolution began in 1989, dissidents tried to realize their dream of entering into a dialogue with a reformed SED regime rather than leading a revolution to seize power from it.

Yet the East German people identified more with West Germany than their own country. A 'common-sense' German identity led most citizens of the GDR to put more emphasis on the material prosperity and political freedoms of the West than on the ideals of official anti-fascism which in practice were heavily manipulated by the SED. The relatively high living standards in East Germany had not dampened popular discontent. Political dissatisfaction was also high. The sense of 'relative deprivation' among many East Germans was high because two-thirds of the people compared themselves to West Germans not others in the Soviet bloc.[73] Equally, if not more important, was the fact that while communist states such as Poland and Hungary had a strong national legitimacy, the GDR had both an unpopular *regime* and an unloved *state*. Popular dissatisfaction with the regime was further increased by its failure to adopt the economic and political reforms that its socialist neighbours were carrying out. This resistance to change, in turn, can largely be explained by the SED's fear of exposing its fragile hold on a people whom it had to lock in behind the Wall. Already 'virtual citizens' of the Federal Republic due to the provisions of the Basic Law, retrospective polls show that even before protests began most East Germans wanted to live in a unified German state.[74]

The full breadth of opposition to the GDR as a communist regime and as an artificial state took unusual forms, which included 'exit'. The existence of a freer and wealthier West German state led some of those opposed to communism and looking for a better life simply to leave the country through emigration, a generally illegal and usually very risky business after the building of the Wall. Before the mass protests of autumn 1989, 'exit' (illegal emigration) and 'voice' (public opposition) roughly correspond to the hostility of the general population wanting to get rid of the SED regime and the GDR as a state, on the one hand, and opposition groups' loyalty to the 'better' East German anti-fascist state despite their criticisms of the regime's flaws, on the other. (This statement must be modified in that would-be 'exiters' in the latter half of the 1980s began organizing their own opposition 'voice' groups.) But the citizen movement opposition wanted to have little to do with those East Germans who did not share their loyalty to the state. Yet it was the emigrants in their hundreds of thousands who undermined the SED regime in a matter of months in the summer and autumn of 1989 by 'voting with their feet' once reforms elsewhere in Eastern Europe made a mass departure possible. Protests led by the pro-GDR dissidents began only as a reaction to mass emigration. These 'loyal' oppositionists tried unsuccessfully to save a state that most East Germans wanted to dissolve in a process of reunification as quickly as possible. The most enthusiastic revolutionaries, then, were those who had already emigrated or wanted to live in what they (unlike most dissidents) considered the 'better Germany', the Federal Republic.

Notes

1 Rose, R., Zapf, W., Seifert, W. and Page, E., 'Germans in Comparative Perspective', *Studies in Public Policy*, No. 218 (Glasgow: Centre for the Study of Public Policy, University of Strathclyde, 1993). These survey results are discussed below.
2 Kopstein, J., *The Politics of Economic Decline in East Germany, 1945–1989*

(Chapel Hill: The University of North Carolina Press, 1997) p. 197 and p. 5.

3 The most famous commentary on this event was Bertolt Brecht's secret poem: 'After the uprising of the 17th June/ The Secretary of the Writers' Union/ Had leaflets distributed in the Stalinalle/ Stating that the people/ Had forfeited the confidence of the government/ And could win it back only/ By redoubled efforts. Would it not be easier/ In that case for the government/ To dissolve the people/ And elect another?' Quoted in: Turner, H. A., Jr., *Germany from Partition to Reunification* (New Haven: Yale University Press, 1992) pp. 80–1.

4 No representative surveys were permitted by an SED regime which did not want to know too much about the true views of its own population. Yet by the late 1980s even sectoral surveys (factory workers, young people, etc.) of carefully selected interviewees began to reveal widespread discontent. For an overview of these surveys see Gensicke, T., *Mentalitätsentwicklungen im Osten Deutschlands seit den 70er Jahren: Vorstellung und Erläuterung von Ergebnissen einiger empirischer Untersuchungen in der DDR und in den neuen Bundesländern von 1977 bis 1991* (Speyer: Forschungsinstitut für Öffentliche Verwaltung bei der Hochschule für Verwaltungswissenschaften Speyer, 1992). The most important pre-revolution poll was conducted by the Zentralinstitut für Jugendforschung in Leipzig, which showed severe declines in youth identification with the GDR after 1985. See Friedrich, W., 'Mentalitätswandlungen der Jugend in der DDR', *Aus Politik und Zeitgeschichte* B 16–17 (1990) pp. 26–41.

5 *1980 World Bank Atlas*, cited in Childs, D., *The GDR: Moscow's German Ally* (London: George Allen and Unwin, 1983) p. 147. The GDR's economic decline had become so obvious by 1988 that international estimates were revised, with the country slipping to 26th place among the industrialized nations, Ramet, S. P., *Social Currents in Eastern Europe* (Durham, N.C.: Duke University Press, 1991) p. 51.

6 Ash, T. G., *'Und willst du nicht mein Bruder sein ...': Die DDR heute* (Hamburg: Spiegel Verlag, 1981) p. 191.

7 Voigt, D., Belitz-Demiriz, H. and Meck, S., 'Die innerdeutsche Wanderung und der Vereinigungsprozess: Sozialdemographische Struktur und Einstellungen von Flüchtlingen/berseidlern aus der DDR vor and nach der Grenzöffnung', *Deutschland Archiv*, No. 23 (May 1990) p. 736 and Hilmer R. and Kühler, A., 'Die DDR läuft der Zeit davon: Die Übersiedler/Flüchtlingswelle im Sommer 1989', *Deutschland Archiv*, No. 22 (December 1989) p. 1385.

8 Opp, K-D., Voss, P. and Gern, C., *Die volkseigene Revolution* (Stuttgart: Klett-Cotta, 1993), ch. 3.

9 *Ibid.*, p. 25.

10 Friedrich, *op. cit.* (1990).

11 Survey data are analysed in Opp *et al.*, *op. cit.* (1993) pp. 93–5 and pp. 346–7.

12 *Ibid.*, p. 95.

13 *Ibid.*, pp. 93–5.

14 *Ibid.*, ch. 5, and Thompson, M. R., 'Why and How East Germans Rebelled', *Theory and Society*, Vol. 25, No. 2 (April 1996) pp. 270–2.

15 Rose *et al.*, *op. cit.* (1993).

16 Offe, C., *Der Tunnel am Ende des Lichts: Erkundungen der politischen Transformation in Neuen Osten* (Frankfurt am Main: Campus, 1994) pp. 249–50.

17 Offe, C., 'Prosperity, Nation, Republic', *German Politics and Society*, No. 22 (1991) p. 26.

18 Kopstein, *op. cit.* (1997) p. 4.

19 Rüddenklau, W., *Störenfried: DDR-Opposition 1986–1989* (Berlin: Basis, 1992) pp. 12–13.

20 Meuschel, S., *Legitimation und Parteiherrschaft in der DDR* (Frankfurt am Main: Suhrkamp, 1992) p. 279.

21 Danyel, J. (ed.), *Die geteilte Vergangenheit. Zum Nationalsozialismus und Widerstand in den beiden deutschen Staaten* (Berlin: Akadamie Verlag, 1995) p. 45, cited in Kocka, J. and Sabrow, M., 'Die doppelte Vergangenheit: Der gemeinsame Blick auf die geteilte Geschichte', in *Funkkolleg: Deutschland im Umbruch, Heft 2* (Tübingen: DIFF, 1997), p. 6/13.

22 On the SED's two-track approach to history, which distinguished between 'carriers' (*Träger*) of reaction and progress in the German past, see Meuschel, *op. cit.* (1992) pp. 67ff.

23 Quoted in Deuerlein, E., *DDR 1945–1970. Geschichte und Bestandsaufnahme* (Munich: Deutscher Taschenbuch Verlag, 1971) p. 194, cited in Kocka and Sabrow, *op. cit.* (1997) p. 6/12.

24 Bude, H., 'Das Ende einer tragischen Gesellschaft', in Joas, H. and Kohli, M. (eds.), *Der Zusammenbruch der DDR.* (Frankfurt am Main: Suhrkamp, 1993) pp. 270–1.

25 Bessel, R., 'How the Gestapo policed the Third Reich', *Times Literary Supplement*, 8 March 1991, cited in Pond, E., *Beyond the Wall: Germany's Road to Unification* (Washington, D.C.: The Brookings Institution, 1993), p. 80. In addition to the 85,000 official employees, the *Stasi* had over 100,000 'unofficial collaborators' (*Inoffizielle Mitarbeiter*, or IMs). In 1983, 1.2 million people in the GDR were armed, including 400,000 Soviet troops, the National People's Army, border guards and an armed militia. This works out to 11 soldiers/1km². Asmus, R. D., 'Is there a Peace Movement in the GDR?', *Orbis* (Summer 1983), p. 305.

26 Quoted in Bude, *op. cit.* (1993) p. 270.

27 Member of the *Bundestag* and former East German oppositionist Gerd Poppe testifying in Enquete-Kommission, *'Aufarbeitung von Geschichte und Folgen der SED-Diktatur in Deutschland': Ideologie, Integration und Disziplinierung, III, 1* (Baden-Baden: Nomos, 1995), p. 144.

28 *Ibid.*

29 Joppke, C., 'Intellectuals, Nationalism, and the Exit from Communism: The Case of East Germany'. Paper presented at the Annual Meeting of the American Sociological Association, (Miami: August 1993).

30 Cited in Joppke, C., *East German Dissidents and the Revolution of 1989: Social Movement in a Leninist Regime* (Basingstoke: Macmillan, 1995) pp. 72–3. Seven GDR judges and prosecutors were tried in Frankfurt (Oder) in 1997, charged with violating East German law in the course of their prosecution of Havemann in the 1970s and early 1980s. He had been held under house arrest for five years until his death and charged with 'endangering public order' and violating currency laws. Though sharply criticizing the behav-

iour of these GDR justice officials, the court found them not guilty. Writing in Der Spiegel, No. 41, 6 October 1997. 'Freispruch als Schuldspruch', pp. 254–6, Wolf Biermann says his friend Robert Havemann was denied justice by three German states: by the Nazi regime which sentenced him to death in 1943, by the GDR, and finally by the Federal Republic. Of course, a very different point can also be made: that while Havemann was denied basic legal due process by the Nazis and the SED, his East German persecutors received the benefit of a fair trial.

31 Linz, J. J., 'Opposition to and under an Authoritarian Regime', in Dahl, R. (ed.), *Regimes and Oppositions* (New Haven: Yale University Press, 1973).

32 Besides those already mentioned, returnees to East Germany included Bertolt Brecht, Anna Seghers, Heinrich Mann, Arnold Zwieg, Alfred Kantorowicz and Ernst Bloch.

33 Heym, S., *Schwarzenberg* (Munich: C. Bertelsmann, 1984).

34 On the size of the GDR opposition, see Mitter, A. and Wolle, S. (eds.), *Ich liebe euch doch alle!* (Berlin: Basis Druck, 1190) pp. 47–8, who quote a secret Stasi document. The Czechoslovak secret service estimates are contained in Urban, J., 'The Powerlessness of the Powerful' (manuscript: Prague, November 1992) p. 22, cited in Linz, J. J. and Stepan, A., *Democratic Transitions and Consolidation: Eastern Europe, Southern Europe and Latin America* (Baltimore: Johns Hopkins University Press, 1996) p. 321. On the Charter 77 signatories, see Bradley, J. F. N., *Czechoslovakia's Velvet Revolution: A Political Analysis*. (Boulder: East European Monographs, Columbia University Press, 1992) p. 21.

35 Torpey, J., *Intellectuals, Socialism, and Dissent: The East German Opposition and its Legacy* (Minneapolis: University of Minnesota Press, 1995) p. 208 suggests that 'the marginal intellectuals [of the opposition] in the GDR cultivated an isolated and, to most of their compatriots, quixotic existence.'

36 It is beyond the scope of this essay to discuss in detail the role of the *Stasi* in undermining opposition in the GDR. The point that must be made is that the *Stasi* did not just observe the opposition, but actively attempted to manipulate and steer it. In the context of détente, and its German version Ostpolitik, outright repression was no longer an option, making the *Stasi's* work even more important than it had been before the 1970s. By 1989 the *Stasi* had infiltrated virtually every opposition group, no matter how small. In fact, there were sometimes more *Stasi* informers in a particular organization than genuine oppositionists. For a general account of the *Stasi*, see Gill, D. and Schröter, U., *Das Ministerium für Staatssicherheit: Anatomie des Mielke-Imperiums* (Reinbek bei Hamburg: Rowohlt, 1993). For a recent English language version, see Childs, D. and Popplewell, R., *The Stasi: The East German Intelligence and Security Service* (New York: New York University Press, 1996). Its omnipresence has even led to the absurd claim that the *Stasi* itself organized the 1989 revolution (and thus its own destruction!). See Broder, H. M., 'Eine schöne Revolution', *Die Zeit*, 10 January 1992, p. 41. The Stasi, which compulsively wrote down everything, left no traces of such a 'plot'. It may well be, however, that the *Stasi* lost control of some of its informers in the heat of the revolution. For a fascinating account of 'idealism' among some informers, see Joppke, *op. cit.* (1995) pp. 117–21.

37 There is good reason to believe that Havemann would not have. In the late 1960s, for example, he believed that only Ulbricht could reform the GDR because he 'could successfully cope with [the] complicated task [of liberalizing the country] without jeopardizing the existence of the GDR.' Quoted in Brandt, W., *The Search for a Third Way*, p. 262, cited in Joppke, *op. cit.* (1995) p. 63.

38 Pelikan, J., 'Warum ist es schwer, ein Kommunist in der DDR zu sein?', in Jäckel, H. (ed.), *Ein Marxist in der DDR: Für Robert Havemann* (Munich: Piper, 1980) p. 50.

39 Rüddenklau, *op. cit.* (1992) p. 15.

40 Grunenberg, A., *Antifaschismus – ein deutscher Mythos* (Reinbek bei Hamburg: Rowohlt, 1993), and Keller, C. (ed.), *Antifaschismus, Geschichte und Neubewertung* (Berlin: Aufbau, 1996) with a selection of articles by leading authorities on anti-fascism.

41 Wolf, C., *Im Dialog: Aktuelle Text* (Frankfurt am Main: Luchterhand, 1990) p. 136.

42 I experienced an example of this popular scepticism while teaching at the Dresden University of Technology in the early 1990s. Discovering that the building in which I taught had a GDR-built monument to German and Eastern European resistance fighters who had died when this edifice had been a *Gestapo* prison, I suggested to several students that it might be worthwhile to organize a class tour. They quickly replied that such tours had been required of them in the old East German days. The mixture of boredom, officiousness, and propaganda that they associated with these meetings made them highly sceptical of any further tours.

43 Rüddenklau, *op. cit.* (1992) p. 13.

44 Cited in *ibid.*, pp. 112–13.

45 Joppke, *op. cit.* (1995) pp. 130–1. Ironically, several oppositionists arrested after the 1988 demonstration – an answer to the official 'Luxemburg–Liebknecht combat demonstration' which used Rosa Luxemburg's slogan 'freedom is always the freedom of those who dissent' against the SED – chose to go into exile in West Germany rather than face imprisonment. This pragmatic willingness to accept 'exit' in adverse situations has proved a source of embarrassment to the opposition.

46 Fricke, K. W., *Opposition und Widerstand in der DDR: Ein politischer Report* (Köln: Verlag Wissenschaft und Politik, 1984) p. 217.

47 The best text in English is Kopstein, *op. cit.* (1997). Kopstein dismisses the importance of the 'national question' in the failure of economic reforms. However, it must be asked in comparative perspective why reforms were undertaken in Czechoslovakia until the crushing of the Prague Spring, in Hungary until 1989 and, beginning in the mid-1980s, in the Soviet Union itself. Kopstein's arguments about the SED's fear of antagonizing the working class should apply to all socialist countries. But the SED was particularly wary given the proximity of West Germany to which workers could flee as well as its population size in comparison to the FRG is even after the Wall was built. It is also clear that the SED leadership's own fear of reform was in large part due to the perceived need to distinguish itself from capitalist West Germany.

48 Stiftung Archiv der Parteien und Massenorganisationen der DDR im

Bundesarchiv, SED IV A2/2021/153 cited in Kopstein, *op. cit.* (1997) p. 66.

49   Reuth, R. G. and Bönte, A., *Das Komplott: Wie es wirklich zur deutschen Einheit kam* (Munich: Piper, 1993) pp. 40–6.

50   Quoted in Grasnow, V. and Jarausch, K. H. (eds.), *Die deutsche Vereinigung: Dokumente zu Bürgerbewegung, Annäherung und Beitritt* (Cologne: Wissenschaft und Politik, 1991) p. 57.

51   Beck, U., 'Opposition in Deutschland', in Giesen, B. and Leggewie, C. (eds.), *Experiment Vereinigung: Ein sozialer Grossversuch.* (Berlin: Rotburch Verlag, 1991) p. 24.

52   Hirschman, A., 'Exit, Voice and the Fate of the GDR: An Essay in Conceptual History,' *World Politics*, Vol. 45, No. 2 (1993) pp. 173–202. Hirschman defines 'exit' and 'voice' as 'two contrasting responses of consumers or members of organizations to what they sense as deterioration in the quality of the goods they buy or the services and benefits they receive. Exit is the act of simply leaving generally because a better good or service or benefit is believed to be provided by another firm or organization ... Voice is the act of complaining or of organising to complain or to protest' (pp. 175–6).

53   The Neues Forum was the only 'mass-based' opposition group: over 200,000 people signed its founding appeal and it played a leading role in many rallies throughout the country. The second largest organization was the Sozialdemokratische Partei (SDP), later SPD after it merged with the West German social democrats: it claimed 10,000 members. Other groups were small and drew largely on a limited clientele, particularly church pastors and peace activists: the best known were the Demokratischer Aufbruch (Democratic Awakening), Demokratie Jetzt (Democracy Now), Vereinigte Linke (United Left) and the Grüne Partei (Green Party). Knabe, H., 'Politische Opposition in der DDR: Ursprüngen, Programmatik, Perspektiven', *Aus Politik und Zeitgeschichte*, B 1–2, 5 January 1990, pp. 26–8. For an encyclopaedic study on the GDR opposition, see Neubert, E., *Geschichte der Opposition in der DDR 1949–1989* (Bonn: Bundeszentrale für Politische Bildung, 1997).

54   Hirschman's analysis misses this point. He assumes 'exit' is an individual and 'voice' a collective activity. But in their effort to leave the country, would-be emigrants formed 'opposition' groups demanding the right of free passage. This is a much neglected area of research on the GDR revolution. One of the few – and best – analyses is by Joppke, *op. cit.* (1995) pp. 127–32.

55   Joppke, *op. cit.* (1995) p. 59.

56   In a semi-autobiographical account, Reich, J., *Rückkehr nach Europa: Bericht zur neuen Lage der deutschen Nation* (München: Carl Hanser, 1991) pp. 171–203, Jens Reich describes his political awakening.

57   For the text of Heym and Wolf's speeches on 4 November 1989, see Schüddenkopf, C. (ed.), *'Wir sind das Volk!' Flugschriften, Aufrufe und Texte* (Reinbek bei Hamburg: Rowohlt, 1990) pp. 207–8 and 213–15. The 'Für unser Land' appeal is reprinted in Prokop, S. (ed.), *Die kurze Zeit der Utopie: Die 'zwiete DDR' im vergessenen Jahr 1989/90* (Berlin: Elefanted Press, 1994) pp. 214–19. Also see in the same book the article by Wuttke, C., '"Für unser Land!": Ein Aufruf im Gegenzug', pp. 88–99.

58 Torpey, J., 'Two Movements, not a Revolution: Exodus and Opposition in the East German Transformation, 1989–1990', *German Politics and Society*, Vol. 26 (Summer 1992) p. 30.

59 Opp *et al.*, *op. cit.* (1993) p. 104.

60 The most thorough academic account is by Friedheim, D. V. 'Democratic Transition through Regime Collapse: East Germany in 1989' (PhD Dissertation, Yale University, December 1997); Ch. 6. Although much has been written about the Leipzig events, an incomplete archival record of state documents has made it difficult to offer a definitive history. Friedheim suggests these public records were 'cleaned up' sometime after October 1989. The surviving archives, however, point to a plan to crack down violently on the demonstrations that was derailed only at the last minute.

61 Pond, *op. cit.* (1993) pp. 117–20.

62 Friedheim, *op. cit.* (1997) pp. 315–47.

63 Ibid., chs. 4 and 6. Friedheim's excellent study is based on over 100 interviews with members of 'Secret Crisis Teams' who made the decision whether to employ force against demonstrators and archival work in Dresden, Leipzig and Berlin.

64 For example, in Dresden the opposition pioneered the practice of silent marches with demonstrators carrying candles. Holding a candle in one hand and shielding it from the wind with the other symbolized the opposition's concern not to start a *'Handgreiflicher Streit'* (i.e. a violent conflict) with the authorities.

65 Pond, *op. cit.* (1993) p. 134.

66 Quoted in TAZ Journal, *DDR Journal zur Novemberrevolution* (Berlin: Die Tageszeitung, 1990), p. 126, cited in Joppke, *op. cit.* (1995) p. 160.

67 *Ibid.*

68 'Beitrag der 13. Autonomen Gruppe zum Kongreß der Vereinigten Linken am 25. und 26. November in Berlin,' reprinted in Schüddenkopf, *op. cit.* (1990) p. 239.

69 See the references in Joppke, *op. cit.* (1995) p. 241, nn. 104 and 105. The idea of round table talks was first mentioned in a speech by oppositionist Wolgang Ullmann on 27 October 1989.

70 Glaessner, G-J., *Der schwierige Weg zur Demokratie: Vom Ende der DDR zur deutschen Einheit.* (Opladen: Westdeutscher Verlag, 1991) p. 93

71 Turner, *op. cit.* (1992) p. 246.

72 Leading East German dissident Bärbel Bohley told a government commission investigating the GDR past: 'We did not so much think of ourselves as oppositionists as that we were treated [by the regime] as oppositionists.' She added that the opposition had wished for a 'great societal dialogue' ('großer gesellschaftlicher Dialog') with even the most hard-line elements of the regime. This included discussions with members of the state secret police (called Stasi). 'Even the *Stasi* wants to be saved,' she claimed in quasi-religious tones. Enquete-Kommission, *'Aufarbeitung von Geschichte und Folgen der SED-Diktatur in Deutschland': Widerstand, Opposition, Revolution, VII, I* (Baden-Baden: Nomos, 1995) pp. 278–9.

73 Opp *et al.*, *op. cit.* (1993) p. 95.

74 *Ibid.*, p. 104.

2

'Nostalgia' in Germany's New Federal States as a Political and Cultural Phenomenon of the Transformation Process

Norbert Kapferer

Introduction

Germany was reunited on 3 October 1990. This event was well planned and organized by the West German government and the administrative machinery, based on a contract drawn up between the FRG and the GDR.

Two comments on this historical moment are memorable:[1]

> Now everything that belongs together will grow together.
> (Willy Brandt, Mayor of Berlin in the 1960s and Chancellor of the Federal Republic of Germany, 1969–74)[2]

> The Germans are now the happiest people in the whole wide world.
> (Walter Momper, former governing mayor of West Berlin)

Several years after reunification, these statements, declared in happier days, seem over-optimistic, and the opposite may now be true.

In the meantime millions of East and West Germans made contact with each other; billions of Deutschmarks were transferred from the old to the new federal states, but the gulf between East and West Germans in terms of human relationships is greater now than during the years of separation.[3]

Germans in the East and the West might have been happy for a while, but things changed very quickly, and when the thrill of the 'fall of the Wall' had passed, the German will for unification was tested by cold reality. In other words, West Germans welcomed reunification enthusiastically as long as their standard of living was unaffected by its costs. Their honeymoon happiness soon turned to indifference and apathy, or even anger and regret once the costs were known.

East Germans became disillusioned with this rapid change of heart in the western half of the country and were shocked by the unexpected burdens and the impact of unification on their personal lives. Faced with the necessity to change their way of life totally in the new market economy, many started looking back to the 'good old days' of 'real existing socialism' in the German Democratic Republic (GDR).

This remarkable phenomenon soon earned a name in the media throughout Germany: 'GDR nostalgia'.[4]

Nostalgia is generally defined as a fashion statement: driving vintage cars, for example, or wearing old-fashioned clothes, or buying furniture of the 1950s, etc.

Psychologists interpret 'nostalgia' as an unconscious wish for a return to the 'good old days', when the world was still well-ordered, easy to understand and not complicated and problematic as it is today.

From a psychological point of view this 'longing for the past' also seemed to be based on a myth, or on a mythologization of the past.

The question now is, how can we explain 'GDR nostalgia' as a political and cultural phenomenon? Are there any consequences for the ongoing process of unification in Germany?

The hypothesis is that 'GDR nostalgia' constitutes one aspect of the transformation process and is also a result of the unplanned and rapid reunification after a period of more than 40 years of division.

As a political and cultural phenomenon it has to be analysed by different means: psychological, sociological and philosophical approaches.

First, I will try to describe the political situation in 1989/90 during the unexpectedly speedy reunification, as well as the phenomenon itself, the rise of 'GDR nostalgia' and its official organization, the Party of Democratic Socialism (PDS).

An unexpectedly speedy reunification

On both sides of the Wall/border, people once believed in the indestructibility of the German language and culture, or trusted in a sense of unity. While East Germans could not express their feelings in public, West German representatives often talked about our 'brothers and sisters in the East' and some took an oath on the deepest, most fervent wish of all Germans to unify.[5]

Apart from the fact that the will to reunite was enshrined in West

Germany's Basic Law, few people after the 1960s, really believed in the possibility of unification, and no one seriously thought about the costs, or about the other consequences.

The collapse of the communist regime in East Germany was quite unexpected, the result of political and economic developments and events, which no one could have foreseen. To name but a few: the decline of the Soviet Union as a superpower from the early 1980s; political reform in Eastern European states like Poland and Hungary and the Soviet Union itself under Mikhail Gorbachev; the hard-line resistance of the ruling political class in East Germany against reform; the stagnation of the planned economy in the GDR; the lifting of the 'Iron Curtain' between Hungary and Austria; the flight of thousands of East Germans to the West, etc.[6]

The government of General Secretary Erich Honecker was forced to resign because of the flight of thousands and the demonstrations in East Germany demanding reform and democracy.[7]

The ruling Communist Party (SED) no longer had the authority to stabilize the situation and create a new order. No one was able to slow, let alone halt, the trajectory of the ongoing velvet revolution.[8]

To begin with some of the organized democratic opposition groups would have opted for a separate 'democratic-socialist' state, while others wanted a confederation between the two German states, with reunification being achieved in the long run.[9]

Neither viewpoint had a chance under the circumstances. The majority of East Germans were no longer willing to accept socialist dogma and, in March 1990, voted in the very first (and last) free and democratic elections in the history of the GDR for the fastest route to reunification. The East Germans were eager to embrace Western democracy and the possibility of a Western standard of living, as soon as possible.[10]

In retrospect there was no alternative to the pace of reunification. The West German government had little time to calculate the international and national risks of a long or short run to reunification since they faced the risk of losing reunification altogether.[11]

The decision was made, but people on both sides underestimated the enormous problems of reuniting after 40 years of separation, after living in different political, economic, social and cultural societies. Language, cultural ties, family connections and goodwill could not span the massive alienation and the different mentalities, the result of different experiences, life conditions and life-styles, values, beliefs, etc.[12]

No one in Germany – neither in the East nor in the West – was prepared for this historical moment, thus no one could have anticipated that the reunion of 'brothers and sisters' could turn into a confrontation of strangers. Very soon after the fall of the Wall, and after the opening of the border, people were talking about a new barrier between East and West Germans, the 'wall in the mind'.[13] Its current manifestation among East Germans is often said to be a tendency to romanticize the recent past and to emphasize certain alleged achievements of the former GDR, especially in the field of social welfare.

The rise of 'GDR nostalgia'

'GDR nostalgia' developed over four periods after the political change in East Germany, and these periods cannot be isolated from one another. The first period began before reunification, starting with the October/November events in 1989, and this period can be described as an optimistic and self-critical one; East Germans used and enjoyed their new-found freedom of expression, criticized their 'deformed' language, the 'double talk', their restricted lives, the lies of daily propaganda, etc. They railed against the Communist Party, against the leading politicians, cadres, secret service (*Stasi*) agents, etc., and looked forward to a democratic future.[14] Most of the opinions published at that time expressed the desire of different people (writers, intellectuals, 'SED' party members, workers, clerks, etc.) to put an end to their 'GDR' history.

Very soon after reunification in October 1990, a rising dissatisfaction was commented on in the media throughout Germany: a dissatisfaction about the practical consequences of the transformation. The people of the new federal states were especially disillusioned with the politics of the 'Treuhand',[15] the sharp rise of unemployment, the 'dismantling of social services', the 'closing of academies, cultural institutes and youth clubs', the 'renaming of streets and places', the 'destruction of memorial buildings and symbols of "Real existing socialism"', the 'arrogance of West German managers' and, last but not least, the 'total discrediting of and discrimination against everything coming from the East'.[16]

In this period of transformation, which marked the end of solidarity after the 'fall-of-the-Wall optimism', letters to newspapers, magazines, radio and TV talk shows were full of East Germans arguing that whilst they welcomed the political change and reunification, they now felt that they were being treated by the West Germans like a vanquished foe.

From a psychological point of view, this second period demonstrated the switch from a lost identity to the feeling of being somebody, of having something to lose, which was their own and therefore worth keeping.[17]

In the third period, between 1991 and 1992, East Germans started to defend themselves – not the political system they used to live in, but their former existence as people with distinctly different life experiences, lifestyles, respectable values, beliefs and traditions. Arguing against critics and accusations from the West, they claimed to be hard-working like the West Germans, and had also created something good and important in the previous forty years.[18] Thus was the time when the media were full of statements about the burdens of the rotten heritage of the socialist state and the enormous costs of unification.[19]

The fourth period can be characterized as the move from self-defence to self-maintenance. A typical comment was often heard was: 'Until now we did not know that we have a "GDR identity"'.[20] East Germans had become self-assured enough to criticize what in their view had gone wrong following reunification.

A survey taken in late summer of 1993 showed that a majority, ranging from 56 per cent to 96 per cent of East Germans believed that the former 'real existing socialism' of the 'GDR' was stronger than West Germany in such domains as job security, child care, law and order, social security, education, sex discrimination, human rights, social justice and social solidarity.[21]

In an opinion poll conducted by the Allensbach Institute in March 1990, 61 per cent answered that they now felt more like a 'German' than a citizen of the 'GDR', while only 32 per cent claimed that they still felt more like a GDR citizen. But in January 1992, 60 per cent identified themselves as East Germans against only 35 per cent as solely Germans.[22]

The Party of Democratic Socialism (PDS) as the 'GDR nostalgia' party

As in some other former socialist states (Russia, Hungary, Poland)[23] the post-Communist/Socialist Party made a remarkable comeback in the new federal states of Germany.

The PDS, the successor party to the old Communist/Socialist Party of the GDR, had no alternative but to accept reunification.[24]

As a very well-organized reservoir for different communist/socialist groups, however (old Stalinists, Marxist-Leninists, post-communist reformers, etc.), the PDS soon started to defend what they called the 'true humanistic socialist ideas', the 'good communist/socialist traditions' like 'anti-fascism', not to forget the social achievements of 'real existing socialism' of the past.[25]

During election campaigns the leaders or representatives of the PDS did not simply glorify or justify the old communist regime of East Germany, but they used well-known anti-capitalistic rhetoric against the market economy and paraded old communist resentments against private property, pluralism of interests and civil parliamentarism in society.[26]

In defending 'socialist values' against the 'now ruling "elbow" society' of aggressive individualism, PDS propaganda mobilized those nostalgic sentiments, employing the myths of solidarity, social security and humanity as practised ideals in the former GDR.

The remarkable success of the PDS is another sign of the rise of GDR nostalgia in the new federal states. In the first all-German elections for the Bundestag in December 1990, the PDS secured only 9.9 per cent in the new federal states, while the Christian Democrats (CDU) won 43.4 per cent, followed by the Social Democrats (SPD) with 23.6 per cent and the Free Democrats (FDP) with 13.3 per cent.[27] But in the second free and democratic all-German elections in October 1994, 10.6 per cent of the East Germans voted for the PDS, 38.5 per cent for the CDU and 31.9 per cent for the SPD. [28]

After the local elections in the capital of Germany, in the city of Berlin, the PDS became the largest party (36.3 per cent) in the eastern districts, followed by the CDU (23.6 per cent) and the 'SPD' (20.2 per cent).[29]

The overall results of the all-German Bundestag elections of October 1994 (CDU: 45.0 per cent; SPD: 38.3 per cent; Bündnis 90/Die Grünen: 6.5 per cent; PDS: 4.1 per cent; FDP: 3.3 per cent) and the overall results of the local elections in Berlin of October 1995 (CDU: 37.4 per cent; SPD: 23.6 per cent; PDS: 14.6 per cent; Bündnis 90/Die Grünen: 13.2 per cent) showed that the PDS is a growing political force in the eastern regions of Germany with very little influence in the West (only 0.9 per cent in the old federal states) and only 1.7 per cent in the western districts of Berlin.

Jürgen W. Falten and Markus Klein, who analysed the PDS voters in the 1994 all-German elections for the Bundestag found that 90 per cent of them were 'GDR-Nostalgiens. They answered that the former GDR had 'more good sides than bad' or 'both good and bad sides'. In Falter and Kleins' view, more than 80 per cent of the PDS voters can be described as 'socialists'.[30]

The extent of GDR nostalgia cannot be calculated precisely. But one thing is certain: far more than 18 per cent of East German voters are unable to think of themselves as citizens of the new Federal Republic of Germany, nor are they willing to accept the rules of a market economy and a pluralistic society.

Dissatisfaction with the chosen (political, economic) path to reunification might be the main reason, but a growing GDR nostalgia also has a psychological, sociological and a philosophical background.

The GDR identity

From a Western point of view, people in the former GDR lived behind the Wall/closed border like prisoners, always ready to escape if the opportunity arose, and longing for freedom, and for the benefits of democracy in a competitive, wealthy society like West Germany.

Political observers and social scientists in the West maintained that compared to the West Germans, people in the GDR had no real identity, but only a false one. Most of them felt like 'handicapped Germans'.[31]

There was also the well-known theory that the GDR was nothing but a 'niche society' ('Nischen-Gesellschaft'), in which everybody looked for a small private niche to live their private life.[32]

Today we know better, that most of those ideas or theories about the non-existent 'GDR identity' were wrong, and based on prejudice. They all underestimated the fact of 40–45 years' experience and the process of social learning at all levels of this particular socialist society.

The 'prison cell' idea ignored the fact that people who spend many years in prison learn to appreciate and use the positive aspects of their unnatural situation. Free again and challenged by the problem of reorganizing their lives unaided, they miss their warm cell and prison solidarity.

But people in the former GDR were not prisoners, because nobody can keep 15 million under arrest for 30 or 45 years. 'Real existing socialism' was not only a freedom-restricting political system with a communist ideology backed by mass propaganda, but also a way of life, a plan or a project in unique circumstances. Generations grew up in this part of Germany learning to live in a controlled and closed society, developing their own strategies and means to a special type of self-determination in their jobs and in their private life without commiting themselves politcally.[33]

One cannot compare the GDR with a prison cell, but one can compare it to an extremely authoritarian old people's home, especially after the 1970s, which followed the totalitarian Stalinist period. On the one hand, the majority of East Germans might not have wanted to accept their (political) restrictions, but they felt comfortable with the illusion of a lifelong solid and secure existence. Indeed, in the mid-1980s, a few hundred East Germans who had risked their lives to flee to the West wanted to return to the GDR, because they felt like 'strangers' in the free West.

The ideological influence and identity

The ideological influence was massive and a normal part of everyday life in the GDR from kindergarten to all further educational institutions including youth organizations, the armed forces and professional training.[34]

Most of the well-paid jobs were only available to party members or to those who thought and spoke in ideological terms. From a Western point of view it seemed that Marxist-Leninist ideology and daily propaganda by the media did not really touch the people. Political observers and social scientists believed in a natural resistance against those orders to think.

This assessment was not wrong in every respect. There is very little left of the Marxism-Leninism and the 'SED ideology' among intellectuals. East German philosophers no longer call themselves 'Marxists-Leninists' or 'Communists' but 'Socialists', or just 'Marxists'.[35] For those intellectuals who once belonged to the ideology producers and propagandists, their 'new' orientation is nothing but an exercise in saving their philosophical identity.

But what about the victims of 'SED ideology' and mass propaganda? What do they think about 'communism/socialism' after the 'Peaceful Revolution' and the collapse of 'real existing socialism' in Europe?

Opinion researchers found that the dream of a socialist Utopia has not been wholly abandoned; the statement 'Socialism did not fail, but was brought down by incompetent politicians' was held by 67 per cent of East German respondents in a survey undertaken in February and March 1990.[36] In 1991, 75 per cent of East Germans thought that 'socialism is a good idea that had been carried out badly'.[37]

This remarkable finding must have something to do with the influence of ideology over the years, which in my opinion can be described as a teaching method: What many East Germans first learned was to perceive reality in totalitarian categories, or to simplify complex facts or phenomena as 'good or bad', 'black or white'.

It is often remarked that this way of thinking can be compared with religious dogma: political philosophers like Eric Voeglin have pointed out that the communist ideology has a 'Gnostic character' and performs the function of a compensation religion ('Ersatzreligion').[38] My thesis is that the ideological influence in the former GDR was at least as effective and survived partly the collapse of the communist regime because of that religious aspect.

The religious background in the atheistic state

The majority of people in East Germany once belonged to the Protestant Church. This part of Germany was the cradle of the sixteenth-century Protestant Reformation, the outcome of which was the division of the Christian Church. That means that Protestantism as a fundamental religious movement has a long and strong tradition there, and has deeper roots than one might imagine.

Protestantism is not only a Christian faith, but a more than 300-year culture. People living in this region might not believe in God, but they grew up with a Protestant education, spiritualizing the Protestant world-view (*Weltanschauung*), the specific Protestant ethics and Protestant values like asceticism, subordination, feelings of solidarity, a sense of mission vis-à-vis others (*Sendungsbewußtsein*), conscientiousness, introspection, etc.

These Protestant values are also well known outside the religious context as typical Prussian values. In other words: Prussian identity and Prussian culture are Protestant through and through.[39]

One may ask, therefore, what has this to do with the communist/ socialist regime in East Germany, which was atheistic and furthermore anti-Prussian?

There is no doubt that the official ideology and the education in the former GDR was atheistic combined with anti-fascism! But behind the anti-fascist and the anti-Prussian image and attitude, the communists mobilized typical Prussian military traditions, their law and order mentality, and used the pre-existing authoritarian structures. Like the Nazis between 1933 and 1945, the SED perverted Prussian traditions for their very own power interests.

In the late 1940s and 1950s, the communist regime persecuted the Protestant Church and Christianity, but from the 1960s the leaders of the SED changed their politics from confrontation to co-operation. The Protestant Church in the GDR, standing in the long Prussian tradition of state church, was willing and able to accept the (atheistic) socialist state. While the Catholic or Orthodox Churches in Eastern Europe were in opposition to the communist regimes, the Protestant Church collaborated as a 'church within socialism'.

The basis of this co-operation was a kind of declaration that socialism and Protestantism shared common values and beliefs.[40]

There is an ongoing controversy in this country surrounding the questions: Did the Protestant Church stabilize the communist regime, or was this religious institution a focal point for opposition groups?

In my opinion both questions have to be answered with a 'yes'!

Erhard Neubert called the political change in the former GDR a 'Protestant revolution', because the majority of the autumn 1989 activists were Protestants, but their perspective was a 'democratic socialism'.[41]

The proximity of Protestantism and socialism was noticed long ago: politically committed Protestants very often sympathized in the past with socialist or Marxist ideas,[42] not to forget also with Nazi ideas. Hitler's NSDAP had far more Protestants as members and voters than Catholics. The one and only Nazi church movement, the 'German Christians' ('Deutsche Christen'), was a movement within the Protestant Church.[43]

Max Weber, the famous German sociologist, wrote at the beginning of the twentieth century about the congruence between the Protestant ethics of Calvinism (which are very different from Luther's) and the 'spirit of capitalism'.[44]

When talking about 'Protestant ethics' one should be clear about which denomination one means: Luther's or Calvin's. I believe that there are striking similarities between Marxist/socialist ethics and Lutheran ethics.

Karl Marx's philosophy has Protestant roots like utopian romantic philosophy and – above all – the German Idealism of Fichte and Hegel. Typical of both Marxism and Protestantism is their extreme moralistic rigour.

For atheistic people with a Protestant background like the people in the former GDR, Marxism or socialism could act as a compensation religion: Religious beliefs and promises of 'salvation' are recycled as a materialistic expectation of the 'classless society'.

Communism means 'salvation' from all evil on earth, from the 'sins' of 'egoism', 'greed for money', 'lack of consideration', 'hate', 'aggression', and so on. Socialism is a hard and painful path to the 'Promised Land' and the people had to follow the orders from above, from the one and only party, which could never err in showing the right way.

GDR nostalgia – a reaction of social alienation

GDR nostalgia is – like the nostalgias in the other post-communist countries – a standard phenomenon of the rapid and dramatic political, economic, social and cultural change in the period of transformation.

For more than 30 per cent of East Germans, the experience of reunification was a mixture of deliverance, confusion, disappointment and fear. Together with the deliverance from a dictatorship, and from an authoritarian regime, a familiar world of 'real existing socialism' with its real existing habits, myths, utopias and belief systems, was shattered.

In the turbulence of change, the sense of deliverance turned into alienation, because nothing from the past seemed to survive the transformation process.

From a psychological point of view, GDR nostalgia is a 'normal' act of self-defence against the widespread opinion in the West that unification should mean total absorption because there is nothing worth keeping from the former GDR. This reaction means that nobody can accept the argument that everything in the past is meaningless, and worthless. In this case, GDR nostalgia is also a survival method in a new social world, which preserves some small packets of personal identity.

GDR nostalgia is a political phenomenon, but there is no reason for political fears, because the majority of East Germans still favour reunification and nobody wants to go back, except a minority of die-hard communists, who exploit nostalgia to further their own interests.

Maybe it is impossible to prevent social phenomena such as GDR nostalgia in the period of transformation after the breakdown of a political system. But one thing can be learned from the German experience.

The more one respects people as human beings with their own history, life-experience and personal qualities, the less one has to face feelings of alienation when the missing community returns through the process of reunification.

Notes

1 Von Münch, I. (ed.), *Dokumente der Wiedervereinigung Deutschlands* (Stuttgart, 1991).
2 Brandt, W., *Was zusammengehört ... Reden zu Deutschland* (Bonn, 1990).
3 Sommer, T. (ed.), 'Vereint, doch nicht eins, Deutschland fünf Jahre nach der Wiedervereinigung', *Zeitpunkte, Sonderheft des Wochen-magazins 'Die Zeit'* (Hamburg, 1995).
4 The word 'Ostalgia' (from 'east' for East Germany and 'Nostalgia') was used for the first time by a journalist of the political magazine *Der Spiegel*.
5 Benz, W., Plum, G. and Röder, W., *Einheit der Nation, Diskussionen und Konzeptionen zur Deutschlandpolitik der großen Parteien seit 1945* (Stuttgart-Bad Cannstat, 1978).
6 Blanke, T. and Erd, R. (eds.), *DDR – Ein Staat vergent* (Frankfurt am Main, 1990); Weber, H., *Aufbau und Fall einer Diktatur. Kritische Beiträge zur Geschichte der DDR*; Andert, R. and Herzberg, W., *Der Sturz, Erich Honecker im Kreuzverhör* (Berlin, 1990).
7 Andert, and Herzberg, *op. cit.* (1990).
8 Wewer, G. (ed.), *DDR – Von der friedlichen Revolution zur deutscher Wiedervereinigung* (Leverkusen, 1990).
9 Schüddekopf, C., 'Wir sind das Volk', in Schüddekopf, C. (ed.) *Aufrufe und Texte einer Revolution* (Reinbek, 1990); Musiolek, B. and Wuttke, C. (eds.), *Parteien und politische Bewegungen im letzten Jahr der DDR* (Berlin, 1991).
10 Gibowski, W., 'Demokratischer Neubeginn in der DDR Dokumentation und Analyse der Wahl vom 18, März 1990', *Zeitschrift für Parlamentsfragen*, Vol. 21, No. 1 (1990).
11 Von Dohnahny, K., *Das deutsche Wagnis. Europas Schlüssel zum Frieden* (München, 1990).
12 Veen, H. J., 'Zwei Identitäten in Deutschland? Nationale Zugehörigkeit, politische Prioritäten und Wertorientierungen der West-und Ostdeutschen', in Jäger, W., Muhleisen, H. O. and Veen, H. J., *Republik und Dritte Welt. Festschrift für Dieter Oberndörfer* (München, 1994).
13 Maaz, H. J., 'Die psychologische Mauer, Stolpersteine auf dem langen Weg zur Deutschen Vereinigung', in *Der Tagesspiegel*, 29 September 1991. Lingemann, H. D. and Hofferbert, R., 'Germany: A new "wall in mind"', *Journal of Democracy*, No. 1 (1994).
14 Bohley, B. *et al.*, *40 Jahre DDR ... und die Bürfer melden sich zu Wort* (Berlin, 1989); Hauschild, J., 'Hier ändert sich manches schneller als man glaubt', *Süddeutsche Zeitung*, 10 January 1990.
15 Artzt, M. and Suhr, H., *Der Treuhandskandal. Wie Ostdeutschland geschlachtet wurde* (Frankfurt am Main, 1991).
16 Maaz, J., *Das gestürzte Volk, Die unglückliche Einheit* (Berlin, 1991).
17 Telschik, H., *329 Tage, Innenansichten der Eintigung* (Berlin, 1991).
18 Bender, P., *Unsere Erbschaft, Was war die DDR-Was bleibt von ihr?* (Hamburg, 1992).
19 Noe, K., *Mark für Markt, Mark für Macht, Die Republik hat sich übernommen* (Bonn, 1991).
20 Hardtwig, W. and Winkler, A. (eds.), *Deutsche Entfremdung, Zum Befinden in Ost und West* (München, 1994).

21 Hilmer, R. and Müller-Hilmer, R., 'Es wächst zusammen', *Die Zeit*, 20 October 1993.

22 Noelle-Neumann, E. and Köcher, R. (eds.), *Allensbacher Jahrbuch für Demoskopie 1984–1992* (München, 1993).

23 Kapferer, N., 'Disintegration or reintegration of Eastern Europe? The Future of Russia, Hungary and Poland Seen from the West', in the Korean-German Conference, *Pacific Rim Studies*, Vol. 7 (Taegu: Kyungpook National University, 1994).

24 Falkner, T., 'Von der SED zur PDS, Weitere Gedanken eines Beteiligten', *Deutschland Archiv*, Vol. 24, No. 1 (1991).

25 Moreau, P. and Lang, J., *Was will die PDS?* (Frankfurt am Main, 1994).

26 Programm der 'Partei des demokratischen Sozialismus' (PDS) 1992.

27 Statistisches Bundesamt, *Statistisches Jahrbuch 1991*.

28 Statistisches Bundesamt, *Statistisches Jahrbuch 1995*.

29 *Landeswahllei erbericht für Oktober 1995* (Berlin: Statistischen Landesamt, 1995).

30 Falter, J. W. and Klein, M., 'Die Wähler der PDS bei der Bundestagswahl 1994: Zwischen Ideologie, Neigung und Protest', *Aus Politik und Zeitgeschichte*, 23 December 1994, B 51–2.

31 Weidenfeld, W. (ed.), *Die Identität der Deutschen* (München, 1983).

32 Gaus, G., *Wo Deutschland liegt. Eine Ortsbestimmung* (Hamburg, 1983).

33 Claussen, B. (ed.), *Politische Sozialisation Jugendlicher in Ost und West* (Bonn, 1989); Büchner, P. and Kermann Krüger, H. (ed.), *Aufwachsen Hüben und Drüben, Deutsch-Deutsche Kindheit und Jugend vor und nach der Vereinigung* (Opladen, 1991).

34 Enquete-Kommission 'Aufarbeitung von Geschichte und Folgen der SED-Diktatur in Deutschland', in *Rolle und Bedeutung der Ideologie, Integrativer Faktoren und disziplinierender Prakitken in Staat und Gesellschaft der DDR*, Vol. 2 (Frankfurt am Main, 1995).

35 Kapferer, N., *Das Feindbild der marxistisch-leninistischen Philosophie der DDR 1945–1988* (Darmstadt, 1990); Kapferer, N. (ed.), *Innenansichten ostdeutscher Philosopher* (Darmstadt, 1994).

36 Noelle-Neumann, E., 'The German Revolution: The historic experiment of the division and unification of a nation reflected in survey Research findings', *International Journal of Public Opinion Research*, No. 3 (1991).

37 Westle, B., 'Unterstützung des politischen Systems des vereinten Deutschlands', in Mohler, P. and Bandilla, W. (eds.), *Einstellungen und Verhalten der Bundesbürger in Ost und West* (Opladen, 1992).

38 Voegelin, E., 'Religionsersatz, Die gnostischen Massenbewegungen unserer Zeit', *Wort und Wahrheit*, No. 15 (1960); Voegelin, R., *Die politischen Religionen* (München, 1993).

39 *Preußen. Versuch einer Bilanz*, 5 volumes (Hamburg, 1981).

40 Enquete-Kommission, 'Aufarbeitung von Geschichte und Folgen der SED-Diktatur in Deutschland', in *Rolle und Selbstverständnis der Kirchen in den verschiedenen Phasen der SED-Diktatur*, Vol. 4 (Frankfurt am Main, 1995).

41 Neubert, E., *Eine protestantische Revolution* (Osnabrück, 1990).

42 Tillich, P., *Die sozialistische Entscheidung* (Berlin, 1980).

43 Scholder, K., *Die Kirchen und das 'Dritte Reich'* (Berlin, 1988).

44 Weber, M., *Die protestantische Ethik, Eine Aufsatzsammlung.*

3

German (Re)Unification: Habermas and his Critics[1]

Howard Williams, Colin Wight and Catherine Bishop

Intellectual changes go hand-in-hand with political changes. Ideas shape the political landscape and intellectual developments are often themselves a reflection of political transformations. These two processes are particularly apparent in the context of German (re)unification: the early illusions of many East Germans of a capitalist Utopia and economic paradise in the West driving the process and the intellectual responses and controversies within the general (re)unification debate contributing to, and possibly shaping, the process. In this essay we shall analyse the response of a prominent German social and political theorist – Jürgen Habermas – to the process of (re)unification in Germany and address some of the criticisms of his interventions.

The link between contemporary Germany and Habermas's work is manifold. First, Germany is perhaps the most obvious practical testing-ground for a German social theorist. Second, Germany's unique (re)unification experience is an important test for democratization, and provides a microcosm of European and global democratization processes. Third, (re)unification has specifically questioned issues close to the heart of Habermas's writings: legitimacy, the constitution, public debate and social discourse, national and post-national identity and German patriotism, history and historiography. (Re)unification, then, poses a unique challenge to the political and constitutional consensus which characterized the former Federal Republic – a consensus now considerably weakened within a more heterogeneous society as a result of the (re)unification process and the transitional nature of German politics since 1989.

As a major philosopher and sociological theorist of the 1960s–90s, Habermas has continuously taken part in German political and public life, taking account of both normative debates and controversies concerning the historical situation of the German people. Typically seen by critics as high-minded and impractical, Habermas has, in fact, engaged himself over the last three decades with the main theoretical debates: the positivism debate of the 1960s (*Positivismusstreit*); Gadamer and the hermeneutics of social theory; Luhmann and systems theory; Lyotard and (post)modernity; the historians' debate about Germany's Nazi past (*Historikerstreit*), whilst, at the same time, retaining an interest and willingness to engage in current political debates. Now Habermas is confronted by German (re)unification, a setting of rapidly developing and changing events, and a potential challenge to his theory. Previous questions, social issues and legitimation difficulties all recur in the 1990s with renewed and acute urgency. How does Habermas's thinking stand up to this latest and perhaps most important test, and can it help us to understand the complexities of post-(re)unification German politics? It is our belief that in Habermas's essays on these themes we find a mirror of the political life processes that are at present determining the future, not only of Germany, but also of Europe itself.

Coming to terms with the past: (re)unification and the *Historikerstreit* revisited

The *Historikerstreit* was an intellectual and political dispute which preceded (re)unification and centred on notions of German identity and issues of historical responsibility, and as such, had many similarities with the present day post-(re)unification debate. Habermas's intervention in this debate criticized attempts by historians, such as Stürmer, Hillgruber and Nolte, to level German history in an attempt to pave the way for a return to a more conventional, nationalist identity. Habermas argued that these historians were attempting to accomplish what politicians could not achieve, namely to aid a positive exegesis of the past providing legitimation for politically conservative policies of the present. He argued, for example, that the attempt to 'relativize' Auschwitz and view it as part of the 'normal' history of a European state, rather than an aberration of a particular state, was being used for politically conservative purposes. His claims remain acutely pertinent in post-(re)unification Germany, particularly in the light of political 'manipulation' as demonstrated in the *Literaturstreit*[2] and the seeming relativization of all pre-1989 German history by some historians.

   Less than a decade ago, attempts to rewrite German history appeared to have failed. Yet today, in post-(re)unification Germany, historians such as Nolte, Weissmann and Schöllgen are again accorded widespread credence when they expound on the continuity of the Bismarckian tradition, or attempt to relativize the Nazis' mass crimes within the context of the modernizing achievements of German industry.[3] As Ian Kershaw has put it, 'Confining Hitler to history ... which had still not been possible at the time of the Historikerstreit, has however become more imaginable as a consequence of Unification'.[4] In his article of March 1990 – 'Der DM-Nationalismus' – Habermas picks up this theme and elaborates a position which reflects Adorno's postwar comments:

> With that dreadful break in its continuity [Auschwitz] the Germans have forfeited the possibility of constituting their political identity in any other way except on universalist principles of state citizenship, in light of which its national tradition can no longer remain unexamined, but can only be critically and self-critically appropriated.[5]

Auschwitz is a symbol of the need to learn the lessons of history: 'In order to learn from history, we must not push away or suppress unsolved problems.'[6] Auschwitz, for Habermas, remains a fixed point in German history, a point which should ensure there can be no return to a traditional form of German national identity, an event once and for all, which like the birth of Christ in Christianity, provides an eternal historical point of reference.

Essentially, the *Historikerstreit*, which began in the mid- to late 1980s, was concerned with the problem of overcoming the past (*Vergangenheitsbewältigung*) and issues of normalization (*Normalisierung*) in Germany, and these themes have re-emerged in a mutated form in German Historiography post-(re)unification. First, de-Stasification is linked with de-Nazification under the all-encompassing category of extinguishing totalitarianism; and second, perceptions of the former West German Republic (FRG) are radically altered; the 'new' historians now seeing it as 40 years of abnormality in German history. This results in a sense of relief in 'bidding farewell to the old Federal Republic'.[7] The historian Weissmann, for example, argues that 'Despite post-war "shifts to the West", the new Germany should resemble the former Germany and not the divided nations of the FRG and GDR.'[8] On this account, then, the former West German republic is seen to be a pathological interim, and 'normality' is that which preceded it.[9]

Habermas opposes both these historiographical developments. With regard to the former, he points out the differences between 1945 and 1989, arguing that comparisons between the *Stasi* and the Gestapo and between Erich Honecker's regime and Hitler's Third Reich are misconceived. In response to the latter, Habermas highlights the advantages and significant democratic progress of the former Federal Republic which should not now be abandoned, discredited or forgotten in (re)unification. In his 'Nachwort' (May 1993) to the interviews of 1991–2 with Michael Haller, Habermas regrets the displacements in time and space, which have transformed the global geopolitical landscape and which now are moving the Federal Republic from its peripheral position within that landscape, back towards its former central position within Europe.[10]

Habermas's approach to these issues was to advocate pluralism in historiography. Avoiding any one particular viewpoint and encouraging multiple interpretations, would, he argued, prevent any one conventional, national consciousness, ideology and identity from emerging. His position seems, to a certain extent, to be vindicated by many postwar historical writings, where the diversity of perspectives provided an opportunity at last to understand the German historical heritage in all its complexity. The result was a reflective, critical discussion that would otherwise be impossible in a situation where one-dimensional historiography was allied with state power.

In his article of April 1992 Habermas explicitly links (re)unification with the problem of dealing with the past.[11] This is an issue which is central to German history in the twentieth century and critical to the whole question of responsibility, identity and legitimacy in post-(re)unification Germany. Habermas attempts to clarify this particular debate by separating the process onto two different levels. These two levels are the objective and the subjective. In the objective process, reproaches and criticism should remain on a public and official political level, aimed at the systemic situation and not the issue of individual culpability. The subjective process involves a personal ethical-political working through of the past, which itself subdivides into two spheres: first, at a formal judicial level, and second, at an informal personal level of self-examination. For Habermas it is necessary for the German people to confront the unpleasant past: self-reflection (*Selbstreflexion*) is essential for self-understanding (*Selbstverständigung*). Through this process, self-delusion must be avoided, and the personal, subjective view should always be considered in its wider ethical-political context. Through this process it might be possible to ensure that individuals alone are not held to be solely accountable.

However, Habermas's calls for full public debate and a pluralist discourse would not automatically prevent the re-emergence of traditional forms of national identity, the rise of violence in the East, or West, nor silence views of extremist politicians or historians. A fuller public debate would entail increased participation from the extremes and increased participation by right-wing thinkers and historians, such as Franz Schönhuber, David Irving and Ernst Nolte, might not assist in promoting Habermas's goals. Open public debate can, at times, be a two-edged sword.

Normalization is another issue that has been a recurrent problem for Germany since 1945, and which seems to have become particularly acute again since (re)unification. Broadly put, Habermas sees two possibilities emerging. On the one hand, the (re)unified Germany can continue the move towards political civilization, begun since 1945, or the old 'special consciousness' may simply renew itself in another form.[12] He argues strongly in favour of the former and demonstrates his allegiance to the general ethos and political principles of the former West German Republic, in contrast to what he sees as the repressive delegitimizing tendencies of the former East German regime.[13] In his view the best that occurred within the pre-1989 polity should not be given up by the post-(re)unification state. For Habermas, the Westernization of the Federal Republic in the postwar period is essentially an emancipatory process: 'I have always found the increasing intellectual openness that became possible after 1945 towards Western traditions as liberating.'[14]

Despite its faults (argues Habermas), Western liberalism encourages public debate, allows the formation of independent social groups and safeguards the independence of the educational sphere. A continual vigilance is necessary to sustain these features of Western society, but clearly they would not emerge in a totalitarian society. The neo-conservatives, despite their clear distaste of the former East German regime, misunderstand this and are in danger of repeating the mistakes of the past through their calls for a return to 'normality'. A normality, that is, with Germany once again dominant in the middle of Europe.[15]

For Habermas, the very raising of the normalization question is itself a tool of political manipulation which obscures the 'real' (re)unification debate.[16] In his view the new-found concept of political 'normality', evident since (re)unification, is a tool for securing short-term political legitimacy. But Habermas is keen to point out the insecurities, distortions and delegitimization dangers that this might cause in the long term. He rejects this new form of historical consciousness,[17] exemplified in Maria Zens's account of the German revisionists' view of history: 'We Germans' should become normal again, and that means 'as we were before'.[18] For Habermas, this 'return to normality' entails a particular vision of Germany, which he would rather see confined to the wastelands of history.

Constitutional patriotism: a non-national national identity?

For the historian Ian Kershaw constitutional patriotism is 'the back-bone of anti-nationalist left-liberal intellectual positions of the 1960s and 1970s' and represents an 'intellectual "paradigm shift"'. Its development accompanied the political transformation of the early 1980s and signified the rejection of the 'critical history' approach to the German past.[19] As a leading thinker on the left in Germany, Habermas takes up this theme and gives 'constitutional patriotism' a new slant and a new place in the intellectual-political debate on German identity post-1989. Habermas uses his notion of 'constitutional patriotism' to support his vision of a future post-national, multicultural, constitutional state, as well as to try to preserve the political achievements of the Federal Republic against what he sees as a re-traditionalizing, regressive tendency emerging in post-(re)unification Germany.

The term 'constitutional patriotism' was first used by Dolf Sternberger, a liberal political theorist, who used it with regard to the political-social reality of the German polity, which he viewed as the 'living constitution'.[20] This 'living constitution' represents the process of conflict and consensus in diverse organizational and institutional forms, which Sternberger claimed were the determinants of civic-social politics in the modern constitutional state. Sternberger regarded this new form of patriotism as based on the Western model of the 'nation of state-citizens', and stressed the constitutional focus of German political culture and identity. Habermas reinterpreted Sternberger's concept within the realm of discourse theory and used it to support his vision of a post-national identity, ironically inverting Sternberger's wider hopes for a return to pre-national identity.

Sternberger's politico-cultural 'living constitution' was redefined according to Habermas's discourse theory, into a universally conceived, subjectless communicating community of constitutional interpreters. Habermas regards the idea – and indeed the actuality of constitutional patriotism – as one of the major developments in the former West German Republic, which he argues should be maintained after (re)unification. He opposes any trends that attempt to negate such postwar developments and which advocate a return to traditional forms of patriotism or ethnic nationalism. Habermas's objective of constitutional patriotism involves identification with the civic state-nation, or *Staatsbürgernation*,[21] rather than the historic, linguistic, cultural or inherited social system, described by Habermas as an ethical community of fate, or *ethnische Schicksalsgemeinschaft*.[22]

Habermas does not want to see the pre-(re)unification, post-national model of identity assigned to the past, and rejects any nationally based conventional form of patriotism. In his essay 'Eine Art Schadensabwicklung' (A Kind of Settlement of Damages), he addresses the connection between nationalism and identity, claiming that nationalism is, in essence, 'a specifically modern form of collective identity' with three characteristics.[23] First, at least in the case of European versions, it is opposed to older religious identities, appealing to all sectors of a society. Second, nationalism combines a common cultural heritage; language, literature, history, with a governmental form of state hegemony. Third, national consciousness demonstrates a tension between universalism and particularism (democracy and freedom versus national state interests). Habermas is principally concerned with twentieth-century examples of the third characteristic, that of the tension between the universal and the particular, as manifest in the extreme one-sided national identity of Nazi Germany.

Habermas's writings since (re)unification have tended to suggest that understanding this lack of balance between universalism and particularism may provide an opportunity for the Federal Republic, and now the new Germany, to realize a nationalism of universal values, which he translates into the concept of constitutional patriotism. Thus, the postwar era in Germany, represents, for Habermas, a decisive rejection of dominant accounts of national identity and anti-Western traditions that engendered National Socialism in favour of a new type of identity – constitutional patriotism – which he describes as 'the only patriotism that does not alienate us from the West'.

In his pre-unification writings Habermas provides various reasons for the decline of the particularism of German nationalism. These range from the diminishing importance of the military as a component of nationalist sentiment, the lessons of the invidious barbarism of the concentration camps, the dramatic progress in mass communications, and mass tourism which promotes cultural heterogeneity and international integration on a scientific and academic level. In Habermas's view, this goes far beyond the narrow security agenda of the anti-communist rationale of the NATO military alliance, affirming notions of political community, democracy and enlightenment, as well as security interests. Habermas describes this as 'the greatest intellectual achievement of our postwar period'. This use of the adjective 'intellectual' to describe an essentially political achievement signifies Habermas's continuing commitment to intellectual endeavour and its relationship to praxis and morality in his thought.

Yet, Habermas's aspiration for a republican Germany moving away from particularist tendencies towards universalist precepts seems increasingly unlikely in contemporary post-(re)unification Germany. The present rise of particularism, seen in the resurgence of nationalism since the fall of the Berlin Wall in November 1989, has once again unbalanced the components of national identity and, moreover, this phenomenon is not confined within the borders of post-(re)unification Germany. Habermas regrets this tendency and warns against the sacrifice of universalist values hard won in the Federal Republic, in favour of the particularlist values which survived, albeit in a perverted form, in the socialism of East Germany.

In his various articles, interviews and essays Habermas has argued in favour of accomplishing (re)unification on the basis of universalist principles, founding (re)unification not on Article 23, but on Article 146 of the West German Constitution. He contends that this would avoid the colonization of the East by the West only through the development of a new Constitution, written and approved by all in a nationwide discourse and referendum.

Habermas here touched on a very important point. The original West German Constitution of 1949 was originally conceived as a temporary measure in the peculiar situation of a divided Germany. It was seen as a means by which the zones occupied by the Western powers (USA, France and Britain) might establish their own political order. Under Article 23 other German states might join the Federal Republic as they saw fit. Ultimately, Article 146 envisaged the whole arrangement coming to an end through the free creation of a new constitution by all the German people. The irony of the (re)unification process under Helmut Kohl is that a temporary measure and the constitutional document relating to it, the Basic Law, was transformed into a 'permanent temporary measure'. In Habermas's eyes this crucially affects the legitimacy of the new and extended Federal Republic.

The battle for universalism in the (re)unification process, however, seems to have been lost before the public debate ever began. Whilst Chancellor Kohl's government seemed, on the one hand, to dictate the tempo and terms of (re)unification, it was also driven by the momentum of the situation and the general geopolitical situation. In May 1993, Habermas attacked the politically hamstrung discussion over a new Constitution, which was framed within vague government appeals to national sentiment, itself a consequence of their short-term 'Hand-in-den-Mund-Politik'. Habermas rejects these hand-to-mouth policies of the Kohl government as being far from legitimate or legitimising.[24] What is more, he also criticized the SPD opposition as unwilling and unable to provide alternatives or to amplify and encourage broad discussion of the issues, despite the opposition of SPD leader Oskar Lafontaine to rapid (re)unification.

Habermas sees the ideal of a 'post-nation-state political commonwealth' threatened by notions of the nation-state, nationality and ethnicity. These phenomena represent obstacles to his aim of three-tiered integration in a new setting: a multicultural society, a federal Germany and a united European community (which, for Habermas, would probably include Central and eventually Eastern Europe). To Habermas's regret Chancellor Kohl stressed a national morality based on ethnicity, rather than the French Republican notion of a nation based on citizenship. A national identity should, according to Habermas, be based on republican self-understanding and constitutional patriotism. These Kantian goals being a necessary constituent of a legitimate state system in his eyes.

Moreover, Habermas contends that the nation may well be historically obsolete, and in his 'Nachwort' of May 1993, states that 'Multiculturalism is not an option, it is a necessity.' Dismissing nations as artificial structures he argues, 'the nations which support nation-states are highly artificial constructions ... fictitious units ... the result of violent processes of homogenisation.'[25] He hereby rejects 'natural' evolutionary accounts of national identity based on factors such as, tribal-type blood ties, religious convictions, state organisation, and language:

> The post-traditional identity loses its substantial, its natural character, it exists only in the modus of the public, of the discursive dispute over the interpretation of a constitutional patriotism respectively concretised under our historical conditions.[26]

To reinforce his point Habermas refers to Paul Kennedy's recent work on the future of the modern state system and argues that 'even the classical nation-states will be unable to cope with the challenges of the 21st century'.[27] In some ways these claims by Habermas and Kennedy have been addressed by the German Green Party, which promotes the idea of a domestic world politics (*Weltinnenpolitik*), and envisages a world beyond nation-state boundaries, in which co-operation takes place in an international institutional setting.[28] Such ideas have also had their impact on the SPD, through Lafontaine (*Deutsche Wahrheiten*, 1992), who sees the fundamental question as being a matter of where to draw the line – if at all – between the national and the international levels.

Habermas views the acceptance of constitutional patriotism by the former Federal Republic as an important step towards, and even a vindication of, his notion of a post-national multicultural society. But, as noted above, this has been challenged since (re)unification by a resurgent nationalism, one form of which Habermas defines as economic nationalism. The question of constitutional patriotism versus economic nationalism raises questions concerning of the role of economics in a Federal Republican or all-German identity, a role that has been undergoing radical change since 1989.

Habermas's comments on economic nationalism, however, tend to be too dismissive. Timothy Garton-Ash's less factional approach, in contrast, situates economics within a complex of values tied up in the symbolism of the German currency. On this reading what the East Germans wanted was 'first the DM of course, but not just the DM, also the free press, the rule of law, local self-government, and federal democracy'.[29]

In short, for the East Germans, the acquisition of the new currency was inextricably linked with the end of totalitarianism and the rule of terror. The Deutschmark, then, was a symbol, although not only a symbol, of the ideals of the West. Habermas is well aware of this bundle of values, but he sees it as loaded with history and liable to explode at any moment. Christopher Türcke has criticized Habermas's discussion of economic nationalism as being naive, arguing that (re)unification *has* been a predominantly economic process.[30] In Türcke's Fukuyamar-esque eyes there is no alternative to the market economy, and thus there was no alternative to how reunification could proceed. The market economy penetrates every part of society, and everything is a question of 'demand' and consequently 'supply', even social philosophy. Habermas's proposed debate on the constitution is a non-debate for Türcke. Whatever the debate discusses and concludes, the constitution is *not* the deciding factor materially or psychologically, and is of little importance to the market economy. Moreover it *cannot* solve the problems of society, which in Türcke's eyes are simply the downside of capitalism: poverty and misery. There is little choice (i.e. little democracy) in a market economy. One cannot accept part of it and reject other parts, it comes as a whole:

> But now that they, i.e. the GDR citizens, can choose democratically, what sort of a choice do they really have? Can they choose to accept the advantages of a market economy whilst rejecting the disadvantages? That would be like trying to bring up a tiger as a vegetarian.[31]

The role of economic achievements, or pride in the 'The German Miracle', is one of four factors identified by Hans Mommsen as being constitutive of West German national consciousness.[32] For Habermas, this pride explains how perceptions of the economic situation now constitute an integral component of national identity, but – and in agreement with Mommsen's analysis – there are other factors in this sense of identity. There has been, for instance, a trend away from economic pride towards pride in the idea of democracy itself in the Federal Republic in the 1980s, and this is backed up Honolka's 1987 survey.[33] Habermas is disturbed by what he interprets as a destabilization strategy led by the CDU with its 'Deutschmark–nationalism'; the helter-skelter collapse of the East German regime brought about by the apparent generosity of Western aid prejudicing the prospects for successful (re)unification.

A German state cannot be founded only on 'pre-political' values of culture and national history, it must instead be a *Staatsbürgernation* and in this sense a 'non-nationalistic nation'. This is the main thrust of Habermas's work *Die nachholende Revolution* (The Rectifying Revolution) in which Habermas argues for the emergence of a German identity based on the model of constitutional patriotism. An identity that would preserve the normative strengths of what has already been achieved in a continuing dialogical development of a political culture of the state-citizen in a constitutional state. On this account, then, the constitution is never simply a product but always a product-in-process.

Habermas's idea of 'constitutional patriotism' has been claimed to be little more than an 'abstract patriotism' which is, in effect, little more than a form of national patriotism for the new Germany. For neo-conservative revisionist historians and right-wing thinkers only a national-based patriotism can guarantee the socio-cultural stability of the modern political-ethical polity. Moreover, they can envisage no alternative to this form of national identity and dismiss Habermas's proposal as either an abstract utopian ideal or simply a form of patriotism based on national identity, however he may describe it.

Karl-Heinz Weissmann, for example, highlights the deep roots of the nation and nation-state in European history and its stabilizing achievements since the Middle Ages.[34] He points out that despite much criticism, there is no recognizable alternative to the nation-state. Even those in favour of a federal Europe (*Bundesstaat*) work on the basis of nations and the nation-state as the fundamental components of that federal structure. Weissmann dismisses multicultural societies and citizens societies (*Staatsbürgernationen*) as artificially constructed forms, and sees the national form as the vital ingredient for international co-operation in the future in both Europe and the world.

Habermas's attack on the contemporary relevance of the nation does, however, seem difficult to sustain in the face of recent developments in world politics. It is difficult to imagine a member of the IRA, the various ethnic factions in Bosnia or the people of the Baltic Republics granting much credence to the view that ethnicity is outdated. Likewise, there is an inherent paradox in Habermas's treatment of 'economic nationalism' which he criticizes as playing too great a role in the CDU's approach to unification. He contrasts this to an ideal of a new constitutional settlement which would attract the consent of all the people. But these ideal constitutional arrangements would be found within one state and would of their nature exclude citizens of other states. This might well constitute a barrier between the national and international that Habermas expressly hopes to avoid. A well-ordered domestic state may well fuel the flames of international rivalry and Habermas does not properly acknowledge. This is a difficulty which made even Rousseau despair of the possibility of international harmony.

That is, that Habermas's universalist notions fail to take into account the unique historical, cultural and social position the Germans now find themselves in. However, much of this criticism is perhaps based on the wrongly held assumption that constitutional patriotism's *raison d'être* was as a substitute for the lack of a genuine national consciousness in the West German state. It is wrong to see

Habermas as advocating only one form of identity, that of constitutional patriotism, and his notion of a three-tiered form of post-(re)unification German society – a multicultural society, a federal Germany and a united European community – is clear evidence of this. Habermas recognizes that individual citizens will have many identities and a Habermasian reading of constitutional patriotism should not be seen as suggesting the complete supplanting of primordial forms of identity, but more correctly, as a reordering of priorities, in which national identity is displaced from its previously central position. Moreover, this reordering of priorities ensures that constitutional patriotism can never be viewed as simply a reformulated form of national identity. Our first social instincts need reshaping and re-educating if they are to allow us properly to come to terms with the modern world.

Legitimacy and political culture

The negative effects of rushing (re)unification can be already seen in the dangerous linking of economics and emotions in the elections of March 1990 by Chancellor Kohl's CDU government, and by the quasi-imperialist connotations inherent in the eastward expansion of the Deutschmark's territories. According to Habermas, from the very beginning Chancellor Kohl (from the Ten Point Declaration[35]) seemed to be pushing towards traditional nation-state unity and utilizing empty European and nationalist rhetoric. Kohl was accused by Ralf Dahrendorf of an unfortunate predilection for the word 'Vaterland', with all its Wagnerian echoes.[36] From Habermas's universalist point of view, Chancellor Kohl's policies and approach seemed short-sighted and unable to achieve legitimacy, being imposed rather than arising from full and open discussion. (From Habermas's standpoint, Chancellor Kohl wanted to use nationalist rhetoric and the new nationalist sentiments as a means of political legitimacy and in many ways his weak-willed short-term stance recalls Pascal's phrase: 'Being unable to make what is just strong, we have made what is strong just.')

Habermas places great importance on the potential significance of the Constitution in this new situation. He fears that the CDU's tactics have sidestepped the proper constitutional processes. He had hoped that the Constitution of a new unified Germany, in accordance with Article 146 of the Basic Law, would be discussed in depth and then put before the people so that a majority decision 'can be taken as a conscious act towards a republican self-understanding for future generations'.[37] In other words, this majority decision would form a legitimate republican basis on which to continue building towards constitutional patriotism and which would incorporate the opinions of the populace of East Germany. Indeed, constitutional legitimacy would depend on such inclusion. Such a process would follow in the direction of a multicultural, post-national community, and lead away from the present tendency to rewrite the past.

In all his articles and interviews Habermas points out instances where reflection and debate have indeed been curtailed in the (re)unification process. Suggesting that the themes of the debate have been imposed from above, leaving only abstention and apathy as possible options from below, Habermas points to missed opportunities for political discourse and thus legitimacy in the unification process, which have assisted the recent resurgent nationalist tendency. He thinks a hasty annexation of the GDR would not be compatible with a free decision of the entire German people. Despite the stability of the proven constitution of the former Federal Republic, Habermas feels opportunities to improve and legitimise the constitution, and of state (re)unification, may have been missed. This is evident, because the constitution of the present unified Germany has not been chosen democratically by a majority, either in 1945 or 1989. To Habermas, 1989 provided a chance for the majority to participate in constituting a nation of state-citizens, a chance that was clearly not present between 1945 and 1949. In December 1992, Habermas denounced the contract that Herr Schäuble concluded as being 'no substitute for the social contract which should have been publicly negotiated in a constitutional debate'.[38] It is not the 'social contract which the citizens of two states should have negotiated together, in order to clarify the conditions and position of their joint future'.[39]

Habermas has a clear constitutional focus in the unification debate and for him German unity is seen to be a constitutional task.[40] Furthermore, Habermas implies that the immaturity of the German nation that led to the Constitution being imported and imposed from outside Germany in 1945 has been preserved and maintained in the new arrangements. This lack of political maturity can now be seen in other spheres. Habermas attacks the handling of German involvement in UN peacekeeping operations, of which the Greens are also highly critical. He also questions the way in which issues of immigration and asylum were hastily drawn into public discussion.[41] As such, a 'real' asylum debate never took place, only a government-led debate on prejudices and side issues. There was no need to make this into a debate on the constitution,[42] at a time when so much was already at stake and the proliferation of issues only served to confuse the public. Every alteration to the Constitution undertaken without full and open public debate undermines that Constitution and the political culture associated with it (i.e. constitutional patriotism). Habermas repeatedly highlights the consequences of stifling discussion, and asks, 'Why [does] the debate over self-understanding never [get] going?'[43] Habermas accuses the government of continually moving the goal-posts, of exploiting moods and conditions for their purposes, and failing to provide any long-term policy or stability, thus warning of the delegitimizing effects upon politics and the constitution.[44]

He criticizes the precipitate (re)unification process which has brought about the lack of a willed and conscious connection to a common future within post-(re)unification Germany. Administrative pressures have engendered practices that have been given priority over social and political considerations of justice, with the short-term objective of winning an election in the old Federal Republic, foreclosing on the possibility of a sensible discussion of the all-German alternatives.[45] This negative prognosis of the long-term repercussions of short-term decisionism is evident in the sense of despair felt by many East German people, expressed in the writings of Schorlemmer: 'The way in which young people have now been treated will have long-term effects for their relation to our democratic state and its capability to react flexibly to their life interests. They experience the state once again as tutelage.'[46]

The present lack of Renan-style classical national solidarity in Germany and the turn away from constitutional patriotism must be considered in the context of political culture, specifically in relation to the differing cultural positions of East and West Germany. This has been demonstrated in the issue as what to do with the *Stasi* files. The *Stasi* debate has highlighted differences between recent West German cultural and social development and the cultural and social legacy of East Germans. Whereas the West has shown a certain eagerness to open up the *Stasi* files, the people of the East have, to a certain extent, been reluctant. Despite their keenness to open the *Stasi* files publicly, the West has not been without their prejudices and accusations, often directly contradicting their rational justification for openness. The East Germans are clearly confused in coming under such close scrutiny. On the one hand, they may have naively believed that the West would discuss the *Stasi* past sympathetically, avoiding any immediate indiscriminate recriminations. On the other hand, they may well have been reluctant to open up, at any level, the files at the Gauck-Behörde, and feel that they have been proved right by the ensuing débâcle in the media, in the judiciary and the public sphere in general.

Habermas's former pupil, Axel Honneth, commented on this retributive component of the (re)unification process, including the trial of East German intelligence and academia. He perceived a colonization process which had given birth to a system of unequal exchange of moral power, an echo perhaps of the regrettable mood of victim's justice (*Siegerjustiz*) at Nuremberg in 1945–6 now seen in a (re)unification context. He states: 'In my view, what would have been best was a very open public moral debate in the former GDR, a chance we have gambled away.'[47]

There is also a gulf in perceptions between East and West of the role of the Constitution in the formation of political culture. The West Germans have developed a consciousness of the success of the Federal Republic, which has become a symbol of democracy and stability. It is doubtful that East Germans share the same sentiments towards the Constitution. They certainly do not share the historical experience of its birth and subsequent development. This Constitution is not 'theirs', they are not familiar with it and it has now been 'imposed' on them externally by the West Germans. This is a point addressed by Michael Minkenberg's article 'The Wall after the Wall' in which Minkenberg supports Habermas's desire to see greater public involvement with a constitutional debate and a referendum.

Where there should be full political discourse, the East Germans have lost their voice, their spokesmen and their *own* public political sphere. The theologian, writer and politician Friedrich Schorlemmer gives voice to these issues, claiming 'We East Germans have progressively less to say. Hardly anyone speaks now.'[48] This is of particular concern when public figures in the East, such as politicians, writers and other intellectuals are often savagely discredited and silenced by the West German media, sometimes to the benefit of the CDU. The treatment of Gunter Grass, whose recent novels have been deeply critical of the reunification process, is a clear example of this quasi-censorship.

There are real issues and concerns if the process of (re)unification fails to take account of East German sensibilities. The customs and practices of the previous East German society are perhaps too deeply embedded to be removed legislatively from above through an imposition of Western laws and culture; the East cannot become a mirror image of the former West German Republic. The danger of not having adopted a more gradual approach might be that the problems of legitimacy might be excessively multiplied in the new situation. Habermas argues that the swift administrative takeover has indeed swept a great deal under the carpet.

There is no automatic means of transferring to the East the same levels of rights and democracy as the West has enjoyed. Notions of rights and democracy in the East were embedded in their existing, although differing practices. In Habermas's terms the rights corresponded to different cultural forms. These represent potential grounds for friction if not handled sympathetically through the opening up of discourse. Habermas's own theory of justice claims that the possibility of a resolution of conflicts within communities of a similar cultural type is real, and logically this must also apply to conflicts between communities, albeit ones with different cultural heritages. For Habermas, progress towards the determination of justice depends on a democratic consensus, and not upon an imposed solution. The processes of (re)unification must, of necessity, involve the people of the former East Germany. Following Habermas's model it seems that the German people have to strive not only for consensus, but also for a common, cross-cultural perception of justice.

Conclusion

Habermas pleads for rational discourse at a time when it is arguably most vital to the future of democracy, stability and legitimacy in Germany. He clearly wishes to preserve what was best in the former Federal Republic and the progress made towards constitutional patriotism, with his ultimate goal being a post-national, post-traditional, post-conventional, multicultural society. Yet, while the new Germany has inherited the institutions of the old Federal Republic and many of its constitutional assumptions, it does not, and cannot, operate within the same close, sometimes suffocating, consensus. The question remains as to whether Germany can attain a kind of normality, and as to which constitutional, (post-)national direction the unified state is now heading. Both questions are not only of deep concern to Germans, but also to the people of all other European states and beyond.

Habermas believes (re)unification carries the possibility of a regressive re-traditionalizing tendency, and it is his role – indeed, it is the specific role of the intellectual – to bring into the public arena just these concerns. This is not to say that Habermas believes that he, or any other intellectual, can lay claim to be in possession of absolute truth, but he does believe that the role of an intellectual within a society is to open up public debate through arguments and criticism. It is only in the light of this belief that his interventions into the debates about conservative revisionist accounts of history and (re)unification make sense. Indeed, Habermas's political writings display a remarkable consistency with his theoretical and philosophical works. Moral discourse is public discourse, and as such, changes the nature of political discourse. Habermas is, we argue, clearly attempting to map out an intellectual terrain where political conflicts are always located within the context of a set of definable norms, which are themselves open to critical scrutiny. As with Kant, he does not believe that the philosophers rule, but he does believe they should publicly be heard.

(Re)unification, then, is a moral issue, not simply a procedural process fraught with practical and material problems, and the specific form of a post-(re)unification German identity is a clear example of this. Moreover, whilst he displays little regret about the demise of the former GDR he is concerned about the fate of its former citizens, and this again highlights the nature of the relationship between the political and moral spheres. For Habermas, what the former East German people need are not simply matters of lifestyle and economic security, although these are clearly important, but also a sense of involvement which, he hopes, would lead to the legitimizing of emerging political institutions. It is this latter issue, that of the level, or lack, of involvement of the East German people, which has led to his critique of the tempo of the (re)unification process, which he sees as being largely dictated by the Federal government in Bonn, rather than as the result of a German-wide public debate. Without such a public debate the legitimacy of the process is brought into doubt and *a fortiori* the Constitution itself.

Yet, it is all very well to attack the breakneck process of German reunification, but there are strong arguments that the internal structural reform sought by many East German intellectuals, such as Christa Wolf, Günter Grass and Stefan Heym, will be impossible given the inherent inefficiences of East Germany and the corruption of the communist system as a whole. Habermas seems to have avoided drawing these conclusions and is perhaps open to the charge of having failed to rethink Marxism and socialism directly, or to examine fully what went wrong and what these 'socialist' regimes failed to get right. Likewise, although Habermas does seem to have neglected detailed analysis of the East German experience, we must respect this omission, for many lesser West Germans have commented upon, assumed and judged the former East Germany from a position of ignorance, unqualified by their 'West' Germanness. But it still remains that Habermas, like many others on the Left, has not confronted the challenge presented by contemporary reality to socialism itself.

Moreover, although Habermas's articles and interviews since 1989 recognize and discuss concrete issues (asylum, economics [the Deutschmark], the Gulf War, new historiography, identity, the *Stasi* past, Europe, and so on), this does not automatically imply that he deals with them practically and realistically. He often discusses idealized situations which are unfortunately distanced from contemporary reality. For example, he speaks of unbiased and full public debate, a new Constitution, the ideal speech situation, morality and legitimacy with little apparent regard for the role of force and circumstance in public life and the charge of idealism is a difficult one to avoid.

Habermas's comments on events since Chancellor Kohl's Ten-Point Plan for (re)unification do, however, show a wider alertness to the rapidly changing environment in East, West, and Central Europe. His complex and diverse theories may not provide all the answers, but they at least do not avoid all the questions. His post-(re)unification writings reflect the need for debate and the struggle for many of the voices in the new German society to be heard, as he continues to polemicize not already within a debate, but for a full debate in the first place.

Notes

1 The choice of the term reunification here, as opposed to the more common term unification, is intended to signify the ambiguities inherent within the debate. The question is precisely one of whether the process should be seen as a coming together of two separate entities or the reunifying of two entities which were previously one: a question of moving forward or moving back.

2 The sudden, unexpected collapse of the GDR and the publicity surrounding its numerous human rights violations have now exposed some East German authors to the charge of collaboration. In 1990 Christa Wolf, a respected author of international renown in the East and West, published a short story, 'Was bleibt' (What remains), written in 1979 and revised in October–November 1989. The story describes her fear and anger while being under surveillance by the secret police; it also discusses her inability to break decisively with her government. The piece unleashed a wide-

ranging debate regarding the culpability of writers who had remained in the GDR. The dispute reached new heights when allegations of *Stasi* involvement by Wolf in the late 1960s hit the headlines, beginning a media sensation that ran and ran. Wolf became a target for journalists and politicians, and her pro-GDR anti-unification speeches in 1989–90 had obviously won her few friends in the Western public sphere. Thus prominent East Germans have been publicly discredited on the one hand as writers, and on the other hand, as people who stood up to unification processes and supported internal structural reforms of East Germany as an independent or confederative state in itself, (i.e. not Chancellor Kohl's policy).

3   Of course, as Bauman has pointed out, this may be precisely the problem. see Z. Bauman *Modernity and the Holocaust* (Oxford: Polity, 1989)

4   Ian Kershaw, *Germany's Present, Germany's Past* (1992 Bithell Memorial Lecture, Institute of Germanic Studies, London).

5   J. Habermas, 'Der DM Nationalismus', *Die Zeit*, 30 March 1990.

6   J. Habermas, 'Aus der Geschichte lernen?', *Sinn und Form*, March/April 1994, p. 189: 'Um aus der Geschichte zu lernen, dürfen wir ungelöste Probleme nicht wegschieben und verdrängen; wir müssen uns für kritische Erfahrungen offenhalten'.

7   J. Habermas, 'Die zweite Lebenslüge der Bundesrepublik', *Die Zeit*, 11 December 1992.

8   K. Weissmann, *Rückruf in die Geschichte: Die deutsche Herausforderung: Alte Gefahren – neue Chancen* (Berlin, Ullstein, 1992) p. 192.

9   *Ibid.,* p. 192.

10 Nachwort in M. Haller, *Jürgen Habermas: Vergangenheit als Zukunft. Das alte Deutschland im neuen Europa?* (Munich: Piper, 1993) p. 204.

11 J. Habermas, 'Bemerkungen zu einer verworrenen Diskussion: Was bedeutet "Aufarbeitung der Vergangenheit" heute? Mit bekannter Gründlichkeit streiten sich Deutsche über den Umgang mit dem stalinistischen Erbe. Eine auf Stasi-Geschichten verkürzte DDR-Geschichte dient als Steinbruch für Würfbeschosse', *Die Zeit*, 3 April 1992.

12 M. Haller, *Jürgen Habermas: Vergangenheit als Zukunft*, p. 204.

13 M. Haller, *Jürgen Habermas: The Past as Future* (Oxford: Polity Press, 1994), pp. 33–34.

14 J. Habermas and Christa Wolf, 'Vom Gepäck deutscher Geschichte', 26 November 1991, p. 145, in C. Wolf, *Auf dem Weg nach Tabu* (Köln, Kiepenheuer und Witsch, 1994). Habermas states, 'Diese Westorientierung hat keine Verkrümmung der deutschen Seele bedeutet, sondern die Einübung in den aufrechten Gang' (This Western orientation did not in any way damage or undermine the German soul, but taught it how to be upright). Habermas mentions in particular the 'enlightened' influences, such as the American pragmatists Peirce and Dewey, as well as the law of reason (*Vernunftrecht*) from the seventeenth and eighteenth centuries right up to its present-day representatives Rawls and Dworkin, and including analytical philosophy, French positivism and the social-scientific thinking of French and American thinkers including Durkheim and Parsons. It encouraged open debate on previously suppressed or marginalized thinkers: Kant as an exponent of the Enlightenment, Hegel as a radical

interpreter and not opponent of the French Revolution, Marx and Western Marxism, Freud and the Freudian Left, the Vienna Circle, Wittgenstein, and so on.

15 J. Habermas, 'Das deutsche Sonderbewußtsein': 'Seitdem [1989] zelebrieren sie den "Abschied" von der alten Bundesrepublik und die "Rückkehr" zu den deutschen Kontinuitäten einer 'Vormacht in der Mitte Europas .... Das deutsche Sonderbewußtsein regeneriert sich von Stunde zu Stunde .... Der ganze intellektuelle Müll, den wir uns vom Halse geschafft haben, wird wiederaufarbeitet, und das mit dem avantgardistischen Gestus, für das Neue Deutschland die neuen Antworten parat zu haben'. Habermas talks of old recurring German regressions in his letter to Christa Wolf, 26 November 1991 (C. Wolf, *Auf dem Weg nach Tabu*, Köln, Kiepenheuer und Witsch, 1994, p. 141) that 'Etwas von den Mentalitäten der 30er und 40er Jahre scheint konserviert worden zu sein' (Something of the mentalities of the 30s and 40s seems to have been conserved). Habermas's concerns in this respect have been echoed by others. This idea of preserving the polity and approaches of the old Federal Republic was echoed by the Green Minister Joschka Fischer, who stated in *Der Spiegel* 1993, p. 20: 'It is very important to preserve the inheritance of the former FRG in the united Germany which kept a distinct distance from German jingoism and nationalism'. And at their autumn party conference held in October 1993 in Bonn, the Bündnis '90/Die Grünen declared that: 'The Greens want to maintain the democratic qualities which grew during the 40 years of the FRG and apply them in particular to foreign policy. They oppose the current redefinition of Germany by means of rejecting her postwar developments. This process of redefinition was already underway before 1989–90 through the Historians' debate, Bitburg, the Chancellor's visit to Ernst Jünger and so on. Such tendencies have meanwhile gained influence on government policies. This is seen as an attack on the republican achievements of the former West German state.'

16 J. Habermas, 'Die zweite Lebenslüge der Bundesrepublik: Wir sind wieder 'normal' geworden – Die Lebenslüge der Adenauer-Zeit war: Wir alle sind Demokraten', *Die Zeit*, December 1992.

17 G. Schöllgen, *Angst vor der Macht: Die Deutschen und ihre Aussenpolitik* (Berlin: Ullstein, 1993).

18 M. Zens, 'Vergangenheit verlegen: Wiederherstellung nationaler Große im Hause Ullstein', *Blätter für deutsche und internationale Politik*, 11/93 (November 1993), pp. 1364–75.

19 Ian Kershaw, *Germany's Present, Germany's Past* (1992 Bithell Memorial Lecture, Institute of Germanic Studies, London, 1992).

20 D. Sternberger, *Verfassungspatriotismus, Schriften X* (Frankfurt-Main: Insel, 1977).

21 P. Glotz, 'Der Ulrich der Deutschen: 'Staatsbürgernation oder ethnische Schicksalsgemeinschaft' – Jürgen Habermas über 'Die nachholende Revolution', *Die Zeit*, 18 May 1990.

22 P. Glotz, 'Der Ulrich der Deutschen'.

23 J. Habermas, *Eine Art Schadensabwicklung* (Frankfurt am Main: Suhrkamp Verlag, 1987)

24 M. Haller, *Jürgen Habermas: Vergangenheit als Zukunft*, pp. 196 and 201–2.

25   M. Haller, *Jürgen Habermas: Vergangenheit als Zukunft*, p. 214, 'Die Nationen, auf die sich Nationalstaaten zu stützen scheinen, sind höchst artifizielle Gebilde ... fiktive Einheiten ... das Ergebnis gewaltsamer Homogenisierungsprozesse'.

26   J. Habermas, 'Der DM-Nationalismus', *Die nachholende Revolution*, p. 220. 'Die posttraditionale Identität verliert ihren substantiellen, ihren unbefangenen Charakter; sie *besteht* nur im Modus des öffentlichen, des diskursiven Streites um die Interpretation eines unter unseren historischen Bedingungen jeweils konkretisierten Verfassungspatriotismus.'

27   P. Kennedy, *Preparing for the 21st Century* (New York: Random House, 1993) p. 131: 'global changes call into question the usefulness of the nation-state itself. The key autonomous actor in political and international affairs for the past few centuries appears not just to be losing its control and integrity, but to be the *wrong sort* of unit to handle the newer circumstances. For some problems, it is too large to operate effectively; for others, it is too small. In consequence, there are pressures for a 'relocation of authority' both upward and downward, creating structures that might respond better to today's and tomorrow's forces for change.'

28   *Die außerordentliche Bundesversammlung von Bündnis 90/Die Grünen* 9 October 1993, Bonn A12, p. 2: 'Unter Berücksichtigung der radikal geänderten weltpolitischen Lage, in der das Aufflammen nationalistischer und völkischer Tendenzen einhergeht mit einer immer stärker werdenden gegenseitigen Abhängigkeit der einzelnen Staaten, ist eine durchgreifende Neuorientierung der internationalen Politik notwendig....' A14, p. 2: 'Nationalismus muß als solcher gebrandmarkt werden.'

29   T. Garten-Ash, in R. Dahrendorf, *Reflections on the Revolution in Europe* (London: Chatto & Windus, 1990) p. 121.

30   C. Türcke, 'Selbstzufriedenheit der Demokratie. Was es kostet, intellektuelles Gewissen der Nation zu sein – eine Antwort an Jürgen Habermas', *Die Zeit*, 13 April 1990, p. 65.

31   Türcke, 'Selbstzufriedenheit der Demokratie', p. 65: 'Aber nun, wo sie [die DDR-Bürger] die demokratische Wahl haben, was haben sie das für eine Wahl? Die Vorteile der Marktwirtschaft zu übernehmen, die Nachteile draußenzuhalten? Das wäre, als wollte man einen Tiger zum Vegetarier erziehen.'

32   The four determining factors in West German national consciousness are: a redefined view of past and present history; anti-communism; orientation towards the West, especially USA; pride in German economic achievements. See H. Honolka, *Die Bundesrepublik auf der Suche nach ihre Identität* (München: C.H. Beck, 1987).

33   H. Honolka, *Die Bundesrepublik auf der Suche nach ihrer Identität* (Munich: C. H. Beck, 1987), quoted in J. Habermas, 'Der DM-Nationalismus'.

34   K.-H. Weissmann, 'Wiederkehr eines Totgesagten. Der Nationalstaat am Ende des 20 Jahrhunderts', *Aus Politik und Zeitgeschichte*, 2 April 1993, B/14/93, pp. 3–10.

35   Chancellor Kohl, Ten-Point Programme for Overcoming the Division of Germany and Europe presented to the Bundestag on 28 November 1989, translated in H. James and M. Stone (eds.), *When the Wall Came Down* (London: Routledge, 1992) pp. 33–41.

36   R. Dahrendorf, *Reflections on the Revolution in Europe: In a Letter Intended to Have Been Sent to a Gentleman in Warsaw* (London: Chatto and Windus,1990), p. 118.

37   J. Habermas, 'Der DM-Nationalismus', *Die nachholende Revolution*, p. 218: 'zu einem bewußt vollzogenen Akt [wird], um den sich das republikanische Selbstverständnis künftiger Generationen wird kristallisieren können'.

38   J. Habermas, 'Die zweite Lebenslüge'.

39   M. Haller, *Jürgen Habermas: Vergangenheit als Zukunft*, p. 196: 'Gesellschaftsvertrag, den die Bürger zweier Staaten miteinander hätten aushandeln müssen, um die Bedingungen zu kennen, unter denen man füreinander einstehen will'. Habermas talks of 'das ungleiche Zwillingspaar Schäuble/Krause' (the unequal twins) in his letter to Christa Wolf of 26 November 1991, C. Wolf, *Auf dem Wag nach Tabu*, p. 140 (Köln, Kiepenheuer und Witsch, 1994)

40   J. Habermas, 'Die andere Zerstörung der Vernunft', *Die Zeit*, 10 May 1991, p. 63. (It is perhaps worth considering the parallel between the title of this article by Habermas and the title of Lukács' work *'Die Zerstörung der Vernunft'*, written in 1955.)

41   M. Haller, *Jürgen Habermas: Vergangenheit als Zukunft*, p. 200.

42   J. Habermas, 'Die zweite Lebenslüge'.

43   M. Haller, *Jürgen Habermas: Vergangenheit als Zukunft*, p. 205.

44   M. Haller, *Jürgen Habermas: Vergangenheit als Zukunft*, p. 205.

45   M. Haller, *Jürgen Habermas: Vergangenheit als Zukunft*, pp. 197 and 194.

46   F. Schorlemmer, *Wahrheit in der Versöhnung. Nachschläge und Vorschläge eines Ostdeutschen* (Munich: Knaur, 1992) p. 246.

47   An interview by the editors with Axel Honneth in *Radical Philosophy*, 1993, p. 41.

48   F. Schorlemmer, *Wahrheit in der Versöhnung*, p. 244.

4
Truism and Taboo: the Rhetoric of the Berlin Republic

Maria Zens

Introduction

This chapter aims to explain elements of Germany's post-unification 'historical culture'. I will refer to the turbulent reception of Daniel Goldhagen's *Hitler's Willing Executioners* in order to highlight problems of moral, political and historiographic discussion in Germany, certain shifts in the interpretation of National Socialism as conveyed by a phalanx of right-wing historians and corresponding shifts in political norms as set out in Wolfgang Schäuble's *Und der Zukunft zugewandt*,[1] which can be seen to represent the ideological basis of the national wing of the CDU. These elements are linked by the enhanced importance of 'nation' as an integrative political concept.

I

It is very rare for an historiographic study to become a best-seller whose sales exceed those of popular fiction and books on how to pay less tax alike. Daniel Jonah Goldhagen's *Hitler's Willing Executioners*[2] managed to do just that. In this book – based on his doctoral thesis – Goldhagen argues that it was a deep-seated and widely accepted anti-Semitism that made ordinary Germans (and not primarily the notorious SS members) brutalize and murder Jews. Goldhagen presents as his basic thesis that, in the eyes of these perpetrators of the genocide, what they did was not only justified, it was just. Thus they were the willing and not coerced executioners of Nazi politics. Goldhagen's argument centres on what he persuasively describes as 'eliminatory anti-Semitism' as the cultural basis of the Holocaust. In reconstructing the omnipresence of pre-existing anti-Semitic prejudice he postulates that the way had already been paved to Auschwitz. Demonstrating that the murderers came from the middle of German society – demo-graphically, socially, ideologically speaking – he concludes that they were representative also in their actions. In dwelling on the represen-tativeness of 'eliminatory anti-Semitism', Goldhagen sharpens Christopher Browning's notion of the 'ordinary man' to that of 'ordi-nary Germans' and locates the genocidal impulse in German political culture. He explicitly wants to give an ideological interpretation of the Holocaust, arguing 'that consciousness determined being'.[3] What obviously follows from this is a renewed emphasis on the aspect of personal responsibility, methodologically speaking a concentration on voluntarism and the individual actor rather than political structures and the machinery of the state. In the following I do not intend to discuss the validity of Goldhagen's thesis or reconstruct the historio-graphic debate; in the context of Germany's post-unification historical culture it is the structure of the book's reception, how various sections of the public reacted, which is of interest.

In association with the book's publication in Germany, Goldhagen took part in a number of panel discussions, where he confronted his critics. He received a lot of attention and remarkable support from the public for forcefully reopening a moral debate about the Holocaust and the question of the individual and collective guilt of those ordi-nary Germans without whom the Nazis could not have sustained their regime.

The critical reception of Goldhagen's book was wide-ranging: from right-wing howls of protest against the promoter of German self-hatred to scholarly critiques of his methodology and hypothesis, which among others came from some of the most eminent scholars of advanced social history in Germany, who certainly cannot be accused of having radically changed the position they took in the 1980s *Historikerstreit*.[4] On the other hand, Goldhagen has received wide acclaim from the public; thousands attended his lectures, and the more he was criticized, the more support he got, especially from the generation of young to middle-aged Germans. The arguments for and against the American's moral judgement thus highlight important aspects of Germany's historical culture, the interwovenness of moral-ity and politics, and the fragile structure of the historico-political field in post-unification Germany.

The book's highly controversial reception made clear not only how closely connected aspects of morals, politics and history in Germany are, but also how deeply any discussion of the Holocaust affects today's politics. Regardless of all programmatic efforts to consider the

Nazi past as a closed book, the subject remains a minefield.

A typology of reactions to Goldhagen's book would cover the following: (1) historiographic criticism, which ignores the political dimension of the book; (2) political criticism, which ignores the historiographic dimension of the book; (3) political criticism, which takes Goldhagen's historiographical flaws as an excuse to dispose of his moral critique as well; (4) moral acclaim, which declares the historiographical impact to be of secondary importance; (5) political acclaim which applauds the book's power to reopen the discussion and declares its actual content to be of secondary importance; (6) the view which argues that by describing the ugly German of the Nazi past Goldhagen brings out the good German of today by attracting thousands of people to his lectures thereby serving as a focus for all those who have felt uncomfortable with 'normalization' gaining ground; (7) moral criticism along the lines of the *Schlußstrich* argument, which argues that the burden of the past should eventually be lifted; (8) popular acclaim for Goldhagen's ability to put history into simple words and so render it accessible; finally (9) some critics – in simple terms but nevertheless with good reasons – argue that Goldhagen's book went straight to the heart of the problem of German national identity, which had been opened up by the 1989/90 transformation. A commentator in the *Süddeutsche Zeitung* writes: '[Germany] is a country searching for its national identity. Goldhagen's book comes at the right moment. The reactions and non-reactions ... show how necessary this kind of excavation is.'[5]

Many compared the discussion to the *Historikerstreit*, in both positive and negative terms, either to highlight the political dimension or to deny the latter's weight. But one essential difference compared to the debate that took place a decade ago is immediate: almost right from the start Goldhagen's book received overwhelming public attention, whereas the 1980s *Historikerstreit* – although published in the newspapers and not in scholarly journals – remained very much a specialists' controversy. Although both discussions seem to be primarily significant as an historico-political positioning in the process of identity-building, their appeal has been quite different. The obvious reasons for this are that they differ with regard to their primary formulation of the question. Whereas the historians' debate tackled the historico-political controversy, by making the debate more accessible, Goldhagen – and his opponents follow him here – focuses on the question of individual moral responsibility and the absence of a sense of guilt at the individual level. This perspective makes it easier to reach the public because it relies on a publicly relevant category and relates to every individual's self-awareness.

The criticisms levelled against the book when it first appeared helped not least in strengthening the support Goldhagen received from his audience. Thus, political criticism from the Right as well as methodological criticism from the Centre of academia struck many as being inappropriate: the first as morally wrong, the second as academically too scholastic.

The public appeal of Goldhagen's book is sometimes equated with the response to movies or TV productions on the Holocaust. Obviously such a comparison is equivocal, it probably will not please Goldhagen as a scholar, and surely most critics meant this in a derogatory sense. But others regard it as a strength: Josef Joffe, for example, editor of the *Süddeutsche Zeitung*, who is 'semi-critical' (which also means 'semi-supportive') of the book sums up:

> Neither the theorizing Goldhagen nor the academia who has tilled the ground for decades will like this: The book is in line with Holocaust and *Schindler's List*. Only when the horror gets a name and a face, does it capture people's minds in a way myriads of footnotes will not.[6]

Joffe rightly points to a tension which may have disturbed some of the historians who have distanced themselves from Goldhagen. The tension between the rightly or wrongly alleged lack of academic rigour and the overwhelming public impact poses a problem for critical history which, in the tradition of the Enlightenment, turns its back on social responsibility. But beyond the historiographic details at stake there remains the performative achievement. Goldhagen set something in motion, a public process, which some believe they could have initiated better – and probably believe they should have.

Some social historians have criticized Goldhagen's cultural approach and regard his adaptation of Clifford George's concept of 'thick description' to be inappropriate to the subject matter and prefer more nuanced methods of historical reconstruction. They criticize Goldhagen's disregard for political institutions and structures. And there are further criticisms: Goldhagen does not present any new material or new arguments, and in analysing his primary data he falls short of the meticulous study by Christopher Browning,[7] and argues monocausally in postulating a direct line from the ideology of anti-Semitism to Auschwitz.

Hannes Heer, for instance, a historian at the Hamburger Institut für Sozialforschung, who was responsible for a strongly criticized touring exhibition on the crimes of the Wehrmacht, is profoundly uneasy with Goldhagen's presentation of anti-Semitism, which he regards as one-dimensional. Heer compares it to a 'comic strip' in which you cannot find anything of the explosive historical situation or the cultural roots of anti-Semitism that made the genocide possible.[8] Equally critical is another commentator who argues that the way Goldhagen sets out his argument undermines his case and those who have laboured to uncover more facts and who stress remembrance as against neglect of the past:

> Criticism of Goldhagen is mainly found among those social groups that have always resisted the suppression of the past. With his simplification Goldhagen has done them a disservice.[9]

One of the most eminent social historians, Hans-Ulrich Wehler, is equally harsh in his verdict. He regards the political function to be a deficiency and supervening on scholarly rigour. He also sees a correspondence between ignorance of research findings and the acclaim for Goldhagen's book:

> The Goldhagen controversy has obviously long taken a political dimension. Some quarters of the American public are exploiting a quasi-academic justification to voice profound resentment and prejudice. The less the complex results of research are known the more enthusiastic the applause.[10]

As a result two phenomena coincide in the reception of the book. First, a scholarly/academic critique, and second, popular acclaim for a book which does not exonerate the Germans but rather discloses the guilt of many 'ordinary' individual people who became Hitler's helpers. But now it is the duty of every school of thought to present its findings and make them accessible to the public. And this surely represents one of the inadequacies in some of Goldhagen's critics. With his historiographic best-seller Goldhagen has accomplished something which in recent years could not have been achieved by meticulous and collaborative research – with the exception of the Wehrmacht exhibition – namely, making the Holocaust a public issue by means of a popular and entertaining portrayal. Even if Goldhagen might not be able to give a satisfactory answer to the question 'How could this have happened?', he undoubtedly manages to move the question of responsibility of all Germans straight to the heart of the discussion. As one commentator put it: 'The so-called Goldhagen debate may be an historical debate as well. Above all, it is a debate on morals and responsibility.'[11]

The acclaim Goldhagen received might be one reason why some of his early critics, if they did not revise their assessment, modified it. Hans Mommsen for instance, one of the best known German historians and mentor of German research on National Socialism, who had sharply criticized Goldhagen's study, at least acknowledges that the American has posed central questions in a new way:

> The attention that Daniel Goldhagen's prize-winning book on 'Hitler's Willing Executioners' receives [not only] in the United States but also in other Western countries, shows that the emotional effects of the German genocide of the Jews after decades still remain. In whatever sense this book is evaluated – which in many respects falls short of the achieved results of research – it forces us once again to confront the question why in a developed and highly civilised country like ours the relapse into barbarism, into the systematic liquidation of millions of people, above all Jews, could happen without any serious attempts to stop this crime.[12]

Nevertheless Mommsen is critical of what he regards as uncritical acclaim of Goldhagen's moral judgement; in his view an ahistoric acclaim is facile and shows 'a new German irrationalism – a twisted national feeling which is articulated through confessions of guilt'.[13]

Goldhagen has publicly put on the agenda what for long had been a taboo: that the distinction between 'criminal Nazis' and 'normal Germans' is mistaken[14] – an insight that was also conveyed by the previously mentioned exhibition on the Wehrmacht and is precisely why both the exhibition and the book caused such an uproar.

Of course, Goldhagen has become the moral target of the Right. A current argument is that his book simply promotes German self-hatred and a fatal preoccupation with a long gone past, but some go much further than this. One commentator in the right-wing journal *Criticon* simply shifts responsibility for the Holocaust. In his view, the Germans did not know about the Holocaust, whereas the Western democracies should have known and reacted. Rather than confronting the question of German guilt he shifts responsibility for it:

Maybe Goldhagen's main problem is that he asks the wrong questions. More important would be how far and how the secrecy in Germany worked. And if the foreign countries knew more about the Holocaust, why didn't they do anything to save the Jews? Goldhagen does not ask these questions. He prefers to hold on to his more simple questions and simplistic answers.[15]

So what can we learn from reactions to Goldhagen's book? The pre-occupation with the Nazi era can obviously focus on questions of morals, politics, historiography, and in so doing tends to have different audiences: children who challenge their fathers, a community of citizens who define their ethical roots, an audience of expert historians. But it can also be seen that these spheres intermingle. This is all the more true since the German preoccupation with the Nazi era is always reflected in the preoccupation with our own history and deeply affects the way we discuss and carry out politics today. Thus, in addition to the explanatory and moral interest we have in what our grandparents did, the ethical discussion centring on the Nazi regime in general and the Holocaust in particular not only shapes the moral self-image of Germany but also serves as a means for civil self-understanding about how democratic politics ought to be conducted, how a community shapes and controls its political institutions, in other words: as a focal point for a self-understanding within a civil society, at best for the sustained development of civic virtues.

Jürgen Habermas put forward a similar argument when he remonstrated against the public use of history 'with a view to the ethical and political self-understanding amongst citizens'.[16] As opposed to the advocates of a politics of history which can only find political recognition in the identification of the past, and for that reason tend to embellish it and make it appear in a better light than it actually was, the critical distance from one's own position – hermeneutic and moral – seems to be the one that promises insight. A critical distance from one's own national history might contribute to a clearer view and develop one's own position, one that is strong enough to dissociate oneself from the errors of the past (also and especially when it is their own). That has nothing to do with self-hatred; it is not even a question of affection (love or hate for one's own country), but rather one of a rational process (recognition of the past and of the political present).

In this sense the popular interest and acclaim Goldhagen received from the German public can only be welcomed. Many ordinary Germans today have demonstrated that they are not willing to draw a line under the political heritage of the Nazi past – and it appears too simplistic to root their interest in a kind of national masochism.

In the Federal Republic of the 1990s coming to terms with the Nazi past is equally a topic which arouses emotional and political turmoil. It can be clearly recognized that the subject cannot be considered closed, that coming to terms with the Nazi dictatorship still takes us into an emotional and political minefield, and that the subject matter still demands that the individual takes a stand. In the future, the moral, ethical and current political question will keep on being inextricably interwoven with research on the Holocaust and National Socialism. As Jürgen Habermas stressed during a prize-giving ceremony for Goldhagen, that does not mean that the researcher of integrity should not (in his research) be led by historico-political ambitions.[17]

The discussion Goldhagen aroused also shows that the subject of political history is affected by competing trends: the discussion about the moral guilt of yesterday's Germans and the political identity of today's German civil society is just one part of it. This part, however, undoubtedly marks the achievement of the federal political culture which ranks among the community of Western civilizations.

II

The historico-political discourse offers its services to political self-understanding in various ways: the boost that the concept of the nation experienced in the Federal Republic after 1989 is supported by attempts at historico-political reorientation. The aim of this reorientation is less to deal with history in a critical and self-reflexive way, than to found a positive tradition where the Federal Republic can continue as a 'self-confident nation'.[18] A whole host of conservative journalists and historians, who – in the clash over the political power of interpretation – keep an eye on diverse publishing places, and are engaged in the search for the lost German nation.

In the political and historiographic guidelines which form the basis of their publications, a catalogue of distortions can be exposed: from a reflexive notion of society to an emphatic notion of the state, from the responsible citizen to the self-contained individual, from the social contract of society to a morally founded community of destiny. The point of reference is the nation: all processes that take their course semi-autonomously in a sophisticated society – including the economy – are being subsumed under this legitimizing superstructure.

These ideas are regularly tied to an understanding of history which is linked to traditional concepts and assigns to the historian the social role of political adviser. Key ideas which are supposed to become politically effective as symbols of identity are extrapolated from the interpretation of national history.

I will outline some of the basic topics raised by a group of national-conservative historians, in particular the attempts to redefine the interpretation of National Socialism and the quest for a new, positive identity for a German nation-state over the last few years. Their writings are much more important for a public opinion as conveyed in conservative papers than they are for academia, but it is precisely their appearance in mass circulation papers, on political platforms or on television which renders them interesting. At first sight it could be argued that these journalists and historians are trying to convey a new German identity or a new German ideology, but in fact they are resurrecting very traditional concepts.

The current notion of the nation is to be given a new profile. The search for a positive historical tradition of the nation-state is equally a part of it, as is the re-evaluation of the so-called 'old Federal Republic' or 'Bonn Republic' and its political principles. Criticism of the *Westbindung*[19] is at the heart of this devaluation of the federal republican political orientation. In addition, it is also a question of the rhetorical rather than political construction of a positive opposite pole. The cleansing of the notion of the 'Right'[20] is liberated from its use in the concept of a New (national) Right by, for example, proving that Hitler was not 'right-wing'.

In this context Rainer Zitelmann's name is prominently noted because he has not only made his name with his own and joint work especially on the subject of National Socialism and modernity, but also as an author and editor of the publishing house Ullstein/Propyläen, where he applied himself to drawing up a publishing programme with the object of 'streamlining the German past'. A group of mostly young authors have come together, adopting in monographs and anthologies different aspects of the historical revisionist project. Ernst Nolte, who instigated the *Historikerstreit* in the 1980s, serves here as a model for a whole range of up-and-coming authors. Some of the authors are academically indebted to Nolte and refer explicitly to his textual and methodological heritage. In addition, the idea of historicization integrates a wide spectrum of national-liberal to national-conservative journalism beyond its direct followers. The group of neo-right-wing academics and journalists is not heterogeneous. In the recurrence of certain buzzwords (e.g.

'historicization'), however, a common motive can be observed.[21] Such buzzwords seem indispensable if one takes the ambition to form a 'new school of thought' seriously.[22] In fact, intimate structures appear: viz.: the numerous affiliations in editing, co-operating, co-authoring and reviewing. In his book *Streitpunkte*[23] Nolte also takes up the theories of this younger generation.

Many of the viewpoints presented – historicization, a positive view of history, the foundation of tradition through national history etc. – sound so familiar. They take positions which caught the attention of the broader public during the *Historikerstreit*. During that debate, however, harsh criticism from academics and public discontent arose over concepts such as 'normality' and 'normalization', which today seem to be political and popular-historiographic benchmarks of reorientation. Politics can hereby count on elements of uncertainty which reunification has produced in almost every political sphere and which also enabled the appearance of a politically vapid but semantically splendid normality to seem welcome. Hereby a revisionist rewriting of history does not only profit from the perceived need for a sense of foundation which was brought about by the trend of the times, but also from a vacuum. This vacuum is brought forward by the frequent inability of established social history, the differentiated knowledge which was brought together by structural and developmental requirements of the Nazi regime over the last decade. Its scrupulous methodology and academic debates failed to touch a non-academic audience. Yards of shelves of research literature on National Socialism still face a certain collective memory which is largely determined by stereotypes. It is uncontested that collective images of the past are always and have to be a synthesis. However, there is a problem of communication/mediation. The didactic deficit of academia often leaves it at the mercy of effective media coverage, whatever its tendency.

The historian's task

The academization of historiography which was accelerated during the 1960s and 1970s has also brought with it a new role for the historian. At the same time the discipline's self-image is hardly identical with the public image which is most likely located between the idea of a free-floating intellectual, a scrupulous academic, a narrator of past times and a helpful political adviser. The new young right-winger tends towards the latter.

It is revealing to cast a glance at the role which the discipline itself assigns to the historian. In the dispute with Gesine Schwan, Karlheinz Weißmann, one of the co-editors of *Westbindung* and defender of the political 'recall into history',[24] makes it clear where he would like to locate the historian's task. Weißmann accuses Schwan, who earlier had critically analysed one of Rainer Zitelmann's essays, thus: 'She wants to prevent the Germans from regaining a healthy self-confidence.'[25] One can thus conclude without difficulty what Weissmann considers his task and that of his supporters: to help the Germans attain exactly that sort of self-confident identity.

Alongside the almost ritual reference to the supposed fact that so far historians have not been working objectively, their own efforts have been directed at creating a store of knowledge which brings out the positive side of German history. This has obviously nothing to do with the emphasis on objectivity and lack of prejudice. Such a value-ridden historiographic programme falls back on a notion which grants history a leading political role and the historian the appropriate power of interpretation. We find the strange mixture of a strong claim for 'objectivity', a political quest for a positive national history and an equally strong claim against established historiography. The requirement of objectivity is trivial, which means that the historian should acknowledge the facts he finds, should not falsify them and when developing his hypothesis should include them appropriately, should justify and disclose how he chose his data both methodologically and textually, and therefore submit them to the scrutiny of others. This is the recognized standard and also the custom in the entire scientific community and as a shared value it does not need special emphasis. Here the word objectivity seems to fall back on a nineteenth-century academic understanding of the word. However absurd the notion of direct access to historical facts might seem if taken literally, it has nevertheless to be noted that their thrust is in the end not methodological but historico-political. The aim is to induce an historiographic paradigm shift – that this might be successful in the academic world is more than questionable – even if Weißmann believes that the days of the '*ancien régime*' in history are numbered.[26] However, the attractiveness of certain revisionist patterns for conservative leading article writers cannot be ignored.

Historicization

One of the keywords that the circle around the right-wing historian Nolte adopted is *historicization*. It was at the heart of an academic debate that was initiated by Martin Broszat[27] and in which well-known personalities such as Saul Friedlander, Dan Diner and Otto Dov Kulka participated. Initially the question was the extent to which the extraordinary nature and moral repulsiveness of the Nazi crimes also prevent the historian from approaching this period academically without being caught up in a – didactically justified – moral gesture. Broszat's postulate of historicization therefore hardly supported a longitudinal transcendence of National Socialism; his intention was rather to prevent the disappearance of the historical facts from memory. As Kershaw sums up:

> The preservation of a critical distance in the case of National Socialism is, in fact, far from being dispensable, a crucial component of the new social history of the Third Reich. But it is precisely the virtue of this new social history located in description and structured analysis of 'everyday' experience that it breaks down the unreflected distance which has traditionally been provided by abstraction such as 'totalitarian rule' and copels a deeper comprehension through greater awareness of the complexity of social reality.[28]

The neo-Right term historicization has little to do with Broszat's concept. Here it is rather a matter of levelling National Socialism into a traditionally suitable historical continuum. Thus the uniqueness of the crimes is to the forefront, not the form of the historical approach. In this sense we should distinguish fundamentally between the assessment of the Nazi era as a 'normal' phase of German history and the application of 'normal' historical methods, and ways of perception to that time. After all, the latter does not need to bring about the former. The singularity of the genocide does not prevent us trying to understand the conditions in which it developed by means of historical tools – also, and especially, if an otherwise incomprehensible element defeats the explanatory power of historical reconstruction.

Modernization

A variation of historicization is to approach National Socialism from a 'modernization' perspective. In this context especially Zitelmann's work on Hitler and an anthology co-edited with Michael Prinz should be mentioned.[29] By making an effort to free the socio-historical notion of modernization of its normative implications, it is being made applicable for labelling societal change under the Nazi rule.

The linking up of the notion of modernization with Nazi rule is therefore also part of the objectification sketched above. A belief in one's own impartial and unprejudiced viewpoint allows us to see the good in the bad and to see it as necessary to academic objectivity. In the end though it is precisely a question of value judgement in so far as objectivity is understood as adding the good to the bad. Thus it is symptomatic, in which terms Rainer Zitelmann attacks previous research, that it did not adequately underline the *positive* sides of National Socialism: 'It is not accidental that those elements which had been perceived as the 'positive' sides of National Socialism by apparently a large part of the population, were only 'discovered' late by researchers. This is especially the case for the Nazi social policies which had long been the unwanted child of contemporary historical research.'[30] The upgrading of National Socialism by attributing modernity to it works particularly well when the question is not about proving socio-structural modernization processes, because this could be refuted, but about modernity appearing merely as a topical reference, as in Weißmann's work: 'The NSDAP was the first German party to carry out cross-class integration. Modernity was the key to their success and such modernity formed equally a substantial momentum of Nazi social politics after Hitler's *Machtergreifung*.'[31] Similar to the notion of historicization, the concept of modernity is enough to strengthen a certain perspective. The intention is not to describe structures of modernity in particular spheres of society (which is, by the way, something National Socialism research has rarely neglected), but rather to consider the whole era – by which it would not only be upgraded but also 'domesticated' in a European historical continuum.

Ian Kershaw emphasized in his critique of the modernity thesis, that it was the duty of historical research to differentiate the accidental from the essential, and that the modernity debate had deviated from this path.[32] In other words, Auschwitz as a point of reference in the debate about National Socialism highlights the essential: the question whether Hitler saw himself as a socio-political revolutionary may be an interesting facet of the individual psychology of the Führer; it will not, however, overthrow the research into the structures of Nazi politics. For all that, considering everyday life under National Socialism is certainly not unimportant, not in the sense of playing it down, but rather as a reference to the fact that the absolute failure of civilizing norms took place against a backdrop of socio-cultural continuity.

The invention of tradition

The objective of constructing a national history requires some amendments. What should a 'straightened out' German history look like?
The breach of civilization that the Nazi dictatorship represents can
only be poorly patched up by the apologists of a German national
history; though this seems to be their aim. Two types of arguments
come to light here: that of diverting negative traditions and that of
emphasizing 'positive' or rather 'neutral' traditions. The elaborate
attempts to detach Germany's previous national history from its
perhaps not necessary but still factual results, leads to a kind of confes-
sion: that there are continuous negative trends of development. These
have often been consolidated under the term *German Sonderweg*[33]
which is now to be faded out of the picture in order not to mark
National Socialism as a catastrophe in the normal nation-state, or at
least not as an endogenous phenomenon. This view ignores that,
beyond morals, history can teach a democratic lesson. This point is
not settled by repetitively resisting a recognition of moral guilt. Even
those who do not feel guilty (and who, of the younger German generation, could have anything like an authentic feeling of guilt?) are
nevertheless in a position to draw democratic and rational lessons
from what happened. The result should generally not be an emphatic
notion of the state, the nation and political leadership, but the idea of
a collective process of will formation which includes a system of political and social responsibility, of control and counter-control. That,
however, is exactly the image that does not fit a right-wing project of
an affective relationship to state and nation. Consequently for many
national-conservative representatives 'constitutional patriotism' – the
approval and loyalty to institutions transparent in their functions – is
a provocation which describes an undesirable social trend away from
the unconscious, emotional sense of community towards the state's
accountability to civil society.

The creation of a positive nationality which confronts rationality
with collective feeling – and from that point of view Weißmann's,
Zitelmann's and others' historiographic efforts are coherent – can
only lie in an exalting past, at best in the promise for a significant
future. A development of thought that is supposed to achieve this has
already been mentioned. The suggestion that Nazism originated in the
earlier phenomenon of Bolshevism perhaps does not produce a causal
connection, however, it does put it forward. Qualifying National
Socialism as a reactive movement as well as equating anti-Bolshevism

with anti-Semitism have been vehemently disputed and hardly any academic follows Nolte's path. Nevertheless, it becomes clear what sort of historico-political options are linked to such an interpretation and why it is so attractive to certain national-conservative projects. The era of Wilhelm II is largely exculpated if the reasons for the Holocaust are to be found outside German national history. The then possible restoration of a Prussian model of virtue integrates in a depreciation of *Westbindung*, which figures only as a non-German result of allied postwar re-education and German self-hatred, in favour of an ideological 'middle way'.

Part of the criticism about the alleged indoctrination is not only a certain anti-intellectualism, which puts feeling before reason, but also the rejection of a democratic understanding of society and the state. With Oswald Spengler, Weißmann argues that the nation is represented by a minority and which one this might be 'is the actual political question within society'.[34] It is not individual equality in the face of and as a member of the state that is the purpose of community life. The aim is the self-preservation of the state structures which are regarded as independent of an everyday legitimization and of benefit to the individual:

> Whilst one caringly turns to some minority, the universal, which is the state, rots. A transformed attitude towards the state is therefore one of the most urgent demand on 'political education'. Without losing the necessary matter-of-factness, that 'impersonal pride' would have to be regained without which no polity has historically survived.[35]

The state is accorded a *raison d'être* beyond the societal consensus: statehood appears as a value in its own right, gaining its justification from the unwavering principle of the nation.

Weißmann also stages the recourse to the 'normal German nation-state': 'Those who wanted to erase terms like "hero", "honour", "Prussianism", "empire" from the vocabulary turned not only against the Nazi ideology which had abused them, but also against the up to then normal understanding of the history of Bismarck's German state.'[36] Here central concepts of Nazi ideology seem to be normal again and therefore reusable. The symbolic starting point is the German Reich of 1870/1 in its Prussian guise.

The readjustment of German national history leads us to the question: which period should serve as the preferred point of reference for a new and self-confident national understanding? National Socialism, of course, cannot be the one, even in its forcefully modernized and relativized form, the old Federal Republic, the 'Bonn Republic' should not be the one. That is the very one that should be overcome. The reversal of the German *Sonderweg* in the 40 years of the Federal Republic's history, the attempt belatedly to democratize a nation which was lagging behind is almost throughout devalued as a time when Germany had to undergo re-education forced upon it from outside. The image is of an 'adult Germany' which is at last shaking off its fetters to take its place in the world of the great powers. The Berlin Republic's self-confident orientation of power is brought face to face with the 'oblivion of power' of the Bonn Republic.

The search for the positive tradition in the Germany of Wilhelm II therefore requires a radical re-evaluation of the *Sonderweg* discussion. The term *Sonderweg* should embrace and explain the development of the 'belated' German nation with its democratic deficit, the burden of an authoritarian state into fascism. This *Sonderweg* – which has semantically and conceptually separated Germany from normality just as the historic Germany broke away from the civilized community – is simply mislaid in the realms of historic reinterpretation. Now the *Sonderweg* is not the development into fascism but rather the way out of the Third Reich leading to the special existence of a semi-sovereign state which regained its 'normal' national status only with reunification.

Here it is not the ideological, political and social continuity from the 'old' to the 'new' Federal Republic that is in the foreground, but the qualitative move from the restrained Federal Republic to the liberated nation-state, Germany.

Normalization

The new, completely sovereign nation which can count on the affective attachment of its easily satisfied members is postulated as normality and its desired development as normalisation. It is not the intentional decision for a community but the love for a nationally founded body that is the motivation of the individual to be part of that body.[37]

During the *Historikerstreit* in the mid-1980s the notions of 'normality' and 'normalization' sparked harsh criticism. Today they serve as points of reference for a number of restructuration processes in current politics: a foreign policy which longs for 'full sovereignty' rather than a supranational security architecture, a dramatic cutback in welfare politics, a return to collective values. And they also guide a new image of German national history, which is quite successfully promoted by a number of conservative journalists and historians. In this context 'normalization' means putting the nation back into its seemingly natural place: the redefinition of what is supposed to found the cohesion of the state bluntly disposes of central elements of the Western idea of constitutional states. Here it is an idea of national identity, it is the entity in which the nation comes together without recurring to an act of will by its members. The social contract as the basis of the modern constitutional state is eliminated. The pre-conscious factor of the nation as a 'community of fate' immunizes this concept against any kind of criticism. As the seemingly ahistoric fact that has 'always been there' the nation finds legitimacy in itself.

The abandonment of collective terms is to be noticed: 'national unity' serves as the symbol of integration for a disintegrated 'society'. Promising a 'natural' solidarity is supposed to create acceptance for individual losses and sacrifices.

Bonds with the West

A central topic which combines reorientation in domestic politics and a shift in the foreign policy agenda is the critique of *Westbindung*. Only the liberation from the shackles of Western integration, which the postwar situation had imposed on Germany, enabled it to become a normal nation-state which is not determined by external orientation. At the end of the twentieth century this seems to be a rather romantic idea, but it nevertheless serves as the symbolic point of reference.

The 1989 break serves as an alibi to go back in geopolitical history. As a result of historic fate Germany finds itself back in the middle of Europe. In this perspective reunification provides a second chance to regain a national identity in Germany's foreign policy. What had not been possible after World War II on the ground of lost morale/morality and power now appears possible: the need to define a new position results in a strengthening of the political nation-state and opens up new possibilities of independent action. In neo-Right discourse this appears to be the 'natural' – which also means the only logical – option. Putting emphasis on traditional foreign policy that had been laid out during the 40 years of the Bonn Republic, and strengthening the *Zivilmacht*[38] aspect and integration into supranational structures (established or to be formed), these concepts portend a withdrawal to power poltics and national interest. At the end of the twentieth century these concepts arguably no longer have the same air of *Realpolitik* that they once may have had.

In the statements of national conservative publicists the term geopolitics plays a central role, although with what impact on foreign political options remains unclear. Again it is the symbolic labelling and attribution that counts. Thus geopolitics is first and foremost marked as the opposite pole of federal republican foreign policy principles. Hence Weißmann proclaims geopolitics the 'science of orientation'.[39] His ally in the debate against *Westbindung*, Jochen Thies, goes *ex negativo* into the matter and complains about two 'handicaps' of foreign politics: the 'suppression of the power politics factor' and the 'lost 1980s'.[40]

The recourse to geopolitics as a methodological and political framework of reference in foreign policy is dominant. Zitelmann/ Weißmann/Großmann, the editors of the programmatic publication *Westbindung*, think that (almost) everybody has to do some rethinking because even conservative academics succumb to 'the mistake that commitments in foreign policy, security and the policy of alliances arise from certain socio-political preferences and options'.[41] This constricts any idea that members of a society (or rather their representatives) can come to an agreement and make decisions regarding foreign policy options. In their view, it is not the norms concept of Western societies that dictate conduct in the world, but the pseudo-deterministic demand of the geopolitical situation: 'In the years to come it will become more and more apparent that the compass [the West oriented political culture] for prospective German situation and condition will not last and will not be able to offer a reliable orientation.'[42]

It becomes apparent how the Federal Republic is explained as a political time-out both in relation to foreign and national policies. It had been especially the integration of Germany into the Western community, which did not deal with all aspects of the *Mittellage*, that is to blame. The 'risks' with a 'total Western integration' is stylized to the totalitarian wrong track of an ignorant elite insensitive towards history and power: 'As a result this commitment to the "Western value community" has almost adopted the character of a utopia intended for the totalitarian indoctrination of the whole society .'[43]

The rhetoric of taboo-breaking

All these thrusts go back to well-known arguments; yet they are accompanied by fanfares which are supposed to proclaim their novelty. Various elements of rhetorical self-positioning recur regularly. There is, for example, the demonstrative linking up of their own position with the political turning-point of 1989. Yet, no reference can be made to a formative role in the transformation process because none of the protagonists of the self-appointed generation of '89 participated in the ideological and political preparation or entourage. 1989 is rather seen as a chance which is 'at last' given to those previously unrecognized and ignored, who have long been denied their rightful place in the historical process. Realizing that they had not been able to get their way in the 'old Federal Republic' enforces, of course, their 'funeral oration'. A new beginning, which with the GDR's implosion draws the postwar period to a close, makes a clean sweep: wartime and the postwar era (in East and West) are being disposed of together, the smooth connection to the pre-past seems possible.

Astonishing, however, is how much effort is put into thrashing the Bonn Republic to death. The Federal Republican past seems not to give way so easily in favour of the new-old emphasis on the nation-state. The requirements of political reality and the persistence of political reason seem to brace themselves against national castles in the air. An indication of this is the repetitive claim of an alleged Left hegemony. The declared opponent of the '89 generation is the '68 generation[44] which is not only guilty of Germany's 'degradation', the national self-hatred, the subjugation of sovereignty and subjection to the norms of Western civilization instead of considering the national particularity of the German geopolitical location, but also successful with it and therefore an obstacle to their personal success and that of the nation. Staging the ideological debate as a conflict between generations, as a requittal with the social and political (fore)fathers who would have almost ruined their chances for the future, is above all a gesture. However, this also says a lot about the self-image of the ageing sons who want to pick up the heritage of their great-grandfathers (Ernst Jünger was not only for his writings but also for the biblical age of over 100 years a leading figure). The radical and revolutionary gesture of the youthful awakening goes hand in hand with yesterday's themes and concepts. Thus the relationship with the generation of '68 remains ambivalent: the attempt to imitate the taboo-breaking awakening is obvious, at the same time there is no comparable success in sight.

Whatever the generation of '68 can be rightfully accused of, the Left hegemony, which the Right wants to attack today, is nevertheless a chimera. One can hardly observe a totalitarian infiltration of society and surely even less politics and the economy with left-wing ideas. Marking society as being infiltrated by the Left shows how far right the New Right positions itself from the fundamental democratic consensual beliefs. How far the broad consensus is vulnerable to attack beyond the limits of party borders is also demonstrated by the fact that progressive exponents of the CDU such as Heiner Geißler who has vehemently spoken up against a renaissance of nationalism, or Rita Süßmuth who has always sought to promote women's issues in her party, are favourite subjects of attack.

The critique of '68 goes beyond the generation conflict: the political movement of the 1960s and their success stand for political orientation. That is why the generation of '68, and what is left of it, is made the internal enemy by the national-conservatives. This construction is hyperbolic in two ways: on the one hand, there can realistically be no talk about a dominance of the intellectual Left neither in the media nor elsewhere; on the other hand, the above-mentioned political positions cannot be confined to the restricted group of the '68 generation. The alleged taboos which Zitelmann and his followers resist are not mysterious, carefully protected and defended irrationalities, they are rather recognized in the middle of society and the basis for everyday action. Indicating totalitarian infiltration and conspiracy theory sounds somewhat absurd in this context. The ambivalent evaluation of the '68 generation – on the one hand, seizing cultural hegemony, on the other, having completely failed – becomes understandable when one is asking about the functional importance of an ideological redefinition. If the old Federal Republic – by which, by the way, not only the Germans but also the European neighbours did well – is dismissed *in toto* as left-wing *Sonderweg*, as a cultural-revolutionary mistake, then the ideological way is free for radical changes. The question as to what is to be maintained of society and politics under the new set-up, does not need to be asked anymore.

After the so-called 'taboos' (the Western consensus of values, concordant foreign policy, participatory democracy, the evaluation of National Socialism) the main point of attack is the danger of a 'multi-cultural-criminal society'.[45] Renouncing multicultural cohabitation and decision-making underlines that the nation is seen as a culturally predetermined community of fate and not based on consent. Rainer

Zitelmann's positioning of the Right sets a similar tone; in addition to 'multiculturalism' it is especially feminism that is declared to be the political enemy of the 'democratic Right'.[46]

Tilting at windmills of such omnipresent taboos puts the defender of the moral right under a political duty to come forward with specific counter-concepts. What we cannot find in the publications of the New Right are alternative political concepts: What should an alternative to a realpolitical, internationally co-ordinated foreign policy look like? How should the economy and individual subsistence work if women give up their employment? Monocultural society and geopolitics?

Still, it is the aim of the New Right to convey the image of intellectual and moral heroism which is known as the very masculine position of very young men. Consequently the figure of taboo-breaking is linked to the 'youth' those writers regularly attribute to themselves. Again, it is a symbolic self-positioning against the established academia, political class, sets of social norms.

III

Much more visible in everyday life is the shift in norms that govern political action: the cutting back of the welfare state has been a feature of the CDU/CSU/FDP government since 1982, but it has radicalized in the aftermath of unification. One reason, of course, is the enormous economic pressure unification has brought about. No one in the political spectrum really doubts that reorganization of the social state and the fiscal system is necessary. However, what is important from the point of view of ideological critique is the justification of these developments: the seemingly new rhetoric follows rather old patterns and steps back – at least in part – from a processual and rational execution of conflicting interest to a less rational, emotive reanimation of truisms of the 1950s, centring on the family, a self-sufficient individual, an elitist view on political and social decision-making and a notion of the state to which more is attributed than simply being the executor and administrator of the collective or majority will of the people, and thus puts it prior to the constitutional sovereign.

All this strongly suggests elements of the national-conservative historiography and the corresponding thrusts regarding political legitimization. If one has, for example, a closer look at the thoughts which Wolfgang Schäuble, leader of the CDU, developed first in his programmatic speech at the CDU party conference in 1993, and then, in more elaborate form, in his book *Und der Zukunft zugewandt*, one can find some of the patterns outlined above (see section II).

Compatible with the emphatic neo-Right concepts of the state Wolfgang Schäuble invoked the state in an ardent speech delivered to the CDU party conference in 1993. The speech emphasized that the nation was not an arrangement of citizens but a 'community of protection and fate' in which every individual had to adapt. The necessary basis for a 'united nation' were 'value convictions'. Schäuble proclaimed the 'recalling our national identity' and especially the *feeling* of national coherence.[47]

This is even stronger in his book which was published the following year. Here the old Federal Republic is portrayed as a decadent feel-good state which led to the neglect of tradition, to political and social irresponsibility and especially to a striking lack of individual willingness to make sacrifices to the state and the community. The not always uncomplicated history of the Federal Republic from 1949 to 1989 is thus designated as a political time-out. A lack of existential challenges that should or could have been taken up, has in the end led to a lack of leading personalities:

> There are hardly any real heroes, any real paragons in the Germany of the 90s. ... Our lack of paragons is due to the times in the first place. A generation that grows up without pressure, without challenges – which is true for all who are alive today, apart from the over 70-year-olds – can never arrive at the weight of a generation who had to stand in situations of existential threat.[48]

What is almost unbelievable about this statement is the fact that Schäuble actually locates the possible conditions of his imaginary heroes during the time of the Third Reich. Of course, during the Nazi dictatorship the people have lived through more existential threats than most of our generation can even imagine. However, many of them have caused the existential threat for others. It is irritating to say the least that the political socialization of all historical events in the fascist era is suggested as the desirable basis for a democratic community in the 1990s. Within this traditional embodiment the normative structuration of the community is questionable: instead of counting on a multitude of informed individuals who as responsible citizens pursue their common business (mutually controlled), Schäuble bets on the hero models, and one can only hope that they are the right ones. Trust, in the incremental accumulation of reason, is not naive but at least a regulative idea, part of every democratic political enterprise. The search for the hero, however, seems to be a substitute satisfaction in politically difficult times.

Schäuble's community therefore does not rest on a contractarian solidarity but on the coexistence of isolated and personally responsible individuals and a framework of traditional values which are vaulted over by an omnipresent declaration of responsibility for the state and an outdated morality. Similar to the historiographic protagonists of a nation-state identity, Schäuble cannot be content with the less emphatic concept of constitutional patriotism:

> A constitutional document cannot alone be sufficient to found a community not only in the minds but also in the hearts of the people. The communitarian sense with which to master difficult times is necessary, too.[49]

It becomes apparent that it is the emotional achievement of national identity that helps us to get over the difficult times, not the administrative and creative competence of the political system. Politics can easily live off such an ideological subsidy, even if politics itself fails. The fact that in Schäuble's conception the state and the government seem all too often to be seen as one and the same, is extremely problematic from a political theory angle. If the government is seen as part or as a function of the state and if the state is seen as transcending society, then the glory of a special legitimization goes, of course, to the government, not only to the political institutions but to the current government itself. The more prosaic and at regular intervals revocable democratic vote takes a back seat.

The image of the state portrayed by Schäuble appears conflicting: on the one hand, he complains of the hypertrophic state which penetrates the spheres of society in a unreasonable way; on the other hand, he demands greater concessions, sacrifices and unquestioned consent of the individual towards this state. Nevertheless it all adds up: the services which the state provides for its citizens should be reduced, the moral and economic input of the individual, however, should be increased.

In other words: at least as far as state care and provision are concerned, a more just redistribution should replace material politics by symbolic politics.

The social cost which, of course, will anyway arise, will have to be covered as neutrally as possible. The moral falling back on unpaid family work has proved successful in this context. A pillar of the orderly community presented by Schäuble is therefore the family which is not only his ideological guarantor of traditional values but also minimizes the real life risks of the individual. Schäuble is aware that this concept corresponds to an ideal and not to the social reality of the 1990s:

> The traditional family consisting of a married couple and children becomes rare, its place is more and more taken by other models like single-households, double income couples without children, homosexual relationships, non-marital relations with children, single parents.[50]

None the less the family is the starting point and above all the goal of conservative and especially national-conservative social politics. It does not have to be explicitly mentioned that linked to this concept are traditional gender roles. The declared aim is the protection of the family (of course only of married couples) which in case of doubt comes before the protection of the individual as tax laws and parental laws duly confirm. A welcome effect of a conservative family-friendly policy is restricting female employment trends (or rather opportunities). These hard facts of social reality and political strategy are regularly linked with a recognition of the family as the 'nucleus' or the 'foundation' of the state and society. Acting against traditional family structures will be denoted – floridly decorated with phrases of tolerance – as acting against a 'natural' order.

The transcendental legitimization of this desired order includes a return to Christian values which – there can be no question of a separation of state and church – serve as the basis of the social order. There is no need for more secular ethics, it is after all not the image of the responsible individual and citizen that serves as the guiding principle. One rather gets the impression that Schäuble longs for a pre-Enlightenment status:

> In former times the basis of the moral and normative consensus of a society were shared beliefs, religious bonds, obedience towards the state and the church. The moral maxims of Christian belief still bear a high degree of commitment in our secular society – one may think of the Ten Commandments. This background of Christian norms in our society still is an essential support for its inner cohesion and its inner peace.[51]

Given the urgent tasks for the future Schäuble demands a return to old virtues:

> It cannot go on like this: without more public spirit, sense of duty and service to the community a liberal state cannot exist for long. These virtues are not old-fashioned, they are necessary if we want to cope with the future.[52]

An old understanding of the state corresponds to the old recital of virtues: the glory that the state cannot obtain as a framework of political institutions and processes is given to it by the nation; the development from the divided state to the united Germany where the nation can regain consciousness. The talk about the nation as a protective community does not only refer to the symbolic power of internal integration but also to the demarcation from the outside.

Here one can find again the patterns of a new self-consciousness: demanding a change in foreign policy, returning to normality, re-entering history, bidding farewell to the childhood of the nation. Understanding the 1989/90 turning point as a chance is not reprehensible. It is, however, irritating how every single historical burden, such as the *Sonderweg* discussion, the GDR and FRG, are being disposed of in one go. Revealing in this context is the phrasing that Schäuble finds for the discussion about the historical classification of National Socialism: it appears to him merely as an 'unpleasant' dispute.[53] It is not history itself that he finds annoying, it is the permanent quarrel about this history.

In his interpretation the fatal connection between nationalism and National Socialism is finally reversed. It is not the common nationalism as a condition of National Socialism that appears worthy of criticism, but the fact that after 1945 the Nazi experience eclipsed German national identity. He characterizes the Federal Republic as 'a country in which a relaxed national identity and a positive notion of the nation could not develop'[54] because Germany's national feelings had been hurt by the degenerate nationalism of National Socialism. Not only does this open the moral debate about what is good and bad nationalism, in the end the nationally thinking German appears as the victim of National Socialism, and the restriction of national pride through the political heritage of the Holocaust as an undeserved burden.

Schäuble's argument aims at the salvation of the nation – which is liberated from the burden of National Socialism – and becomes a positive historical force which realizes itself in the new greater Germany.

Legitimating the nation-state has its repercussion. Clearer than former Chancellor Kohl who is held up as a reliable European, Schäuble, while being split between the nation and Europe, tends towards the nation. The conceptual starting point is the return to the geopolitical formula of Germany's middle position[55] that determine its foreign policy options:

> The East–West conflict had made us Germans a peripheral state; in our back was the Wall. But the position on the periphery has remained an episode: We Germans are back in the middle of Europe.
> ... This position in the centre of Europe weighs on our historic fate.
> ... We Germans bring together East and West.[56]

If the geopolitical situation is as a 'natural' determinant of realpolitical consolidation then the 'new responsibility', on the other hand, plays a role. First, it is noted with pride that we are full members again, then there is the demand to draw the consequences from the new strength.

> Germany has to confront great challenges – not only domestically, but also as far as our global role is concerned. With unification we regained our full national sovereignty. We are regarded as a nation with equal rights by our neighbours and by the world. ... It cannot work out in the long run that we confront the unpleasant and uncomfortable aspects of foreign and security policy only to meet the expectations of others. We ourselves must know and must want to know what to do. The real challenge is to perceive clearly that the capacity to act internationally is indispensable if we want to live up to our national interests.[57]

Giving shape to the new role of the united Germany takes precedence over criticism of the old Federal Republic's foreign policy which now enters into the new Berlin Republic as a mental deficit. As the burden of the old Bonn Republic, Schäuble states 'helplessness in strategic thought and hesitation to take clear decisions', the lack of sovereignty had resulted in 'self-restraint and passivity'.[58] The foreign political 'be-nice-attitude', as Schäuble puts it bluntly, serves as the negative foil for new foreign political action. Foreign observers may find these fears unfounded in the light of the German operation in Croatia and lately in Albania – or they might on the contrary conclude that German foreign policy is being restructured.

The evaluation of the Atlantic alliance ties in well to this classification; in Schäuble's work as well as in Zitelmann *et al.* the *Westbindung* appears as a dispensable option. Its conditions – ideological supremacy of the Western Allies and the Eastern threat – disappeared with the end of the Cold War. To summarize: what Schäuble presents as the political outline for the future is a shopping list of conservative elements that supposedly receive a new dignity but can hardly reveal a new legitimacy. The risks of modern society as well as the political changes of the last years are in the end not resolved within the realm of politics but by going back to old concepts.

The political complexity is reduced in the seemingly self-explaining ideas of the nation, the family and a state in which one believes rather than on which one can rely on. The consolation of only the seemingly known – because what does 'family' or 'nation' mean nowadays? – appears therefore as the happy ending of every modernization crisis. The postulated return to normality appeals to an affective commitment that is supposed to secure, without question, the support for decisions of the political elite. The truistic double structure of their argument is obvious: the retreat to 'normalization' signifies a truism in itself, the retreat to affective basics requires acclaim without exposing the corresponding political decision-making (restructuration of the fiscal system, family politics, which keep women at home, etc.) to critical investigation. So we arrive at legitimization by truism.

Schäuble's political testimony unites a whole range of positions that go beyond the mainstream of the conservative government. They may not be representative, but they mark undoubtedly a national-conservative segment of politics that resembles in many ways the concepts of a group of neo-Right historians and journalists. Their statements cannot be dismissed as academically irrelevant, they rather deserve special attention because of their political strategies of self-assertion.

IV

The decision to move the government from Bonn to Berlin was not only a symbolic tribute to the East Germans. It was also meant to give some credibility to the process of reunification. But there also has been criticism of this decision from the start not only concerning the enormous costs but also the problematic political heritage that is associated with Berlin as a capital. Some critics favoured Bonn as the seat of the working government, standing for functional and pragmatic politics rather that the traditional representation of a nation-state. The notion of the Bonn Republic also means Germany's reintegration into the Western civilized world and stands for a democratic political culture of the postwar state, for modesty in military politics and the attempt to attribute political cohesion to public affairs by a common obligation towards constitutional values. On the other hand, the criticism toward the former capital centres on Bonn's 'provincialism' and its provisional status as a capital. Correspondingly, Berlin is seen as more adequate for a 'grown-up' and unified Germany.

As we have seen, there is a growing effort from the Right to re-emphasize traditional political and social concepts in an emotive rather than a rational way: the nation, power politics, the family, social hierarchy. In this line of argument Bonn is criticized not only for being a provincial town, but the Bonn Republic has been accused of representing a provincial way of doing politics – neglecting national interest, losing control over what is seen as the hypertrophic state, destroying traditional value systems and a positive national identity. And again the years of the old *Bundesrepublik* are marked the real 'special path' in German history, which has to be corrected. But in addition to this, there is an advocation of Berlin which goes beyond the mere announcement of a new stage in the development of a democratic postwar state in Germany. Put on scene as the retrieval of Germany's lost centre, Berlin as the new and old capital serves as a focus to articulate and visualize the new emphasis on the self-confident nation. The usual keyword for this is 'normalization': Germany as a normal nation-state, Germany as a normal military power, Germany as a self-confident power that finally steps out of Hitler's shadow, and a Germany that becomes normal on a domestic level as well. An emphatic reading attributes changes towards the restitution of these 'normal' paradigms to the 'Berlin Republic'. The semantic and ideological opposition between a *'Bonner Republik'* and a *'Berliner Republik'* refers to announced and factual shifts in politics.

Berlin and the 'Berlin Republic' (as Bonn and the 'Bonn Republic') serve as short-hand as 'condensation symbols'[59] in a debate about what kind of republic the *Bundesrepublik* should be. The old republic has been characterized by its federal structure, by a fragmentary and provisional status which had become quite stable and reliable over the decades. One of its most important features has been the orientation towards the West – a Rhenish tradition that is aptly symbolized in the geographic location of the former capital. A return into the Prussian tradition and Wilhelmine pre-history of Germany thus underpins not only a different, not-so-liberal understanding of politics and society, but also a new orientation towards the East – beyond Eastern Germany. As the declared heart of Germany, Berlin also serves centralist tendencies which counter the federalist tradition of the republic.

Symbolic greatness is often called for when politics has to face greater challenges that it is prepared to deal with. The rhetoric of the Berlin Republic appears to combine such evasive nationalism and shifts in current politics that are presented with moral and emotional arguments. Most of them might hope to find public appreciation in a more rational decision-making process.

A debate on what art is allowed to do in the face of politics might illustrate this: When Christo and Jeanne-Claude wrapped the *Reichstag* in Berlin many visitors – international and national – experienced this as an important politico-cultural event, and it in fact attracted thousands of people – many of whom primarily enjoyed the character of a cultural event and would not have visited a political institution, a state building or an instructive exhibition otherwise. Still the veiling of the building unveiled history, whatever fragmentary parts of it were called back into people's minds and were *discussed*. The very traditional artistic means of *Verfremdung* worked well once again. In advance there had been vigorous argument against the display; Wolfgang Schäuble for instance sharply criticized what he regarded as a profound disrespect towards a national symbol. Even a minor subversion like Christo's poses a threat to the unsullied image of a nation which aims to evade historiographic or political or ideological critique. But at the end of the twentieth century it remains an image, and symbols do not come to life.

Translated by Daniela Kroslak

Notes

1 Schäuble, W., *Und der Zukunft zugewandt* (Berlin: Siedler, 1994). Schäuble ironically derives his title from the words of the GDR anthem by Johannes R. Becher.
2 Goldhagen, D. J., *Hitler's Willing Executioners. Ordinary Germans and the Holocaust* (New York: Alfred Knopf, 1996). [Goldhagen, D. J., *Hitlers willige Vollstrecker. Ganz normale Deutsche und der Holocaust.* (Berlin: Siedler, 1996).]

3   *Ibid.*, p. 455. A perspective Goldhagen modifies somewhat as a result of subsequent discussions. He steps back from his hypothesis of ideological determination and also attributes some significance to non-ideological factors such as the framework of totalitarian political institutions. See, 'Die Befassung mit den Tätern mußte kommen. Daniel Jonah Goldhagen und Josef Joffe im Gespräch', *Blätter für deutsche und internationale Politik*, Vol. 41, No. 10 (1996) pp. 1186–96.

4   In English: Historians' Debate; a controversy on the 'singularity' of the Holocaust, in 1986/7. See 'Historikerstreit', *Die Dokumentatim der Kontroverse* (München: Piper 1987).

5   Senocak, Z., 'Das selbstzufriedene Deutschland hat sich als unsicheres und schnell beleidigtes Konstrukt geouted', *Süddeutsche Zeitung*, 19 August 1996.

6   Joffe, J., 'Das Goldhagen-Phänomen', *Süddeutsche Zeitung*, 11 September 1996.

7   Browning, C., *Ordinary Men: Reserve Police Battalion 101 and the Final Solution in Poland* (New York: HarperCollins, 1992). [Browning, C., *Ganz normal Männer. Das Reserve-Polizeibataillon 101 und die 'Endlösung' in Polen.* (Rowchlt: Reinbek, 1996).]

8   Heer, H., 'Die große Tautologie', *Tageszeitung*, 4 September 1996.

9   Heil, J., 'Nicht die Kritiker, der Kritisierte hat versagt', *Süddeutsche Zeitung*, 19 August 1996.

10 Wehler, H.-U., 'Wie ein Stachel im Fleisch', *Die Zeit*, 14 June 1996.

11 Wiedemann, C., 'Im Land der Täter', *Die Woche*, 13 September 1996.

12 Mommsen, H., 'Schuld der Gleichgültigen', *Süddeutsche Zeitung*, 20/21 June 1996.

13 Mommsen, H., quoted by Suchsland, R., 'Neuer Mythos', *Frankfurter Rundschau*, 21 September 1996.

14 Ullrich, V., 'Goldhagen und die Deutschen', *Die Zeit*, 13 September 1996.

15 Maurice de Zayas, A., 'Ein Volk von willigen Henkern?', *Criticon*, No. 150, 1996.

16 Habermas, J., 'Geschichte ist ein Teil von uns. Warum ein Demokratiepreis für Daniel J. Goldhagen', *Die Zeit*, 13 March 1997.

17 *Ibid.*

18 Schwilk, H. and Schacht, U. (eds.), *Die selbstbewußte Nation. 'Anschwellender Bockgesang' und weitere Beiträge zu einer deutschen Debatte* (Berlin: Ullstein, 1994).

19 The critique of *Westbindung* is discussed below. Zitelmann, R., Weißmann, K., Großheim, M. (eds.), *Westbindung. Chancen und Risiken für Deutschland* (Frankfurt am Main: Propyläen, 1993).

20 Zitelmann, R., 'Position und Begriff. Über eine neue demokratische Rechte', in: Schwilk, H. and Schacht, U., *op. cit.*, pp. 163–81.

21 An excellent account of Nolte's theses and how they are taken on and transformed by a new generation of historians is Schneider, M., '"Volkspädagogik" von rechts. Ernst Nolte, die Bemühungen um die Historisierung des Nationalsozialismus und die "selbstbewußte Nation"', *Archiv für Sozialgeschichte*, Vol. 35 (1995) pp. 532–81.

22 Weißmann, K., *Rückruf in die Geschichte. Die deutsche Herausforderung: Alte Gefahren – neue Chancen* (Berlin: Ullstein, 1993), p. 190.

23 Nolte, E., *Streitpunkte. Heutige und künftige Kontroversen um den Nationalsozialismus* (Berlin: Propyläen, 1993).

24 Weißmann, K., *op. cit.*, see note 22.

25 Weißmann, K., 'Auf dem Sonderweg verirrt', *Rheinischer Merkur*, Februrary 28, 1992.

26 *Ibid.*

27 see for instance Broszat, M., 'Was heißt Historisierung des Nationalsozialismus', *Historische Zeitschrift*, 1988, pp. 1–13.

28 Kershaw, I., *The Nazi Dictatorship. Problems and Perspecitves of Interpretation.* (London: Edward Arnold, 3rd edn 1993), p. 193.

29 Zitelmann, R., *Hitler, Selbstverständnis eines Revolutionärs* (Stuttgart: Klett-Cottn, 1989); Prinz, M. and Zitelmann, R. (eds.), *Nationalsozialismus und Modernisierung* (Darmstadt: Wissenschaftliche Buchgesellschaft, 1991).

30 Zitelmann, R., 'Das Erbe der Diktaturen', *Rheinischer Merkur*, 18 January 1991.

31 Weißmann, *op. cit.* (1993) p. 86f.

32 Kershaw, *op. cit.*, pp. 202–6.

33 See below.

34 Weißmann, *op. cit.*, p. 19.

35 Weißmann, *op. cit.*, pp. 159f.

36 Weißmann, *op. cit.*, p. 26.

37 see Seebacher-Brandt, B., 'Norm und Normalität. Über die Liebe zum eigenen Land', in Schwilk and Schacht, *op. cit.*, pp. 43–56.

38 Civilian power.

39 Weißmann, *op. cit.*, p. 65.

40 Thies, J., 'Perspektiven deutscher Außenpolitik', in Zitelmann, Weißmann and Großheim (eds.), *op. cit.*, pp. 523–36, here: p. 527.

41 Zitelmann, R., Weißmann, K. and Großheim, M., *Deutschland und der Westen. Einleitung zu Westbindung*, *op. cit.*, p.14.

42 *Ibid.*

43 Zitelmann, Weißmann and Großheim (eds.), *op. cit.* (1993), p. 10.

44 See for instance Graw, A., 'Dekadenz und Kampf. Über den Irrtum der Gewaltlosigkeit', in Schwilk and Schacht, *op. cit.*, pp. 281–90. Graw calls the generation of '68 somewhat enigmatically 'onanists of the age of consumerism' (p. 283).

45 Bergfleth, G., 'Erde und Heimat. Über das Ende der Ära des Unheils' in Schwilk and Schacht, *op. cit.*, pp. 101–23, p. 102.

46 Zitelmann, *op. cit.* (1994) p. 179f.

47 Schäuble, W. 'Rede vor dem CDU-Parteitag', in CDU-Informationsdienst, *Union in Deutschland*, 16 September 1993, pp. 34–47.

48 *Ibid.*, p. 56.

49 *Ibid.*, p. 221.

50 *Ibid.*, p. 113.

51 *Ibid.*, p. 55.

52 *Ibid.*, p. 53.

53 *Ibid.*, p. 214.

54 *Ibid.*, p. 217.

55 See *ibid.*, p.196.

56 *Ibid.*, p. 189.

57 *Ibid.*, p. 184.
58 *Ibid.*, p. 195.
59 Edelmann, M., *Politik als Rituat. Die Symbolische Funktion Staatlicher Institutionen und politischen Handelus* (Frankfurt am Main Campus, 1976) p. 9.

5

Citizenship and National Identity in Reunified Germany: the Experience of the Turkish Minority

Nicola Piper

Introduction

The 'foreigners issue' (*Ausländerfrage*) has been an important aspect in public discourse for many years. Since political reunification has taken place, however, a shift in priorities can be observed. In particular, the issues of employment and housing now come at the head of public concern in opinion surveys.[1] The presence of 'foreigners and the government's foreigners' policy have none the less remained important topics of public debate. This chapter will, therefore, explore the definitions of citizenship and national identity held by the majority population and the implications these have for 'foreigners', with particular reference to the period following reunification. More precisely, I will examine the question of whether citizenship functions as a mechanism for inclusion and participation of settled, postwar labour migrants of non-European origin and their descendants. The focus will be on the Turkish minority in Germany as it is the largest and one of the most distinct ethnic groups. It is argued that settled immigrants do not enjoy a fully equal status as citizens, despite their long periods of residence and the emergence of subsequent generations raised and/or born in Germany. This is due to the fact that there is a conceptual or ideological link between the processes of racialization and nationalism, made manifest in the intermingling of nationality and citizenship and aggravated in times of 'crisis'.

Rights to citizenship are central to the issue of who should be included in the national society as a participating member with full access to civil, political and social rights – the three main elements to citizenship according to Marshall – and who should be treated as an outsider with limited rights.[2] Exclusion from socio-national membership is also reflected in the nationality and citizenship laws, whereby 'descent' acts as an impediment to the acquisition of citizenship for immigrant 'newcomers'. Moreover, it is not only the dimension of rights and laws that is central to the issue of inclusion, but also the wider dimension of social participation and recognition within society at large. The focus in this chapter will be mainly on the latter dimension, in particular on immigrants' recognition as citizens and legitimate members in identity terms on the part of the indigenous majority.

Empirical data

The empirical data employed in this chapter derive from two different sources: (1) in-depth, open-ended interviews with senior personnel of semi-governmental or non-governmental organizations (half 'indigenous' Germans, half members of an ethnic minority) engaged in *Ausländerarbeit*,[3] conducted during December 1993 and April 1994; (2) secondary analysis of social attitude surveys and opinion polls. The former is designed to provide insights into the viewpoint of ethnic minorities themselves, the latter were consulted to establish broad generalizations on the part of the majority society. A number of surveys and polls mainly conducted during the 1990s were selected to show trends in the general public's attitude towards ethnic minorities. Secondary analysis of existing data is admittedly not a perfect method as I did not design the questions myself, and the questions were not necessarily those that I would have asked – neither in terms of wording, nor in terms of the issues raised. In addition, reliability of some of these surveys and polls has to be questioned as they were often commissioned by government ministries or political parties to serve certain purposes rather than to reflect 'reality'. It is, however, not an easy task to theorize about 'mass discourse', and this method was chosen with the aim of establishing very broad generalizations about, and trends in, the attitudes of the 'indigenous' population to ethnic minorities-related issues.

Citizenship and the effects of nationalism and racism

As the majority of modern states have established a link between citizenship and nationality, nationality is considered as a necessary, if not sufficient, condition for the exercise of citizenship. Thus, in the context of inclusion of immigrants, citizenship raises a number of issues, 'in one case concerning national identity and the historical role of nation-states as the pre-eminent modern form of organization of a political community',[4] and in another, concerning rights and 'liberties' of individuals living in a state.[5] Immigrant peoples' membership of a state might be accorded formal recognition in law, while their presence and participation as full citizens are still questioned within civil society.[6]

Nationalism is understood here as the ideological or discursive articulation of national identity, i.e. as ideologies or 'discourses in which [collective] identities and counter-identities are conceived and through which they are sustained'.[7] In other words, the construct of the 'nation' tends to depict 'the people' with the notion of descent and blood-relatedness, or – as suggested by Arendt – as 'one super-human family that we call "society" and its political form of organization called the nation-state'.[8] As a result, clear boundaries (or lines) are drawn between those who belong and those who do not belong to the socio-national community. 'These lines are essentially established within the laws of nationality, but they are not at all restricted to these formal relationships'.[9] This distinction between belonging and not-belonging, however, is not one of the main purposes of nationalism only, it also serves racism.

The emergence of the nation-state has resulted, or was accompanied by, several forms of collective identity. One such form is nationality as an expression of cultural unity which does not necessarily have to correspond with a sense (or the perception) of being a citizen.[10] National identity derives from the fact that it is a source of individual identity within a 'people' and is seen as the basis of collective solidarity. The 'people' are 'the mass of a population whose boundaries and nature are defined in various ways, but which is usually perceived as larger than any concrete community'.[11] Since the emergence of European nation-states, universalistic and particularistic notions of the 'nation' have tended to co-exist[12] and thus, national identity frequently utilizes ethnic or 'racial' characteristics for self-identification as well as for establishing 'a *natural* division of the world's population into discrete categories'.[13]

A second form of collective identity is citizenship. One of the particular features of an 'identity-as-citizen' is 'the way in which it overlays the other social identities the individual inevitably feels'.[14] These other social identities based on, for instance, class, ethnic or gender divisions, can create intense antagonisms. Citizenship as a political identity, however, can help to generate an awareness of responsibility for conciliating conflicting interests and thus help to appease social antagonisms. However, 'as nationality became associated in the ideology of nationalism with the doctrine of popular sovereignty, it became important that cultural nationality and legal citizenship should correspond'.[15] Hence, the two sources of collective identity, citizenship and nationality, tend to be enmeshed, and thus, counteract the conciliatory function of citizenship by involving exclusionary effects for immigrant minorities.[16] I argue, however, that not only does identity as a citizen tend to be equated with national identity, but also that identity as a 'national' is linked to identity as a 'race'. Thus, the drawing of boundaries between insiders and outsiders of a socio-national community also involves processes of racialization. This is reflected in German law as well as within the perception of society at large.

To sum up, racism and nationalism show certain similarities in that they are both sources of human collective identity and both categorize human populations into discrete groups, each of which is presumed to have unique characters. Both seek to naturalize the differences they construct, and both invoke narratives of origin referencing defined territory as the natural home of a specific racialized group with its defined cultural traits. Hence, it is argued here that the relationship between nationalism and racism – which is regarded as symbiotic whereby neither can be given an absolute priority over the other – has implications for the understanding of citizenship. As identity as a racialized group and as a 'nation' is reflected in the intermingling of nationality and citizenship laws, concrete forms of racialization are perpetuated by the granting, or non-granting, of full citizenship, whereby long-term third country nationals tend to be at a disadvantage politically, socially and often also economically.

The postwar period and identity crises

Usually, the issue of 'identity crisis' is related to an individual, personal level. However, as Macdonald suggests, it is not only individuals who suffer from identity crises, societies can suffer from it too if they have lost touch with their history and their roots.[17] Even majority identities need not necessarily be secure and unambiguous – a fact discussed by Forsythe in the context of German identity.[18] Any question of identity is clearly dependent on the social and political environment of a particular period in time and on the categories available for the drawing of boundaries. These elements – environment and boundaries – are subject to changes and can, therefore, result in crises at the moment of redefinition.

The postwar period has witnessed a number of socio-economic problems, such as the decline of industrial societies, the fading of the labour movement and the downward mobility of the middle classes – circumstances which are responsible in part for increasing national populism and a generally rising sense of insecurity. This is very likely to be attributed to immigrants, thus resulting in strong anti-migrant attitudes.[19] In this context, political debates about nation, nationality and citizenship are activated, and nationalism tends to become weighted with xenophobia and racism.

In Germany, it was the reality of complete destruction in 1945 that caused a radical change in its people's self-perception. The experiences and revelation of the full scale of atrocities during the Third Reich and the division into two separate states resulted in German identity becoming fragile and ambiguous.[20] People's feelings about being German have often been referred to as being bound up with their feelings about their recent past, and have therefore been a rather sensitive and painful topic.[21] Germanness as a positive identity has been described as '*historisch belastet*' (emotionally burdened as a result of the Nazi past).[22] In the wake of the 'economic miracle', any feeling of pride in being German was dominated by so-called 'economic patriotism' (*Wirtschaftspatriotismus*).[23] However, Germans did not actually have to face the issue of national identity until reunification in 1990.

This was also reflected in the interviews with representatives of organizations engaged in *Ausländerarbeit*. There was wide agreement among the interviewees (indigenous Germans as well as Turks) that West Germany had certain identity problems before reunification in 1990 and that this situation has somehow changed since then, in both the East and West. Most interviewees thought that before reunification, national identity was a 'non-subject',[24] it was 'never talked about'[25] or at least 'did not play an important role'.[26] This was explained by reference to Germany's experience with extreme ethnic nationalism during the Nazi period. A member of the Turkish minority expressed this very well:

A distinction has to be made between what national identity has meant in West Germany before and after unification. German identity has surely suffered from its past, and when you came from outside, you noticed that the Germans in the West had a detached attitude towards their nationality or identity. This had without doubt to do with the Nazi past.[27]

The process of reunification, however, has brought vast socio-economic and political changes resulting in a widespread feeling of insecurity. Rising nationalism is said to be one response to this new situation:

> I think [nationalism] also existed before [reunification] only now, [nationalism] is reinforced through the socio-economic crisis ... through the disintegration of family structures ... Radical changes are happening at the moment, resulting in an identity crisis for many.[28]

Meanwhile – between the 'national identity crisis' of the immediate postwar years and the second wave of crisis following reunification – the recruitment of 'guest-workers', in particular of Turkish workers, has largely resulted in their permanent settlement, and thus to the establishment of 'new' ethnic minorities. Until reunification, German policy towards immigrants consisted of maintaining a legal and political distinction between nationals and foreigners. Even today, German policy has hardly changed, treating second and third generations as much as *Ausländer* as the first immigrants.[29] The traditionally ethno-cultural conception of the German nation is still retained in nationality laws (in particular Article 116 of the Basic Law, which offers immediate citizenship to all ethnic 'Germans' in Eastern Europe) and naturalization procedures.[30] The term *Ausländer* and non-recognition as a country of immigration indicate this, as well as the right to nationality continuing to be based on *ius sanguinis* (right of descent).

Reunification entailed a new crisis of national identity in various guises. It is a crisis for West Germany as it has regained full political sovereignty and thus has to redefine its role in European and world politics.[31] The terminology of the 'nation' with a '*völkisch*' (ethnic) identity seems to have been emphasized more than ever since 1945, being fundamentally contradictory to the notion of a republic – an issue raised by Oberndörfer.[32] It is a crisis for East Germany, as it has to come to terms with economic, social and ideological changes created by a new political union of two national identities whose historical paths had been diverging for two generations. Thus, the official self-understanding of the GDR as a 'socialist country' as well as the propagated version of a *Verfassungspatriotismus* in the West are coming to an end, and concern has been expressed over narrow nationalism taking over and resulting in the formation of a 'wrong' new identity.[33]

The reunification process is suggested by most of the interviewees to have triggered rising nationalism and a redefinition of national identity with a stronger ethnic connotations, as explained by one respondent:

> I think that the question of national identity has grown since unification, that this question did not play an important role before, because the West Germans were doing well materialistically. In a way, they had established themselves behind the Wall ... By unifying both German states, a massive process of social sharing has been set off. This is the main reason for me: [This process] has automatically started this exclusion – why do I want to participate in the first place and you only second? – and from this developed: Yes, I am German and that is why we belong together, and the foreigner shall not get anything ... With this social sharing, huge legitimation problems have emerged and they help to re-establish old ideologies – suddenly we are a nation, we have got a national identity, whatever it is ...[34]

The immigrant perspective

For the Turkish minority, too, reunification seems to have resulted in more awareness of their position in Germany, and for the first time this has triggered a stronger, openly expressed claim for 'an expansion of the concept of Germanhood' to reflect the actual composition of German society.[35] The first generation of immigrants in particular have to come to terms with the fact that they have become permanent residents and, thus, part of German society. This was never an issue for those generations born and brought up in Germany. And yet, they too experience identity problems: they actually identify with Germany, but as a result of the exclusiveness of German national identity, the difficulty in obtaining full citizenship rights and rising nationalism/racism, they tend to look back to their ethnic origin as their source of identification.[36] This is well expressed in the following excerpt:

> Unification – that was a turning point for us [the immigrants], too.

Before the *Wende* we never asked ourselves whether we should stay or leave. Now, we ask ourselves whether we *can* stay. [37]

During the rapid process of socio-economic and political reunification, the status of long-term settled immigrants as legitimate citizens has been ignored as they were not given any clear political signs (such as the extension of full citizenship rights) to confirm their belief in having become an established part of German society, as one Turkish respondent explained:

Sections of the [Turkish] community have considered themselves to be an integral part of this society. For them, unification was a shock. ... I would say ... it was actually the political signal which we [the Turks] had expected in those sensitive moments which we did not get. And this was a rather strong 'stab in the back'. And the question arose 'Where do the police stand? Where does this state stand?'[38]

In other words, the immediate incorporation of East Germans did not run parallel to a similar incorporation of former guest-workers and their children. German society as a whole, therefore, missed the chance to redefine its identity as multi-ethnic or multicultural. One step towards that would be the legal redefinition of nationality which is still based on the ethnic or 'racial' concept of *Volk*. One respondent explained this 'missed chance' very well:

For too long West Germany has not taken into consideration any processes of change in the area of migration .... It was realized too late [by the government] that, if I want to integrate these people, that doesn't just mean that they don't stand out [i.e. are assimilated culturally], but If I want them to participate, if they should identify themselves with the nation or republic, with this state – and this is our common ground, you can pray how you want, that is not important – that [opportunity] was missed by not offering them citizenship and political participation.[39]

This means that more than 26 years after the official 'recruitment halt' of guest-workers – when it became clear that a substantial number of foreign workers would stay – provisions and requirements for obtaining citizenship have not been thoroughly facilitated. The revised Foreigners' Law of 1991 had been preceded by a fierce debate among parliamentarians and highly criticized after implementation by activists.[40]

Mass discourse: social attitude surveys and opinion polls

It is not surprising to find relatively high rates of anti-immigrant sentiments in the immediate years after 1973, when it became clear that 'guest-workers' were not guests any more, but about to settle. In a survey of 1975, regarding the issue of equal rights on the job, for instance, 57 per cent of the respondents thought that in times of crisis, foreign workers should be fired first; and 52 per cent did not think that foreigners who had lived a long time in Germany should be able to vote in council or municipal elections.[41] Despite these examples of prejudice and discrimination during the 1970s, Koeh-Arzberger, commenting on the 1980s, found that a generally hostile attitude to foreigners could not be observed and that agreement by the indigenous population with discriminatory statements vis-à-vis foreigners had, rather, decreased.[42] She has, however, also noted that during this period the 'foreigners' issue' (*Ausländerfrage*) was not highly politicized and that the dominant picture of the 'foreigner' in the public's mind was that of a hard-working person who kept a low profile in everyday life. Events in the more recent past, however, have resulted in a polarizing trend of attitudes towards foreigners. Issues relating to 'foreigners' invite people's views more than ever.[43] She also notes that it is difficult to determine whether the increasing polarization of the public's opinion is related to 'objective' perceptions of the situation (such as e.g. the number of foreigners) or to the politicization of this issue based on reports by the mass media.[44]

To gain more insight into changes during the 1990s, I consulted four IPOS[45] social attitude surveys on current domestic affairs (conducted on behalf of the Ministry for the Interior). The first of the IPOS studies (1990) points out that topics related to 'foreigners' living in Germany have gained importance in the public debate over recent years, ranging from advocating inclusion (by granting voting rights, etc.) to the more controversial debate about the number of asylum-seekers.[46] An important role played here in particular is the critical manner with which the *Republikaner* (extreme right-wing party) has presented their 'foreigners policy' since 1989. This has, however, somewhat changed since reunification as public debate has been dominated by other domestic issues relating to national-political developments.[47]

Asked whether foreigners should be allowed to vote, the IPOS 1990 study reveals that 80 per cent replied that only those who have German citizenship should be allowed to do so.[48] There is a difference, however, between supporters of the Green Party and the other parties' supporters: among Green supporters, 50 per cent thought that foreigners should be granted the right to vote, whereas among supporters of all the other parties, the majority was against this (92 per cent of the CDU/CSU, 74 per cent of the SPD, 81 per cent of the FDP and 95 per cent of the *Republikaner*).[49]

In the 1992 IPOS study, the attitudes towards foreigners had scarcely changed.[50] Asked whether they thought the number of foreigners living in Germany was 'all right' or 'not all right', a small majority of respondents in East and West Germany opted for 'not all right' (53 per cent in the West, 51 per cent in the East).[51] Supporters of the SPD were split almost 50:50 on this question, and 60 per cent of the CDU/CSU supporters were against the high numbers of foreigners. Acceptance was somewhat higher among FDP supporters, but much higher among the Greens (78 per cent in the West) and the PDS[52] (78 per cent). The Republikaner showed the lowest levels of acceptance: 83 per cent of their supporters opted for 'not all right'.[53] The next question in the 1992 IPOS study was whether the respondents thought that Germany's economy needs foreign workers or not. It seems that most West Germans have become used to the presence of 'foreign workers' since the late 1950s as two-thirds agreed that the German economy needs foreign workers. In the East, however, two-thirds of the respondents disagreed. It is suggested in this study that this has to be seen in the context of economic restructuring, rationalization of labour and high rates of unemployment, as well as in the context of the limited experience East Germans have had of foreigners.[54] The respondents were then asked how much contact they have with foreigners at work or in the area where they live (p. 85). Thirty per cent in the west had no contact with foreigners whereas in the east, 70 per cent had no contact. The two results are particularly interesting in this context: In the east and west, most supporters of the Green Party said they had contact with foreigners (and are the most liberal minded in this respect), and in the west most supporters of the Republikaner also said they had regular contact with foreigners (82 per cent). The latter, however, are comparatively the most hostile. It seems, therefore, as if political party alliance or prior prejudice can have a greater influence on people's opinion about foreigners than actual contact.

One issue that has clearly dominated public debate since reunification more than a general 'foreigners policy' is asylum-seeking. The IPOS 1993 study, therefore, points out that the 'asylum and foreigners issue' was still perceived as one of the most important problems in Germany since October 1991 (according to research done for the *Politbarometer*).[55] The increasing numbers of asylum-seekers as well as the rising attacks on foreigners around that time demonstrated the importance of this issue.[56] The acceptance of foreigners has, however, only decreased by 1 per cent: 54 per cent now thought that it is not 'all right' that so many foreigners live in Germany (in 1992: 53 per cent). Fewer respondents in the west thought that the German economy needs foreigners (62 per cent) and in the east, this figure was again exactly the opposite. The support of the asylum law in principle has decreased by two points (72 per cent; in 1992: 74 per cent), but the proportion of those who thought the law was being abused has also decreased by 2 per cent.[57]

The 1995 IPOS study states that the 'asylum' issue has lost a lot of its importance since 1993 as the result of the revised asylum law and the reduced numbers of accepted refugees.[58] It now seems as if the most important issue is the availability of jobs. None the less, issues related to the presence of foreigners and asylum-seekers were still among the ten most important topics in domestic politics.[59] General acceptance of foreigners is said to have slightly increased by 3 per cent: 48 per cent of the respondents thought that the number of foreigners in Germany is 'all right' (1993: 45 per cent). Nevertheless more than half of the population (52 per cent) thought that this is not 'all right' (in the east 54 per cent).[60]

With regard to formal citizenship, in both the East (69 per cent) and West (64 per cent), most of the respondents did not support the facilitation of naturalization procedures (and thus the acquisition of German citizenship).[61] However, 54 per cent in the west and 57 per cent in the east thought that in future those who were born in Germany should be granted citizenship, even if one of their parents was not a German citizen.[62] This means that a slight majority would support the addition of the territorial component to the citizenship law. Supporters of the CDU/CSU were less in favour of the *ius soli* than supporters of the SPD and FDP. Identifiers with the Green Party were most in favour. Two-thirds, in the east and west alike would reject the provision of dual nationality (83 per cent even of CDU/CSU supporters, but only 46 per cent of Green supporters).[63] The replies to the issue of citizenship showed that the public largely supports the non-radical stance of the government on this matter.

Commentary

With regard to the issue of citizenship, questions put to German respondents dealt mainly with the formal citizenship of 'foreigners', which reflects the fact that most long-term settled immigrants do not carry a German passport. Broadly, the replies revealed that governmental policies are largely supported: i.e. the restrictive policies on future immigration and existing legislation (concerning, e.g. naturalization procedures most of the respondents were in favour of the *ius soli* principle and rejected dual nationality). It has also been suggested that a slightly more liberal attitude towards settled immigrants has coincided with a steady reduction in numbers of 'newcomers'.

Two observations are particularly interesting. Despite the general trends described above, an increasing polarization of the various political parties' supporters seems to have taken place. Conservative and right-wing party supporters tend to be more 'anti-immigrant' than any of the other parties' supporters. The second observation is that settled immigrants are still seen explicitly as a 'problem' in the way in which questions were put in some of the surveys.

Overall, the surveys show that ethnic minorities do not enjoy an equal status with the indigenous majority in terms of citizenship – formally and/or substantially. However, these surveys fail to address the issue of national identity which has only indirectly been dealt with. This issue needs, therefore, to be looked at in more detail.

Surveys on national identity

In this section, I will discuss whether there is an association between a sense of national pride or identity and exclusionary effects on ethnic minorities. A special international report as part of the British Social Attitudes series compared British and German levels of pride in their country.[64] West Germans according to this report are still conspicuously reluctant to express pride in being German. In 1986, only 20 per cent of the German respondents thought of themselves as 'very proud' compared with 13 per cent as 'not proud at all' (as opposed to 53 per cent of the British ('very proud') and 3 per cent ('not proud at all')). This has changed, however. A Eurobarometer survey of 1995 showed that although the Germans are still the least proud, the percentages of those feeling 'proud' were 45 per cent and 'not proud' 35 per cent[65] (for Britain, 81 per cent opted for 'proud' and 15 per cent for 'not proud').[66] Feelings of strong national pride are concentrated in the 55 and over age group, and six out of ten EU citizens are reported as saying they are proud of their nationality, either because this is seen to be a citizen's duty or because it is simply seen as 'something natural'. 'National identity' was also tested in connection with 'European identity'. Respondents in the six founder member-states of the EU have the highest proportion who say that they see themselves principally as 'Europeans' in addition to their nationality. When all EU respondents are taken together, 10 per cent see themselves as 'European' first and then as a national of their country; 46 per cent first as a national and then as 'European'; and 33 per cent in terms of their nationality only. Germans have the highest figure for 'European first and then nationality' (15 per cent). The answers to these questions are clearly related to national pride. Those who are 'fairly' or 'very' proud of their nationality tend to identify themselves as such, while the less proud respondents tend to identify more with Europe, either additionally or exclusively.

The findings for 1996 reveal a further change with regard to the figures for Germany: only 9 per cent now think of themselves as 'Europeans first and then nationals', 43 per cent as 'nationals first and then European' and 38 per cent as 'nationals only'.[67] There is, therefore, a remarkable increase in those who see themselves in nationality terms only. This must be related to post-reunification developments and an increase in confidence as a 'nation', but is also part of an 'anti-foreigner' atmosphere in the light of huge socio-economic problems, such as rising unemployment. The EU overall average in this matter is worse in 1996 than the year before and this may be related to the increase in membership and the low European consciousness in the new member countries (Sweden in fact has taken the place of Britain as the least European country in terms of identity). So, for whatever reasons, there seems to be an increasing retreat to an emphasis on national identity. This trend might, therefore, indicate rising nationalism. On the other hand, high self-esteem does not automatically have to correspond with a feeling of superiority or a deorgatory attitude to others. However, with respect to more populist right-wing governments – at least in Germany and Britain – nationalism may be increasing at least among supporters of right-wing and conservative parties.

A survey conducted by the *Zentrum fir Türkeistudien* ('The Image of Foreigners in the Eyes of the Public') found that particularly among those people for whom national identity is a very important matter on a personal level there is a tendency to agree with anti-immigrant views (1995:119).[68] A relationship was, therefore, established by the authors between nationalism and racism. The data showed a strong correlation between full agreement with nationalistic statements and prejudice. For example, most respondents agreed with the statement 'Germans should have more rights' and most respondents emphasized the differences between foreigners and Germans based on the 'non-adaptability' of foreigners when asked for the causes of 'inter-ethnic' problems. However, more than one quarter (28.9 per cent), saw the main cause of those problems in the prejudices and ignorance on the part of the indigenous majority – so, here again, a polarization can be noted. Overall, half of the respondents who identified with their nationality were classified as 'prone to prejudice', followed by respondents who identified with the region they live in or who felt principally 'cosmopolitan' or 'European' and who expressed the least anti-immigrant attitudes.[69] In terms of political alliance, the most who expressed rather 'nationalistic' and 'prejudiced' statements were supporters of conservative and right-wing parties, the least nationalistic and prejudiced were supporters of the Green Party.

Concluding remarks

Ethnic minority and immigrant-related issues appear in the surveys reviewed as quite controversial and seem to polarize respondents' views. It has been suggested that the replies to questions in public opinion surveys can be highly influenced by single or multiple events at a particular time and do not, therefore, necessarily indicate long-term changes in attitudes on the part of the respondents.[70]

Shortly after the infamous arson attacks in Mölln and Solingen, for instance, a survey conducted by the Emnid Institute on behalf of the magazine *Der Spiegel* in 1992 found that before the attack in Mölln, only 43 per cent of the respondents disagreed with 'anti-foreigners' attitudes and phrases, but after the attack this rose to 69 per cent. Another survey undertaken in Germany shortly after the attacks resulted in 70 per cent of the indigenous respondents being in favour of granting local voting rights to foreigners which had been rejected four years earlier by 72 per cent of respondents. It might, therefore, be true that it is more plausible to assume that certain events have a strong influence on the responses than that there has been a sudden change in attitude. Hence, events can have a 'shock effect'.[71]

The surveys reviewed show that with regard to general attitudes towards ethnic minorities, fluctuations are quite slight. Instead of seeing these fluctuations as a result of particular incidents, however,

Koeh-Arzberger suggests that an increase in liberal or discriminatory statements is linked to the level of politicization and politicians' rhetoric.[72] It is, thus, questionable – as Koch-Arzberger observes – whether these fluctuations really indicate a change of attitude or whether it is a change of conditions under which it is more acceptable to express discriminatory or hostile opinions (or to even 'act' out intolerance through violence). A climate of more or less acceptability of anti-immigrant statements could again be created by politicians' rhetoric. If they depict foreigners or immigrants as a problem, and if they show sympathy for anti-immigrant attitudes and depict them as justified, it is only to be expected that such views are adopted by the wider public.

On the whole, it can be observed that most respondents support governmental policies which underpin the hypothesis by the *Zentrum für Türkeistudien* that the language used by politicians in the context of asylum and immigration (which is then reproduced by the media) causes and entrenches prejudices vis-à-vis foreigners and immigrants. This is, however, not only true negative attitudes: politicians' rhetoric can also cause more liberal attitudes. This was shown in the case of the future willingness to accept the *ius soli* principle (albeit without the provision for dual nationality) by the German public.

Another proposition relevant in this context is that the asylum and immigration issue (which has loomed larger than more general immigrant-related issues on the agenda of public debate) is used by politicians to divert attention from other, more important, but less easily solvable, socio-economic problems. In other words, the issue of asylum and immigration is inflated into a serious problem more or less deliberately to deflect public attention from other socio-economic problems. Unemployment, or the fear of unemployment, for instance, is often suggested as being the cause of racially discriminatory attitudes. Those attitudes are first directed against non-European immigrants and are expressed in many different ways. This can be well illustrated in the German context. Reporting on the results of a public opinion survey, Ms. Noelle-Neumann wrote in the *Frankfurter Allgemeine Zeitung* of 8 November 1992:

> Economic problems and also resentments in the new Länder towards the West Germans are pushed into the background due to problems of 'floods' of asylum-seekers which then has the effect of uniting the East and the West. Under such circumstances, the worry that more conflicts between East and West Germans could

break out becomes a minor issue. This remarkable result is hardly acknowledged by the public.[73]

More important than the actual socio-economic differences between the East and the West was the issue of the increasing numbers of asylum-seekers. This topic functioned, therefore, as a 'unity construct' to overcome social and psychological problems between the East and West.

A typical German issue is that 'racial' discrimination and prejudice have often been regarded as a more serious problem in the eastern part since unification. The new surveys reviewed here, however, have shown that the East is not fundamentally different from the West.[74] The remaining differences result mainly from the fact – as pointed out in the surveys done on behalf of the Commissioner for Foreigners Affairs in Berlin – that in the East there has been less contact with foreigners at home and abroad.

On the whole, the surveys and polls discussed here have shown that respondents are mostly concerned with members of ethnic or immigrant minorities who belong to the largest groups, who have come for economic reasons (although the public readily forgets that these people were originally invited to come to Germany as workers), and whose lifestyles appear to be very different from indigenous citizens customs or habits. Hostility, prejudice and 'racial' discrimination are, thus, not directed against all ethnic or immigrant minorities alike. This indicates that certain groups are racialized for certain purposes.

Public attitudes show that there is a conceptual link between citizenship (formal and substantive) and nationality with racializing effects on ethnic minorities. This link does not, however, appear in a clear and straightforward way. People often display attitudes in contradictory ways. In particular racial prejudice and discrimination may be expressed on one dimension but not on another related dimension. This is less surprising on the proposition that attitudes can be inconsistent and that people rarely conform to neat descriptions such as 'racist' or 'nationalist'.[75]

At the same time, however, the majority of respondents (even if small in places) adopt views of immigration and ethnic minority-related issues as expressed by the ruling party. In this context, it has been claimed that 'what is most important about public opinion in a broader sense' might be 'that people are willing to acquiesce in what a small set of leading individuals say'.[76] In this way, public opinion needs to be treated essentially as dependent. Career politicians play an important role as they draw 'attention to the existence of problems and the merits of possible solutions'.[77] Their rhetoric usually emphasizes values and goals, rather than facts or analysis, and it often consists of arguments in symbols or slogans that are misleading or incomplete. However, it should not be forgotten that the public's opinion is highly polarized with regard to many, if not most, immigration and ethnic minority related issues.

For immigrants and their children, this means that long periods of residence and the birth of subsequent generations in Germany have not resulted in the removal of serious barriers to formal, let alone substantial, citizenship. Boundaries between the indigenous 'insiders' and immigrants as 'outsiders' are still being drawn, and, since reunification, on clearly racializing terms.

Notes

1 Ausländerbeauftragte des Senats von Berlin, *Deutsche und Türkische Jugendliche in Wichtigen Fragen Einig – Gegenseitige Tolerante Einstellungen Überwiegen* (Berlin: AusIB, 1990a).
2 Marshall, T.H., *Citizenship and Social Class – and Other Essays* (Cambridge: Cambridge University Press, 1950), pp. 19–50.
3 This term is the equivalent of 'race relations field' in English, but clearly indicates a difference in approach and historical background, i.e. 'race' is largely treated as a taboo term in Germany, and former immigrants and their children are still largely treated as 'foreigners' (*Ausländer*), in formal (legal) and substantive terms.
4 Marshall, T.H. and Bottomore, T., *Citizenship and Social Class* (London: Pluto Press, 1992), p. 85.
5 Held, D., 'Between State and Civil Society: Citizenship', in Andrews, G. (ed.), *Citizenship* (London: Lawrence & Wishart, 1991).
6 The term 'civil society' refers to the 'indigenous' majority.
7 Bauman, Z., 'Soil, Blood and Identity', *The Sociological Review*, Vol. 40, No. 4 (1992) pp. 675–701. Quoted on p. 678.
8 Arendt, H., *The Human Condition* (Chicago: University of Chicago Press, 1958), p. 29.
9 Goulbourne, H., *Ethnicity and Nationalism in Post-imperial Britain* (Cambridge: Cambridge University Press, 1991), p. 17.
10 Heater, D., *Citizenship – The Civic Ideology in World History. Politics and Education* (London: Longman, 1990), p. 3.
11 Greenfeld, L., *Five Roads to Modernity* (London: Harvard University Press, 1992), p. 3.
12 Bauman, *op. cit.*, and Räthzel, N., 'Aussiedler and Ausländer: Transforming German National Identity', *Social Identities*. Vol. 1, No. 2 (1995) pp. 263–82.
13 Miles, R., *Racism* (London: Routledge, 1989), p. 62.
14 Heater, *op. cit.* p. 183.

15 *Ibid.* p. 185.
16 Not only for immigrant or ethnic minorities: It should be noted that the concept of citizenship has also been criticized in the context of gender inequalities (Anthias & Yuval-Davis 1992; Meehan 1993; Vogel & Moran 1991).
17 Macdonald, S. (ed.), *Inside European Identities* (Oxford: Berg, 1993), p. 8.
18 Forsythe, D., 'German Identity and the Problem of History', in Tonkin, E., McDonald, M. and Chapman, M. (eds.), *History and Ethnicity* (London: Routledge, 1989), pp. 137–56.
19 Wieviorka, M., 'Racism in Europe: Unity and Diversity', in Rattansi, A. and Westwood, S. (eds.), *Racism, Modernity and Identity – On the Western Front* (Cambridge: Polity Press, 1994).
20 Forsythe, *op. cit.*
21 Habermas, J., *The New Conservatism* (Cambridge: Polity Press, 1989); Maier, C.S., *The Unmasterable Past – History, Holocaust and German National Identity* (London: Harvard University Press, 1988).
22 Forsythe, *op. cit.*, p. 151.
23 Weidenfeld,W. and Korte, K.-R., *Die Deutschen— Profil Einer Nation* (Stuttgart: Klett-Cotta, 1991).
24 Interview with *Türkische Gemeinde, Berlin.*
25 Interview with *TGB Hamburg c.V. (Bund Türkischer Einwanderer).*
26 Interview with *Blindnis Türkischer Einwanderer in Berlin-Brandenburg e.V.*
27 Interview with Amt für Multikulturelle Angelegenheiten der Stadt Frankfurt am Main.
28 *Ibid.*
29 Cohn-Bendit, D. and Schmid, T., *Heimat Babylon – Das Wagnis der multikulturellen Demokratie* (Hamburg: Hoffmann und Campe, 1992).
30 Heckmann, F., *Ethnische, Minderheiten, Volk und Nation. Soziologie inter-Ethnischer Beziehungen* (Stuttgart: Ferdinand Enke Verlag, 1992).
31 Estel, B., 'Grundaspekte der Nation – Ein begrifflich-systematische Untersuchung', *Soziale Welt*, Vol. 42 (1991), pp. 208–31.
32 Oberndörfer, D., *Der Wahn des Nationalen* (Freiburg: Herder Spektrum, 1993).
33 *Ibid.* See also Estel, *op. cit.*
34 Interview with *Blindnis Türkischer Einwanderer in Berlin-Brandenburg e.V.*
35 Leggewie, K. and Senogak, Z., *Deutsche Türken* (Hamburg: Rowohlt, 1993), p. 11.
36 *Ibid.*
37 Interview with *Forum Buntes Deutschland – S.O.S. Rassismus e.V. in Bonn.*
38 Interview with *TGB Hamburg c.V. (Bund Türkischer Einwanderer)*
39 Interview with *Türkische Gemeinde, Berlin.*
40 Cohn-Bendit, and Schmid, *op. cit.*
41 Noelle-Neumann, E. (ed.), *The Germans – Public Opinion Polls. 1967–1980* (London: Greenwood Press, 1981).
42 Koch-Arzberger, C. (1993). 'Die Auslander in den Augen der Deutschen', in Koch-Arzberger, C. (ed.), *Einwanderungsland Hessen? Daten, Fakten, Analysen* (Opladen: Westdeutscher Verlag, 1993), pp. 17–29.
43 *Ibid.*
44 *Ibid.*

45   The abbreviation stands for Institut für praxisorientierte Sozialforschung See, IPOS. Einstellungen zu aktuellen Fragen der Innenpolitik 1990 in der Bundesrepublik Deutschland und in der DDR (Mannheim: IPOS, 1990); IPOS, *Einstellungen zu aktuellen Fragen der Innenpolitik 1992 in Deutschland* (Mannheim: IPOS, 1992); IPOS, *Einstellungen zu aktuellen Fragen der Innenpolitik 1993 in Deutschland* (Mannheim: IPOS, 1993); IPOS, *Einstellungen zu aktuellen Fragen der Innenpolitik 1995 in Deutschland* (Mannheim: IPOS, 1995).

46   *IPOS* (1990), p. 41.

47   A telephone survey (sample: 600 indigenous German youths aged 16–25) conducted in 1990 on behalf of the Commissioner for Foreigners' Affairs in Berlin confirms this. Most Berliners thought that the most important problem the Berlin Senate should deal with is housing (53 per cent), followed by traffic (43 per cent), jobs (35 per cent) and then 'foreigners' policy' (31 per cent) (Ausländerbeauftragte 1990a:15).

48   *Ibid.*, p. 42.

49   The same telephone survey found that only 46 per cent of the respondents are in favour of local voting rights for Turkish residents who are not naturalized (Auslanderbeauftragte 1990a:10). This survey does not include any information on party alliance of the respondents.

50   *IPOS* (1992).

51   *Ibid.*

52   The PDS (Partei des Demokratischen Sozialismus) replaced the former SED and exists only in East Germany.

53   *Ibid.*, pp. 80–1.

54   This is also confirmed by the surveys done in Berlin on behalf of the Commissioner for Foreigners' Affairs (Auslanderbeauftragte, 1990 a and b).

55   *IPOS* (1993).

56   *Ibid.*, p. 78.

57   *Ibid.*, p. 84.

58   *IPOS* (1995), p. 1.

59   *Ibid.*, pp. 10–11.

60   *Ibid.*, pp. 84–6.

61   *Ibid.*, p. 87

62   *Ibid.*, pp. 88–9.

63   *Ibid.*, p. 90.

64   Jowell, R. *et al.* (eds.), *British Social Attitudes – Special International Report (6th Report).* (Aldershot: Gower, 1989).

65   It has to be noted that the Eurobarometer survey offered only two options ('proud' and 'not proud', whereas the British Social Attitude survey had two additional categories ('very proud', 'not proud at all').

66   European Commission, *Eurobarometer No. 42* (Brussels: European Commission 1995), p. 67.

67   European Commission, *Standard Eurobarometer No. 44* (Brussels: European Commission, 1996).

68   Zentrum für Türkeistudien, (ed.) *Das Bild der Ausländer in der Offentlichkeit* (Opladen: Leske & Budrich, 1995).

69   *Ibid.*, pp. 121–2.

70   *Ibid.*

71 *Ibid.*

72 Koch-Arzberger, *op. cit.*

73 Quoted by *Zentrum für Türkeistudien*, 1995: 56.

74 *Ibid.*

75 Jowell, R. and Airey, C. (eds.), *British Social Attitudes – the 1984 Report* (Aldershot: Gower, 1984), p. 7.

76 Margolis, M. and Mauser, G.A. (eds.), *Manipulating Public Opinion – Essays on Public Opinion as a Dependent Variable* (Pacific Grove, Ca.: Brooks/Cole Publishing Company, 1989), p. 3.

77 *Ibid.*, p. 309.

6
The Germans and their Capital: a Plea to Continue the Debate

Werner Süß

Introduction

Between 1989 and 1991, Germany was as taken by surprise by the discussion about its future capital as all of Europe was by the changes in Eastern Europe. West German policy never rescinded the reunification of the divided country, even when the global power structure necessitated a more realistic approach and, since the 1970s, the fact of two German states was accepted. Insisting on Berlin as the capital of a unified Germany was metonymic of the conception of a united country. Since the constitution of the German Bundestag (parliament), the correlation has been reiterated between the political option for the West German Federal Republic of a united Germany and the resulting symbolic function of Berlin.

Considering this unequivocal commitment to Berlin as the capital of a united Germany, questioning Berlin's role as the capital during unification negotiations came as a surprise. Even more so the vehement rejection of Berlin's claims to capital status and the defence of Bonn as the seat of the major governing bodies. The unification agreement left the final provision open. A broad media debate ensued, with the positions colliding with frightening intransigence.

This intransigence may be the underlying reason for not holding a referendum, contrary to earlier parliamentary initiatives, but leaving the decision to parliament. The differences in opinion concerning the German political centre seemed so irreconcilable that a referendum may only have burdened the German unification process with a deep rift between Bonn and Berlin advocates.

The capital debate has been resolved by compromise. A slim majority voted for Berlin as the capital, while Bonn was to remain a site of political importance by virtue of a division of labour. For a few years, cost rationale and administrative blockade tactics were used to try to reverse the decision to Bonn's advantage. But this failed with the passage of the Berlin–Bonn Law and the appointment of a government Ombudsman for the future capital. Since 1994, the decision has become irreversible.

The fact of events has ended the 'Capital debate' for the time being. Berlin and Bonn are preparing for their new roles. Approximately half of the ministries will remain in Bonn as well as a large part of the bureaucracy, and the city will receive reparation payments and compensatory functions. In Berlin, construction work for the arrival of the major governing bodies and their staffs, associations, embassies and other institutions is in high gear. The city can commence its career as the German capital in the year 2000. Despite any division of labour, Berlin will be the true capital in the eyes of the media.

But what course will this career run? Both advocates and adversaries of Berlin put enormous weight – whether out of hope or of fear – on the location change of the centre of political power. Hardly anyone assumed that Berlin would be a mere replica of Bonn or that Bonn would simply be implemented in Berlin. Rather, Berlin has been invested with a multitude of symbolic meanings which will accompany Berlin's career as capital for a long time and ensure that the controversy won't go away. For that reason alone, the debate will be continued and arguments for Berlin or Bonn will continue to be analysed.

The capital controversy from 1989 to 1991 became modified in the wake of the widespread discussion about the 'Berlin Republic'. The term designates the relocation of the government bodies and thus a rupture in the social development of the Federal Republic. One can discern optimistic and fearful standpoints – a capital Berlin as a site of misfortune or of a new sense of responsibility in politics. In both cases, the location of the capital is weighted heavily and the political symbolism highly overdetermined. The term 'Berlin Republic' is under debate, but does it contribute to the ongoing German capital debate, or is it merely divisive and stylizing an opposition that the Bundestag decision should have resolved? How adequate is the term and does it promote understanding of the relationship between the ongoing unification/integration process in Germany and Berlin's role in it as capital? Is the term a mere concession to the sloganeering language of the press and publishing industry, or does it facilitate analysis and enlightenment? The term suggests it does matter from where the republic is governed. The choice of the term 'Berlin Republic' assumes that Berlin won't be Bonn, and implies that Germans will have a different relationship to their capital.

The veracity of this premise will be tested in due time. For the moment, the term is suggestive and belongs to an uncharted language policy and political symbolism in terms of the Germans' capital quest. The controversy about Berlin's historical heritage, about the potential historical legitimacy the city could contribute to the future of a united Germany in the wake of a discontinuous and contradictory recent German history, proves this uncertainty. As of the capital decision in June 1991, Berlin could look back on 120 years in the role of capital. But Berlin's capital status and its meaning for the city and the socio-political development of Germany are just as discontinuous as German history as a whole, and therefore much less clearcut.

Berlin was the capital of the authoritarian Wilhelmine state and of the National Socialists, the capital of a country catching up with industrialization and modernization, an intellectual and cultural centre as well as the symbol of Germans' will for freedom, and finally, the power centre of the Socialist dictatorship. The ruptures outnumber the continuous lines; oppositions and dissent are more dominant than identity-forging elements. Berlin's history is just as disparate as recent German history, so it's not surprising that a lively debate has ensued about the self-understanding of the capital of all Germans.

Berlin stands for the heritage of German history with all its contradictions. But beyond that, can the city refer to certain traditions as progressive input for the future and for the legitimization of itself in its new role as capital? Would these traditions be those of the symbolic function during the postwar era or those of the vital 'golden twenties', or both? Does history outline meanings that Berlin's authenticity in its role as capital must fulfil?

Berlin in German history

Today, Berlin is the largest construction site in Europe, and the second largest in the world. In the area surrounding the Lehrter Station, around Pariser Platz, Potsdamer Platz and Leipziger Platz, but also at other places in the central Mitte district, like Friedrichstrasse, Dorotheenstrasse, at the former Checkpoint Charlie, etc., Berlin's construction is on display, promising a renewed, metropolitan future. The extent of the efforts is understandable, in the light of Berlin's historical importance among European capitals and past metropolises of the world. Against this historical background, the ambitious reconstruction of Berlin's centre to capital standards and to a metropolis goes without saying. Over six decades, first the National Socialist, then the Socialist dictatorships appropriated city spaces. Before its fall, Berlin had a meteoric rise. By the early 1930s, Berlin had become a European world city and the third largest city in the world. 'Golden twenties' Berlin throbbed and was one of the most exciting cities in Europe, a social and political centre in Germany.

Although a centralist system like those in Great Britain or France never developed in Germany, Berlin's importance was equal to those metropolitan capitals. Berlin was the political and economic centre of the German Reich. Berlin was the largest industrial city on the continent and the leading banking and stock exchange site in Germany. Not only were the executive branch of the empire, the Reichstag (parliament), the ministerial administration and the party headquarters located in Berlin, but also the central bank, large corporations and the most important business associations. Most importantly, Berlin was a centre of innovation as the site of large publishing houses and the mass market press. Berlin was an important film and fashion city and became a transit hub for Europe.

Intellectual and artistic life in Berlin was just as important as political and business interests. Berlin became an international culture metropolis and a centre of science and research. Twenty-eight Nobel Prize laureates worked in Berlin, among them Max Planck, Albert Einstein, Werner Heisenberg, Otto Hahn and Robert Koch. Nowhere else were intellect and power in such close proximity as in the former Reich capital.

The memory of 'golden twenties' Berlin is that of only a moment in time. Referring to the pulsating metropolis of the past sheds little light on the relationship between the Germans and Berlin. The late establishment as a nation-state as well as the modalities of Berlin's instatement as the Germans' capital render historical judgement difficult. While other European cities grew into their capital roles successively over a long period of time, Berlin went through this process after 1871 with breathtaking speed.

Berlin was already the intellectual and economic centre of Germany during the first decades of the nineteenth century. While the political climate was dominated by restoration, the industrial revolution took place in Berlin, especially in clothes manufacturing, machinery and the metal industry. Berlin developed into a major railway intersection in Germany. In science and culture, Berlin experienced a golden age. Fichte, Hegel, Schleiermacher and Ranke taught at Berlin universities.

Schinkel and Tieck, Carl Maria von Weber, Albert Lortzing, Felix Mendelssohn-Bartholdy, Heinrich Heine and E.T.A. Hoffmann were the important cultural figures of the day.

Despite all this, however, Berlin was not the centre of Germany. The dissolution of the Holy Roman Empire in 1806 left a power vacuum, that only in the 1860s Berlin would fill, surpassing Vienna, with smaller German states bridging the gap. In this context, the up-and-coming city of Berlin competed with free city-states such as Hamburg, Nuremberg and Frankfurt, and especially with the residential cities and regional metropolises like Dresden, Leipzig, Cologne, Regensburg, Mannheim and Munich. While Berlin grew exponentially after the foundation of the German Empire in 1871, so did other cities and regions in Germany.

Even if they did not reach Berlin's size, a typically German poly-centralism developed which, nevertheless, did not impede Berlin from becoming a world city and the business capital of Germany. The multitude of smaller states and alliances among principalities hindered the crystallization of a political centre in Germany.

German bourgeois society's roots and concentration were not only in Berlin, but also in south-western Germany and along the Rhine. Prussia's feudal society felt more comfortable in Potsdam than in Berlin, the centre of liberalism, the masses and the workers' move-ment. Symptomatic of this situation was Berlin's designation as capital in Versailles, after the announcement of the German army's victory and the enemy's unconditional surrender.

There are numerous other symptoms of feudal reluctance towards Berlin, such as the completion of the Reichstag building 23 years after the Reich's foundation. Even leading lights of German parliamen-tarism later preferred Weimar's small-town quiet to the bustle of the big city Berlin. The basically centralist workers' movement may have been the only socio-political force unequivocally to commit to Berlin. Its radical wing could conceive revolution only as the conquest of the centre of political power.

For many reasons, Germans in the nineteenth century and the first years of the twentieth only reluctantly accepted Berlin as their capital. The residence of Prussian kings was considered, along with Vienna, to be a centre of restoration. Western Germans especially saw Berlin as the seat of the Prussian forces occupying them and Prussian mili-tarism. The behaviour of the Frankfurt Revolutionary Movement of 1848 sheds light on Berlin's precarious role within Germany. The 1848 freedom fighters naturally considered Frankfurt as the seat of a parliamentary German nation. For security reasons, they wanted to crown the Prussian king emperor. Consequently, Berlin would have been the capital. But the Prussian king refused. The national and thus the capital question remained unresolved, and was only finally resolved on a European scale by military victories over Austria, Denmark and France.

During the twentieth century, both world wars were launched from Berlin, and the National Socialists designed a gargantuan capital for the world rule of Germania; consequently, some see Berlin as the historical site of the misfortunes Germany had brought upon the world and as a metonymy of German authoritarianism and militarism. However, in Berlin, the integration of the bourgeoisie, liberalism and the business elite into feudal society took place on a wide scale. And the equation of Prussia with Berlin, of feudal with urban society, does not bear close scrutiny. The political leaders of Prussia were recruited from junkers, the rural nobility, in the eastern Elbe region. The urban society in Berlin, however, was more complex, more contradictory, and on the whole, more liberal.

'Golden twenties' Berlin bears witness to this. The metropolis Berlin was a modern and culturally open city. The republic was declared here by Scheidemann or Liebknecht; Bertolt Brecht, Kurt Tucholsky and Carl von Ossietzky all worked here. The expansion of the underground train lines and the construction of the 'Funkturm' (radio tower) in Berlin were important impulses for the new technological-industrial age.

But the internal dissension of the Weimar Republic, ending with street fights between right and left, Walter Rathenau's assassination and the persecution of Jews, was most painfully evident in Berlin.

The briefly outlined historical conflict sheds light on the quagmire of the German capital debate since 1806. Berlin became the power centre of Germany and a world city. But its capital status was always controversial, even though Berlin had become a metropolitan capital and the most important city in Germany. A symbiosis of political power, economic dynamics and intellectual and cultural force gave Berlin a status comparable to that of London, Paris or New York.

After the Second World War, Berlin – now destroyed – was divided into four zones and it became the seat of the Allied Control Commission. The subsequent long period of division into two halves, one of which was surrounded by a wall, had paradoxical results for Berlin.

On the one hand, the dynamic development of the city was rudely interrupted. The political and business institutions relocated to the western half of the divided nation. Political parties, associations, large corporations and companies moved to West Germany. Berlin became marginal relative to the rest of Germany and especially Western Europe. Berlin lost the role of transit hub and international communications nexus in Germany. Frankfurt has since assumed these roles.

These developments strengthened polycentralism. Hamburg, Frankfurt, Cologne, Stuttgart and Munich have all surpassed Berlin in economic importance during the last decades, not because of the subsidizing of the city, but because of the division of Germany and Europe.

On the other hand, Berlin as a capital and a city in general has never had more unanimous approval than during the division of Germany. After the Berlin blockade and the erection of the Wall, Berlin's and Germany's destinies were entwined. The Berlin question fostered agreement in the Western defence alliance.

Berlin, if only as an object, became a central location of international action and of political and diplomatic connections between Germany and the rest of the world, especially the Allies. After 1945, for the Germans, Berlin became a symbol of steadfastness for the free West and a democratic new beginning. Ernst Reuter's and Willy Brandt's Berlin fostered high regard for the West German half-nation more than provisional seat of the governing bodies in Bonn did.

Nevertheless, Berlin's merely symbolic capital status due to the division of Germany sharply severed the belated establishment process of the nation-state and of a political centre in Germany. Despite any reservations about the Prussian metropolis, Berlin had become the social and political centre of Germany, a European-style capital, while federalism prevented other German regional metropolises from sinking into obscurity. On the contrary, German regional metropolises, too, grew dynamically during the late Industrial Revolution, unhindered by Berlin's fast growth. Nevertheless, the socio-political development impulses culminated in Berlin; Berlin's development into a capital, a metropolitan capital, followed the historical impetus of Germany's belated modernization and establishment as a nation-state. After the rupture in 1945, this relationship existed only virtually. The city lost touch with the society to which it belonged and to any claims to supremacy. Only with considerable effort could West Berlin, as an enclave in Eastern Europe, keep up with developments in Western societies, thus Berlin's designation after 1948 as the uncontested capital of the Germans had no social foundation. For the citizens of the West German half-nation, Berlin became a political symbol and in light of the city's social importance, devolved into a mere tourist attraction.

Considering this background, history is an unreliable witness in the Germans' quest for a political centre. History outlines meanings, no more, no less. 'Golden twenties' Berlin, a metropolis of worldwide impact, lives on in the present imagination. Attempts to put an already mythic matter with little basis in German historical reality into perspective may seem somewhat ludicrous. Especially outside Germany, Berlin's historical importance has naturally entailed the city's function as capital. Within Germany, however, Berlin's loss of importance had more far-reaching consequences. The merely symbolic capital status could not compensate for this loss of importance. Also on a symbolic level, National Socialism left a heritage offering few points of reference for the continuation of the capital debate in terms of recent German history. With the decision of the provisional instatement of Bonn, the capital debate remained unresolved.

Bonn or Berlin? The capital debate, 1989–91

Bonn was never the capital of Germany, not even of the West German half-nation. Bonn was the provisional seat of the governing bodies, deputizing for Berlin until the reunification of Germany. Designating Bonn as provisional made the reasons clear for deciding against Frankfurt after the war. In 1948/49, all the founding fathers of the new republic knew that the choice of Frankfurt as capital would strip Berlin of its capital role. In numerous sessions, the Bundestag was ever more insistent on Berlin's status as the capital of a united Germany.

Only very late, in the 1970s, was Bonn accepted by the political strata as their centre of political power. In the spirit of détente and the acceptance of two German states, Bonn was fashioned into the federal capital and a modern political-administrative centre. The normalization of Bonn was introduced by Willy Brandt and Helmut Schmidt and continued during the Kohl administrations. Bonn was positioned as an intellectual-cultural centre, a symbolic locus of German history and the division of Germany. Bonn actually was to have been remodelled and reinterpreted as the capital of the West German half-nation.

This policy of profiling the old Federal Republic and the political centre more prominently did not imply rescinding the policy of reunification. On the contrary, reunification remained a policy guideline.

Therefore, Berlin's capital status was no longer questioned. Whereas Bonn increasingly symbolized the democratic self-esteem of the West German half-nation, Berlin remained the authentic capital of entire Germany.

The authors of the Berlin Proposal picked up this train of thought during the capital debate in the Bundestag on 21 June 1991, entitling their proposal 'The Completion of German Unification'. The proposal programmatically referred to Germany policy efforts since 1949 and to Berlin's proposed role as capital of a united Germany. But the majority decision of the Bundestag to reinstate Berlin as capital was marked by the subsequent compromise between Berlin and Bonn. Besides unequivocally accepting Berlin as the actual German capital, Bonn remained the centre of the ministerial administration. As the decision was further elaborated, Bonn was accorded the status of an additional centre of political power to Berlin, with not only two-thirds of the ministerial administration, but also about half of the ministries remaining in Bonn.

The compromise is understandable, considering the bitter and irreconcilable differences between advocates of each capital location. During negotiations for the Unification Agreement, Berlin's claim to capital status was surprisingly and fundamentally questioned by some federal states such as Nordrhein-Westfalen. Bonn's recent rise in status was evident in the tenacious clinging to insignia of the West German half-nation. At the same time, the distance of the political administrative staff in the Western federal states from the new German situation became visible. Efforts to maintain the status quo were discernible, taking the emerging united Germany's new geopolitical situation little into account.

In light of this background, Berlin's advocates may have felt defensive from the start. From the perspective of the politically dominant Western Federal Republic, there was little reason to give up either Bonn in its modesty and political efficiency or Berlin as the symbolic capital. That Germans should have a symbolic capital to represent their unity wasn't fundamentally contested, even by Berlin adversaries. They had more substantial matters in mind. The capital controversy had largely become a manifestation of regional egotism of the Western federal states, particularly motivated by civil servants living in the Rhine area. The East/West opposition became an obvious element of the capital debate.

In the context of the debate, one argument in particular, which basically stemmed from regional egotism but also had a connection to the new geopolitical power situation in the united Federal Republic, was significant, namely, the reference to the power advantage of the Western federal states over the Eastern states. All the major functions lie in the West of the Federal Republic, as Wolfgang Thierse observed, correspondingly seeing a power upgrade for Eastern Germany resulting from the relocation from Bonn to Berlin. The population of the former GDR would consider retaining Bonn as capital an affront and a reinforcing of the division instead of overcoming it and the establishment of a new status quo which was also relevant for regional politics.

Thierse's diagnosis is correct. With Berlin, the capital would be located in Eastern Germany, which then could keep up with other centres in Germany such as Hamburg, Munich, Cologne, Düsseldorf and Stuttgart in terms of power politics.

The references to the symbolic implications of the capital location were less substantial. Bonn is the symbol of the Westernization of Germany, of Western democracy and the proximity to the Western neighbours, especially the governing bodies of the European Union. Berlin, by contrast, is the the symbol of an Easternization of German politics, the opening towards the Central Eastern European countries and a recognition of the new geopolitical situation in Europe.

The East/West opposition has been used here forcibly and the political symbolism in general overdetermined. The auxiliary arguments serve to cover up the regional egotism underlying the motives. Furthermore, a Bonn nostalgia is operating, especially in large parts of left-wing intelligentsia, who earlier made no secret of their rejection of Bonn. Most of all, a location specification has been confused with a political project. The question of Western, Eastern or Central Eastern European orientation is political and not symbolic.

The East/West opposition within Germany hereafter played a major role in the capital debate. Nevertheless, it was not the centre of the recent German capital debate, and reducing the capital controversy to West German regional egotism is inadequate. Considering the entire argument repertoire of the debates between 1989 and 1991, it becomes evident that the deep-rooted problems Germans have with their political identity and their new capital underlie the Berlin/Bonn/ East/West oppositions. The question still is: What is the German political centre?

A series of arguments from far off has accompanied the Germans capital quest for over 150 years. Noteworthy arguments include:

- The conflict between centralism and federalism: in this controversy, the metropolis Berlin is equated with centralism, the smaller residential town Bonn with federalism
- The opposition big city/small town, with the big city signifying modernity, contradiction, social tension and the possibility of social experiences; the small town by contrast signifies the possibility of effective and undisturbed constitution of political will and of decision-making
- The question of the capital in the polarity of the denominational axis Catholic/Protestant and the political culture axis Northeast/ Southwest
- The question whether Germany lends itself to a political centre, an old inner German question which led to the suggestion of Kassel or Erfurt as possible capitals. And the question, asked more on a European scale, whether a national capital is even necessary.
- The merging of the capital debate with a debate about Prussia, stylizing Berlin as a symbol of German authoritarianism and Prussian and Protestant dominance

All these arguments played a major role in the capital debate. The stylization of the Berlin/Bonn and East/West oppositions are merely an indicator of the characteristically German insecurity about designating a political centre, stemming from the late establishment as a nation-state. Long-forgotten wounds of German politics and German history were brutally reopened and projected onto the current tensions between East and West.

Evidently, most arguments are anachronistic and don't give deeper insight into the content of German conflicts. This is especially true about the stylization of the denominational opposition. The urbanization of German society has been so far-reaching that the opposition of the big city and the small town, of modernization and idyll, is no longer relevant. This stylization was significant during the class struggle between feudalism and bourgeois society. Mixing the capital debate with a debate about Prussia is also anachronistic. Besides the equation of Berlin with Prussia being inaccurate, the rupture in 1945 should be considered. Prussia and the Prussian heartland were defeated and dissolved. The Prussian Junker power elite as well as the militarism of German political culture were eliminated.

The attempt to cope with German history in the capital debate should not be criticized. But too much has been dependent on location, too much projection has occurred, leading to too many lopsided debates. One must concede, however, that many arguments were born out of worry.

Between 1990 and 1991, there was a widespread fear that Berlin as capital might signify an extreme nationalism and indicate a relapse into the German nationalist state. The West German Left especially was very worried about the capital location of Berlin as a symbol of the German nationalist state.

To this a Federal Republican state mind was contrasted, post-nationalist, universalistic, European and patriotic only towards the Constitution. The accuracy of this self-image is not relevant. The Left has reiterated old arguments in the context of the German's capital quest. But this same Left must concede that the 'state of mind' debate is not tied to place, if one wants to assume that all relevant German cities have this state of mind.

Concerning the connection between the capital debate and the forging of a national identity, the Left formulated a widespread and perhaps typically German misunderstanding, at least when national identity and the symbolization in a political centre, in a capital, is contrasted with European universality.

On the question of whether a capital is even necessary in the wake of European unification, the German misunderstanding becomes even clearer. The assumption emerges here that the political institutions of the European nation-states will be absorbed into a pan-European institutional network and will thus disappear. This is not the case. The national constituting processes will remain dominant. No one is considering abolishing national governments or national parliaments.

In Germany there is a consensus from Jürgen Habermas to Helmut Kohl that political constituting processes should be inspired by European universalism, especially in Germany. But this doesn't render obsolete the question about German identity, about the existence of German interests in world politics and in Europe, as well as about the characteristics of a German political centre of power.

The opposition built up here between a united Europe and its metropolitan capitals isn't viable. Outside Germany, there is no talk of abolishing capitals. On the contrary, in Europe the predominant type of metropolitan capital has remained untouched by integration processes. One look at the uncontested role of European capitals, one look at Stockholm, Lisbon or Prague, at Paris, London or Madrid, at Warsaw, Budapest or Vienna, etc., shows how much the inner German capital debate and Berlin/Bonn compromise have become irrational and even grotesque.

All in all, the capital controversy has not brought about any normative consensus, and its division of labour between Berlin and Bonn has had precarious results. Thus the continuation of the capital debate is assured. Even heavier than its precarious results weighs the superficiality of too many arguments. Mostly, the capital controversy has worked too much along the old lines of conflict in German history. Social developments in Germany and a European context have superseded them. Nation-state and Europe, European unity and European regionalism are not oppositions in the current course of the European integration process. With this background in mind, a Europe of capitals can be accepted, in which the capital Berlin can find a place.

On the way to the 'Berlin Republic'?

The capital debate during 1989 to 1991 and the capital decision of the German Bundestag contributed little to a new German political self-awareness or understanding of the 'political centre' of united Germany, as the following debate about the 'Berlin Republic' versus the 'Bonn Republic' bears witness. Insecurities about the meaning of the location change of the capital already expressed by Berlin adversaries culminated in the question of a *translatio rei publicae*, of an actual foundation act, of a new republic and, in this vein, of an historical rupture. The debate also conjures up memories of the Weimar Republic and its demise, issuing a warning against risking the gains of the Bonn Republic. This perspective becomes all too understandable when leading representatives of Germany warn against such a rupture discussion. Regarding the legal state identity of the old and new Federal Republic, one cannot speak of a historical rupture as in 1933 and 1945/1949.

If one wants to speak of a Berlin Republic, it would follow the constitutional understanding and principles of the Bonn Republic. That entails a certain stability. One should be aware of this relationship when declaring the unification of Germany difficult under economic conditions or in terms of relocation of the political centre of power from Bonn to Berlin. The Berlin Republic has the same philosophy of stability as the Bonn Republic as well as a deeply democratic and freedom-loving self-understanding. This was indeed the base of the international approval of the unification process of the Germans, which European neighbours viewed sceptically.

As late as 1988, there was confusion in France about the increasing acceptance of the two German states entailing a new conception of a neutralist European policy. One year later, the Allied governments consulted each other about the democratic maturity of the Germans, whether one could trust them in times of crisis. The Kohl administration's pushing forward with Western Europe policy after the beginning of the unification process can be seen in this context. The European neighbours' worries about the democratic stability in Germany is based on the governmental modalities of the unification.

Considering this background, contrasting the Bonn Republic with a Berlin Republic seems awkward. The term's use serves more to sharpen the view for the present dynamic of change. In this context, the term Bonn Republic is emblematic for remembering the past of the old Federal Republic. Correspondingly, the term Berlin Republic stands for the erection of something new. It symbolizes the new united German reality and refers to processes of change in the social structures of the Federal Republic.

In this sense, the term's usage has little to do with the locality of the cities Bonn and Berlin. While locality was at the centre of the capital debate at the beginning of the decade and far-reaching conclusions were drawn from the various symbolic contents, the debate about the Berlin Republic is mostly about designating the heritage of the old Federal Republic, of the Bonn Republic, and showing any changes in the future entailing from the location of the political centre of power in Berlin. Governmental continuity aside, is there a shift from a Bonn Republic to a Berlin Republic, and how will they differ?

The answer to that question depends on the designation of the Bonn Republic. Basically, the term stands for the stability and 'economic miracle' society of the old Federal Republic, for the German model as implemented during the second half of the 1970s under the Helmut Schmidt administration. This model has four characteristics: a relatively socially peaceful society, a high consensual level within the elite, high political stability and a pragmatic economic self-understanding. This society still has an impact, its characteristics influencing Germany's further development.

The changes of recent years could be mastered thanks to an astonishing social peace. The revolution of unification took place along stable lines and without extreme offshoots. The mood was festive rather than excited. No nationalist outbreaks occurred. There was no fundamental shift to the right, rather the failure of the governing opposition party to recognize the signs of the times. During this period, there were no mass strikes or student revolts, although one can witness a certain disposition for violence among the very young and the arsonist mentality with right-wing young people. Because of this disposition for violence, the New Right probably won't provide the soil for the renewal of a conservative counter-movement, meaning that there will be no unmanageable conflicts in this society.

Society is still anchored by a consensual elite. The leadership of the most important social organizations and groups is firmly grounded by the freedom-oriented basic principles of the Federal Republic. Even the PDS designates itself within the existing constitutional spectrum and doesn't have obstruction as its goal. It should be considered, however, that the basic consensus within the elite is highly abstract, and underneath that, the elite is very segmented, as Ralf Dahrendorf remarked during the early 1960s.

The resulting weakness for assuming collective leadership responsibility, as Dahrendorf diagnosed back then, could be compensated for a long time by political stability. This stability has much to do with constitutional provisions strengthening the executive and introducing the constructive vote of no confidence, with the conception of a democracy defending itself forcibly if necessary and, most of all, with the role of the party state in the political constitution process.

A disadvantage of this political stability is the governmental-political scene's inability and disinclination for reform. Reformatory impulses usually came from extra-parliamentary protest groups. The political-institutional space by contrast seems static. This space is highly interconnected and has mutated into a complex negotional democracy leading to bureaucratization of the political process on all levels. Political stability and political rigidity are so close that Johannes Gross justifiably speaks of a 'moral dissonance' due to differing development speeds between the political level and society. This 'moral dissonance' is all the more worrying in light of the Bonn Republic's self-presentation as apolitical.

The Bonn Republic's central characteristic is indeed the society's pragmatic economic self-understanding grounded in the success story of the German economic miracle. The Bonn Republic helped Germans to forget major waves of poverty and hunger in 1907, 1917, 1923 and 1947. It brought prosperity to broad sectors of the population and firmly anchored in the German political culture the conception of a society without poverty, a middle class society with few class differences. The current sluggishness towards reforms has to do with the tenacious defence of this guideline of the former West German Federal Republic.

Signs of erosion in the stability and 'economic miracle' society have reached unmonitorable dimensions. Many current and future problems were already responsible for the power changeover from Helmut Schmidt to Helmut Kohl in 1982.

The exhaustion of the West German Federal Republic was under discussion even then. So we actually were no longer living in the cosy Bonn Republic, but in a republic facing great challenges. The events in 1989 and 1990 were additional challenges.

Since then, there is asymmetry in the lifestyles of Western and Eastern Germany. The major social institutions, innovation and communication centres are all metropolitan areas in the West of the Federal Republic. The Eastern cities, especially the new capital Berlin, must still position themselves. The city system of unified Germany is divided and must be brought into equilibrium. In those terms, we have been living in a new Berlin Republic for a long time; in a republic in which shortly Bonn, the old centre of the Federal Republic, will no longer be the origin of aid for Eastern Germany. This aid will come from Berlin, from East German territory. This is merely an image, but a very significant image. Berlin as capital can adapt better to this new united German reality, because the city is an active player in the establishment of a new inner German regional and urban equilibrium.

The new republic in which we live doesn't exhaust itself in the change dynamics resulting from the inner German relationship between East and West. Especially in the Anglo-American press, the term Berlin Republic is entwined with the debate about the economic and business site Germany. This debate shows how much the current change dynamics stir up the self-understanding of the stability society. As with other European societies, the Berlin Republic must muster the strength to remodel traditional institutions. Political culture needs to be readjusted in some fundamental areas, as the debate about the flexibilization of working hours or the remodelling into a service-oriented society clearly indicate.

The new society of mass unemployment is only partly accurate, as mass poverty has yet to occur. Not only the welfare state was effective here; other flexible reaction patterns came into effect. About 60 per cent of the population is in a so-called normal working relationship, while part of the poulation earns its money in working relationships which no longer fit the definition of normal. It makes no sense for the future to continue designating such forms as illegal, inferior part time work or as gaps in someone's resumé. Instead, a new basic understanding must be reached that will challenge traditional power structures and institutional engagement.

Equally dynamic is the changeover to a service-oriented economy in which the virtues of hard work and obedience are no longer central, as they were when Max Weber was examining the industrial economy and the bureaucratic state. The service-oriented economy will have to be more open, friendlier and customer-oriented; it will force society to reappraise traditional ideas. The current widespread privatization of many heretofore public services will be a push in the right direction.

These examples of change in the employment market shed light on the degree of erosion at the social foundation of the economic miracle in Germany. The situation can hardly be mastered by political restraint and pragmatic concession to the self-regulating power of the market. The situation calls for intellectual efforts, for which the metropolitan capital is more suitable than a political administration centre which exercises restraint in consideration of the provincial areas. In this respect, the question of implications or symbolic value of relocating the capital remains relevant.

The question remains whether it makes a difference from where the republic is governed. What will the capital Berlin offer the Federal Republic?

For the moment there are no provable answers to that question. The East and West German populations' reception of the capital is unpredictable. It is known that the population of the former GDR had an ambivalent relationship to its capital, although it should be closer to its heart through the course of unification process than Bonn, for example. In the West of the Federal Republic, one had got used to Berlin as a mere symbol. The capital debate and the included cost rationale probably led to a considerable loss of acceptance of Berlin, so that the West of the Federal Republic was mostly disinterested and apathetic. The relocation of the governing bodies and of associations beginning in 1999 wil probably take many years, with thus both the cost argument and the fear of a change in residence remaining in the mid-term.

Berlin's population is still an unpredictable factor, behaving sceptically and cautiously since 1989/90. The widespread scepticism among Berliners became evident for the first time during the city's campaign for the 2000 Olympic Games. Here massive reservations about Berlin's new role were articulated. And especially in Berlin people are jealous of privileged civil servants whose lives would be sweetened even more through the relocation.

This may result from Berlin's social structure and from the fact Berlin was burdened more than anywhere else in 1989/90 with the costs incurred by the new situation. The quick cancellation of the Berlin subsidy led to a severe drop in the standard of living. In addition, institutions which had hitherto guaranteed job security were restructured. Simultaneously, an explosion of housing costs drove some population sectors below the poverty line.

And both halves of the city experienced a major identity crisis. The former East Berlin had a burdensome heritage as the centre of a dictatorship. West Berlin, showcase of the West, itself became part of the East. It takes time to cope with this reassessment of values.

The question of the new capital's acceptance remains open. This will only strengthen Berlin's often quoted role as melting pot of the unification process. And if Berlin as capital will become a media event as assumed, then Berlin's melting pot role will be dominant in the media as well. Impulses for the unification process will come from Berlin. In addition, Berlin was always a highly politicized city, in stark contrast to Bonn. 'Spaceship Bonn' is proverbial. The city itself has offered few impulses for the creation of a vital political culture. In the quiet of small-town and bourgeois Bonn, a climate of administrative political execution developed, without interfering and questioning. Berlin is not suitable for that. The special situation of the city has influenced the political consciousness of its native and naturalized citizens over the decades. Here the division of Germany and Europe was evident in everyday life. With this heritage, the city is destined to contribute to overcoming this division. Furthermore, Berlin, unlike Bonn, was a central place, always in touch with the corresponding *Zeitgeist*. Changes in political ideologies and trends always left their traces in Berlin.

However, one must take one restriction into account. Germany's powers that be used Berlin less as a sounding board for conflicts and debate about the future. Berlin had become too marginalized through the long period of division and the Western half being surrounded by a wall. Düsseldorf, Frankfurt, Hamburg or Munich seemed more suitable for dialogue about the future or fads. By assuming the role of capital, Berlin will not only catch up but also assume a special role. Starting in the mid-1990s, Berlin has become a political and intellectual forum, where diagnosis of the times and dialogues about the future do take place.

The Federal Republic's social elites probably won't return to Berlin, and Berlin probably won't become a centre for social decision-making. Thus Berlin isn't a centralist metropolis which dominates all other regions. The decentralization and segmentation of power structures in

Germany is too far advanced. The elites won't move to Berlin, but they will spend more time in the city than before. Developments of the last two or three years indicate that under certain circumstances, the capital Berlin could pass as a site of intellectual and decision-making discourse. The ambiance of the city as well as the capital function favours this. In Berlin, the capital will present itself less modestly in old and new buildings and in more ostentatious surroundings than Bonn did. It will be a different representation of the political centre of power, more flamboyant and memorable. The republic will gain more attention in Berlin than in Bonn.

Interest especially from abroad will be directed towards Berlin. The international scene has never understood the internal German debate between Berlin and Bonn. For this scene, with Berlin, a metropolitan capital returns. Expectations of Berlin are high, especially in regard to Berlin's future role in the international East/West dialogue. Berlin has every chance of establishing itself, besides sober Frankfurt, as the centre of the German business community and an international centre. In the wake of globalization and internalization, capitals will communicate more frequently with each other. Capitals remain the site of national will finding and decision-making, even in the wake of a uniting Europe.

If this estimation is correct, Berlin can assume a different role from Bonn's past. It is expected that Berlin will fulfil its capital role in every way, especially intellectually and culturally. It is a moot point whether Berlin's significance equals that of London or Paris. The facts speak against this. But Berlin will be compared to cities like those mentioned. One expects impulses from this city and not just the bureaucratic execution of debates and decisions carried out and made elsewhere. That has to do with the metropolitan flair of this big city. Berlin has great political, cultural and intellectual potential, so that it could, beyond the economic power functions, again become the social centre of Germany. The relocation of the capital is not identical to implementing Bonn in Berlin, however the big city context will stimulate politics.

But these effects don't justify qualifying the locality change as a rupture of the Bonn Republic. United Germany with its capital Berlin is too continuous with the democratic principles of West German society. The different localities are not the defining characteristics. Every speech act about Germany is confronted by uncertainties about language usage. Although united Germany justfiably took over the designation as Federal Republic from the West German half-nation, the difference before and after 1990 is evident, between the 'old' and 'new' republic, between its 'old' and 'new' federal states, between its former division into two states and its current unification.

A strange tension between continuity and rupture exists which remains to be designated. The term 'Berlin Republic' may help by overcoming the heritage of division and contributing to the forging of a united German identity. The capital's change of location made developments in Germany and Europe in 1989/90 more visible. Bonn didn't offer the stage for the display of the changes in Germany, so that Berlin has a chance to appear in a different way as the Germans' authentic capital.

Outlook. A plea for a continuation of the capital debate

The capital controversy, which broke out unexpectedly with the changes in 1989/90, is coming to a close. The division of labour between Bonn and Berlin must be confirmed with the least damage to Berlin's role as capital. Since two-thirds of the ministerial administration will remain in Bonn, the location of the decision-makers in the various levels will be crucial. Without the movers and shakers behind the government and parliamentary machinery, Berlin will at best be a partial capital, a place where decisions are announced but not a site of political power and thus the Germans' political centre. The location is not suitable for reinstating a war of faith which only thinly disguises regional egotist motives with a superficial East/West debate.

Political symbolism is used in debates beyond the locality question. Symptomatic of this is the debate about the term Berlin Republic. Basically, the debate utilizes the opposition between Berlin Republic and Bonn Republic to go deeper and mark the historical space of the capital location change. Analytically speaking, the debate is concerned with precisely designating continuity and rupture in current German developments in their European and worldwide context. The political symbolism serves as an analysis of the tasks of political power and function assignment to the new German capital.

The symbolism operates with the classical understanding of capital functions, in which the political structure and the nation's destiny are evident in the capital. Speaking about the Berlin Republic is not possible without characterizing the capital or the future-oriented parameters of Berlin's role. The debate about the Berlin Republic bears witness to how little the Germans' capital quest has been completed, despite the capital debate. The nature of Berlin's capital role as opposed to Bonn's will depend on the estimated relevance of location for politics and how much weight will placed upon the the influence of the ambience and impulses of the big city Berlin considering the advanced urbanization in Germany.

This question also played a role in the capital controversy, although Berlin's big city qualification was never verified. Instead, historical overdetermination and symbolic overvaluation in equating the big city capital with political centralism blocked the necessary understanding of differences between the locations and of the specific character of Berlin, which at least is no longer considered provincial. The result was a catalogue of things Berlin could or should never be: neither provincial nor central.

It is questionable whether the debate status can be maintained. The expectations towards Berlin's role as capital won't allow that. The city itself essentially needs answers about the depletions that National Socialism, the Socialist dictatorship, the division and walling off have entailed. The political function of the capital isn't relevant, so much as a designation of the social functions beyond that. Berlin lies to the east of Germany. It thus shares the destiny of other federal states and other cities of the East trying to reposition themselves in the geopolitical structure of a united Germany and compete with the functions held by the regional metropolises of the former West German Federal Republic. The high symbolic value of the capital debate concealed rather than revealed this more pragmatic level. The question of Berlin's metropolitan character, its social significance with its dynamics and impulses, and its influence can be more adequately answered with material functional definitions than with political symbolism.

Neither was a dialogue about this opened, nor is there a consensus about starting the discussion and leading it discursively. And yet its presence can be felt in two ways. First, in many specific singular decisions in various social segments on the corporate level, in the media, in conference and trade organizations, concerning cultural subsidies, etc. In each case, these are decisions concerning which resources should be allocated to Berlin, what know-how, what management capacities, which social and functional parameters should accompany the political function of Berlin and enrich it. Market forces and opaque institutional arrangements regulate these processes and prevent the necessary clarification of Berlin's social role as capital.

Secondly, the controversy about the city's status as a metropolis shows how sensitive this topic is within the process of establishing a capital. The press, especially, has registered and given much attention to both the pros and cons of Berlin's attempt through extensive construction to catch up with the metropolitan centres of Europe. Berlin doesn't just entail the relocation of the capital from a small city to a big one, Berlin is also one of the largest cities in Europe. The city is larger than the three next larger German cities, Hamburg, Munich and Cologne, put together. Berlin's size meets every requirement for being considered in the same category as average European capitals and as metropolitan capitals. But the European capital is usually also the social centre of its respective country beyond its political function. The question is how Berlin will fit into this European context.

Berlin is preparing for this, but one can hardly predict how long it will take to overcome the consequences of depletion and marginalization. In any case, the city will need to be patient until the future investments pay off. The concept of a 'metropolitan capital' designates a long-term strategy, which, without society's consensus, especially that of the elite and the social leadership groups in Germany, stands on uncertain ground.

The prerequisite for a further reality check is the recognition that the concept of a 'metropolitan capital' cannot necessarily be equated with any kind of political or social centralism. Berlin's rise has already shown how compatible a world metropolis was with German federalism. The decentralization of power structures and of main social functions has progressed steadily during the last 40 years and is now irreversible. Tension between metropolitan capital status and federalism or polycentralism is basically not expected. Some more centrality for Berlin would be a guideline for carefully compensating the historically caused loss of significance and counteracting the city's devolution into a metropolis of poverty. Berlin is not a normal German city, as critics want to see it; and it has no chance to generate itself as such. The combination of historically designated significance and the international standing of Berlin, of the city's size and the extention of structural distortions make its designation as a normal city seem like a euphemistic idyll, which neither acknowledges the city's capital status, nor offers options for an adequate development perspective for Berlin. Designating Berlin as normal conforms to leaving the capital's further development to market forces and barely communicated institutional arrangements and decisions.

Approaches for a dialogue about the capital Berlin's role beyond its political function will not be gained from a further overdetermination of arguments of political symbolism, because Berlin is as far removed from the development status of the major modern European capitals as it is from any ambition of assuming a central role. The results do not exclude Berlin's return to the context of Europe's metropolitan capitals; they do not immunize it against a new type of symbiosis between intellect and power for the 'location of Germany', for which the big city context of the capital Berlin could offer at least ideally fertile soil. The goal is to make this soil fertile in reality too.

Prerequisite for this is a more profound dialogue beyond any political symbolism about the chances for development in Eastern Germany and its regional metropolises. Here, concrete complementary strategies to the Western regional metropolises need to be developed in which the development opportunities for Berlin are precisely spelled out and in which options for a metropolitan, internationally open future for Berlin are realistically considered. Such a debate must take regional egotism into account instead of concealing it with symbolic overdetermination. The continuing capital quest of the Germans is for more pragmatism than the intellectualism of political symbolism reveals. Even if this pragmatism turns out to be wrong, one must concede that the continued controversy about the status and functionality of the capital will run along very profane material lines carrying social significance.

7
The Debate over Germany's Normality: a Normal German Debate?

Tuomas Forsberg

Introduction

In view of the now popular debate of whether ideas matter in the field of International Relations, German foreign policy can be seen to constitute an excellent case in point. There is probably no other state where foreign policy style and orientation has been seen so much as a result of ideational factors, such as the 'German mind'.[1] Moreover, there is no other state where the prevailing ideas seem to have changed profoundly during the course of history. The whole history of Germany can be seen in terms of a competition of two ideologies, namely that of power and that of spirit.[2]

The course of German foreign policy after unification has been a matter of substantial debate. The debate revolves around the question of whether Germany will remain a state conducting a low-profile foreign policy or if it will become a great power with wider national interests. In the literature of International Relations, people who incline towards liberalism or constructivism argue that Germany's postwar commitment to institutionalism and multilateralism will continue.[3] Germany will remain reluctant to fight for its national interests unilaterally, and it will use soft power rather than act militarily. These views are opposed by those realist voices who expect that as a result of unification and its regained full sovereignty Germany will act more unilaterally, including being less embarrassed to use military force. In John Mearsheimer's much debated analysis, Germany will be forced to adapt to the role of a traditional great power and will eventually go nuclear.[4]

In the light of this debate, the end of the 1990s is in many ways a crucial period. First of all, the change of government will bring into power people who belong to a new, postwar generation to whom year

1968 may have been more significant than 1945. The new Red-Green coalition has declared that foreign policy will not change. Yet, they will have to formulate foreign policy in conditions that are shaped by a different material and ideological background from that of their predecessors. In the same vein, the capital will move from Bonn to Berlin and symbolize the end of the post-World War II Bonn Republic. Finally, Mearsheimer suggests that his prediction will become true only ten years after unification.

The key word to this debate on German foreign policy has been 'normality'.[5] This is because the argument for a more assertive role in world politics has been expressed as a need to normalize Germany's foreign policy. According to the normalization thesis Germany should conduct itself like the other great powers. As Germany has regained its unity and full sovereignty, it is logical that its foreign policy also will become more visible in the global and European arena. For the critics, these attempts at normalization have been seen as a euphemism for the remilitarization of Germany's foreign policy.[6] Yet, they do not argue that Germany should be different. In their view, normalization along the lines of the other great powers means that Germany will be abnormal. Normality in the case of Germany means that it stays loyal to its postwar commitments.

Indeed, the role the notion of normality plays is only understandable against the background of German history, in which divergences from normality have been seen in a negative light. Because Germany has no 'normal' past, the definition of normality is connected to views of the role of the state in international relations. Indeed, although the terms of the debate are peculiarly German, the debate itself is not internal, but depends on the expectations of others of what is normal for Germany, something the Germans cannot define by themselves.

In this essay, I will look at how views of normality are connected to the discourse on the future of German foreign policy. I will start by explaining some dimensions of 'normality'. Then I will present the current mainstream views of Germany's role in international politics and discuss how voices from the Left and Right try to criticize that position without challenging the notion of normality.

Ideas and German foreign policy

If ideas influence foreign policy, what are the ideas likely to be? In the German case two views clash. Several authors have suggested that German cultural deep structure leads to expansionism and authoritarianism. Treitschkean ideas of power politics and Haushoferian concepts of geopolitics brought German foreign policy to a belligerent track in the first half of the twentieth century. Yet German foreign policy has also contained strong pacifist elements. The peaceful tradition of German culture has perhaps been overlooked, except by Herder, for example, who claimed that German destiny was not to conquer, but to be a nation of thinkers and educators.[7] Today, this tradition ties Germany to multilateralism and inhibits its willingness to exercise military power.

Today's debate on the ideas that shape German foreign policy is not easy to depict in a straightforward manner. Although normality has been a key word in the debate, any juxtaposition of two perspectives along the axis of normalization will radically simplify the debate and does not do justice to the multifaceted aspects of the discussion. Therefore, any typology of schools of thought often conceals both the strong consensus as well as the magnitude and diversity of the nuances that are represented in the political debate. One of the best attempts to capture this debate is Hellmann's distinction between five schools of thought: Pragmatic Multilateralists, Europeanists, Eurosceptics, Internationalists and Normalization Nationalists. Among these schools, Internationalists are on the Left, Pragmatic Multilateralists are with Europeanists in the political middle, whereas Eurosceptics and especially Normalization Nationalists represent the political right.[8] Although the positions of the schools of thought are reminiscent of the political debate in many other European countries, it is instructive to see how close the positions, extremist views apart, actually are to each other. This is why a Green Foreign Minister can promise continuity and be seen as a pupil of the former Chancellor. Moreover, although the Normalization Nationalists of the postwar and the post-'68 generation added a new critical voice to the discussion that was conducted between the Centre-Right mainstream and its Left-Green opposition, their position does not depart far from the multilateral and institutionalist premises.

The debate over German foreign policy is naturally not conducted by Germans alone. Although public spheres are still somewhat limited by language and national boundaries, ideas that influence foreign policy decision-making, and especially ideas that are related to national identity, are not necessarily internal to the state (or nation). It is partly true that debates over national identity are conducted in the national discursive spaces, such as in the media, in parliament or between the executives, and draw on historical experiences of the state (or nation) in question. Yet, national identity is formed in a relationship between the image of the self and the image of the other. Similarly as the personal identity of the individual does not develop from the inside out, but from the outside in, nations need reference points in the outside world in order to define their identity.

The German case, in particular, demonstrates that ideas shaping national identity and interests are to a large extent driven from the outside. It is not only that the Federal Republic of Germany has always been very sensitive to comments from abroad. In the past, Nazism too borrowed elements from elsewhere: fascism from Italy, anti-Semitism from France and totalitarian ideology from Russia. The nineteenth-centrury concept of the *Machtstaat* was also cast in terms of international morality (*Sittlichkeit*). Even today the view that Germany should play the role of a great power is often motivated by the expectations of other people. These utterances often enter the German debate. As one participant of the normalization debate argued, 'our eastern neighbours, and not only they, expect from us a clearly conceptualized, unmistakenly formulated and responsibly executed policy that corresponds to the new status of Germany as a European great power'.[9]

The debate being conducted around the notion of normality makes it more than clear that Germans cannot define their role in world politics without reference to the views of others. The definitions of others of what Germans are or should be are increasingly the source of German identity.[10] It is, however, not possible to impose the terms of the debate from outside, as ideas and expectations that are circulated internationally will be filtered into the German debate through the prism of the national tradition and particularities of the current situation. The discussants will always have a choice of what to pick out from the various comments on Germany. Indeed, Germany faces a multiple choice as 'other powers perceive it to be not only the dangerous Fourth Reich in waiting but also the Good Germany, the solution to their own particular problems.'[11]

Dimensions of 'normality'

What does 'normal' mean? When is a state 'normal'? 'At first sight it seems a harmless phrase, one which is aimed at nothing and nobody and which could easily become the basis of a new consensus', writes Wolfram Wette. But 'normality' is nothing but a neutral concept. As Wette points out, it can turn out to be 'a pithy formulation behind which are concealed quite distinct concepts about the possible future role of Germany'.[12]

Of course, there is no such thing as a 'normal state' that would be above some sort of political arbitrariness. The standards for normality have changed continuously throughout the course of history. A good reminder from the late 1980s was that the existence of two German states was justified as a kind of normality.[13] Indeed, talk about normality will ring bells immediately if one is familiar with Foucauldian ideas about the power of discourses. In his view, the boundary between normality and abnormality is arbitrary and defined discursively. In today's world politics, discursive inclusion and exclusion are more virulent means of power than ever before. The definition of normality implies that the power of normal states does not need to be controlled. Yet, any definition of normality is often dependent on hegemonic states, which are themselves retrospectively anything but normal.

But why should one be normal? If the underlying idea of states is that they preserve cultural differences in the world and carry on their own traditions, states should emphasize their differences rather than their similarities. Compared to other states, 'the Germans' obsession with wanting to be perceived as "just like everybody else" may look anomalous'.[14]

The reason why 'normality' is the key concept especially for Germans is to do with the interpretation of the past that the Third Reich and the Second World War were the consequence of a *Sonderweg*, a special anti-Western and anti-democratic path that Germany took in the nineteenth century.[15] This special path was cut after the Second World War and (West) Germany was tied to the Western institutions. For those who now want to leave the political tradition of the postwar *Bundesrepublik* behind to become normal therefore means stepping out of Hitler's shadow. The need to normalize now replaces the former need to reconcile. The political tradition of the 'Bonn Republic' is regarded as an exception which cannot continue following unification. 'Normalization' after unification implies that the quest for establishing German identity changes into a quest for pursuing German interests. Germany's strategic role means that it must put its national interests to serve the international order: The denial of international responsibilities would also be a *Sonderweg*.[16] But for the critics of this view of normality, 'a normal international actor in the still emerging international system of the twenty-first century, may share much in common with a country that pursues restraint, multilateralism and a general avoidance of the use of military force'.[17]

For many people, any quest for a return to normality in Germany evokes the idea of a return to the tradition of a *Machtstaat*. The concept of *Macht,* power, in late nineteenth-century debates was the essence of the German idea of a state. Von Treitschke, who carried on the Machiavellian tradition, argued that the highest moral responsibility of a state is to preserve its power. The duty of individuals is to sacrifice themselves to the higher community of which they are members. The state, in turn, can only aim at moral values, otherwise it would contradict itself. The juxtaposition of politics and morality is a misunderstanding, as morality in this case refers only to positive law. The idea of an eternal peace is regressive, as all progress in history has been associated with wars. In von Treitschke's words, it is precisely political idealism that demands wars.[18]

Yet, a *Machtstaat* is only one possible idea of a 'normal' state. The concept of a *Handelstaat* can be seen as a way to oppose the idea that normality should be seen as a return to power politics. The idea of a commercial state is based on Richard Rosecrance's distinction between a state that aims at welfare through expanding its territory, and a commercial state that tries to achieve the same benefits through commercial exchange.[19] It may be ironical to note that in the German tradition at the beginning of the twentieth century, *Handelstaat* used to be a pejorative term which was used to describe England. Yet today, as Gunther Hellmann argues, German experts agree that the *Handelstaat* concept provides the best description of Germany's current role in international affairs. Nobody wants to return to *Machtstaat* status.

Considering the overwhelming support for the notion of a commercial state as a description of Germany, one should carefully analyse what this concept actually involves. For normalization nationalists, it has different connotations than for integrationists. Indeed, at a closer look, one can actually distinguish between a commercial state that fosters territorially defined national interests and a commercial state that aims at shared benefits. Moreover, along with the notion of a commercial state another notion is often added to the conceptual mix, namely *Zivilmacht*.

The notion of *Zivilmacht*, or 'civilian power', as a description of Germany's role in international politics stems from Hans Maull. For Maull, civilian powers will reflect normality in future world politics. As he has put it, the 'United States will have to evolve into a new type of international power, of which Germany and Japan are already in a sense prototypes: it must become a civilian power'. According to Maull's definition, a civilian power has three crucial attributes. First, it is ready to accept the necessity of cooperation with others in the pursuit of international objectives; second, it concentrates on non-military, primarily economic means to secure national goals; and third, it is willing to develop supranational structures to address critical issues of international management. A civilian power, however, does not stand in direct opposition to military power. Not only can civilian powers resort to military self-defence, but they can also foster common aims through military means. The distinctive factor is, however, that a civilian power does not look for autonomous military options.[20]

In the following section, I will tie the discussion on German foreign policy to these three notions of a normal state. I will present the idea of Germany as a commercial state that is committed to Western institutions as the mainstream view. I will then compare it to the idea of a global civilian state which is put forward by the Left-Green discussants and to the idea of a more nationally oriented great power that is suggested by the 'new democratic Right'.

The mainstream: a western trading state

Very few people think that German foreign policy will remain unchanged following unification, but the mainstream position is that much of the old can be preserved. The most valuable heritage of the Bonn Republic is that Germany is and remains firmly part of Western and global multilateral institutions. Yet, Germany can no longer continue its low-profile policy. It must develop leadership and articulate its national interests. Germany now needs to play an increasing European and global role. This means that Germany must be prepared to be involved in military operations abroad. The use of the military is limited to multilateral operations with a morally grounded aim. National values of security and welfare need not be denied, but global responsibility over questions of the environment, democracy, human rights and stability ought to be given more attention.

A good grasp of this way of thinking can be offered if we look at an article by former Federal President Roman Herzog. In his view the inevitable consequence of the recent changes in world politics is the globalization of Germany's foreign policy. In his view, more responsibility is needed as risk-avoiding action can be more risky than being ready to take risks. Yet, military responsibilities are only a minor part of the tasks. The problems of the twenty-first century are not primarily strategic but can be captured only through a broad definition of security. To solve the problems soft power is more relevant than hard power. Germany's channels of influence in the multilateral concert are primarily economic and moral rather than military.[21]

Germany cannot, however, give up hard power entirely; it is needed to combat future threats of aggression and genocide, not just against Germany but elsewhere in the world too. Besides its immediate national interests of security and welfare, Germany should aim at fostering global free trade, it should contribute to the spreading of democracy to all parts of the world, to building up the United Nations, to setting a new basis for the Atlantic alliance and to completing the European process of unification (*das europäische Einigungswerk vollenden*). In Herzog's view, these aims reflect both the pragmatism of a realist policy of interests and an idealist policy of responsibility. The two are no longer separable.

Volker Rühe, the former Minister for Defence, too, sees the change in terms of increased international responsibility. In his view, the global and regional challenges require concepts of security, which extend national and regional horizons. Community and solidarity, participation and influence are in his view imperatives of German foreign policy. Yet, politics of responsibility is not possible without power. Within this politics of responsibility, Germany should be ready to contribute militarily.[22]

Similarly the new Social Democratic Minister for Defence, Rudolf Scharping, argues that Germany should conduct its foreign policy in a self-conscious but restrained manner. It has to recognize the expectations of other states, but it cannot neglect the fears that they have about Germany either. In the future, Germany should focus on the creation of a stronger European foreign and security policy. In Scharping's view, a Europe that can act globally as an equal partner with the United States can best meet the challenges entailed in quests for peace, democracy and human rights, future-oriented welfare and broad security.[23]

In Hellmann's typology these mainstream German foreign policy-makers from the CDU, FDP as well as the SPD are pragmatic multilateralists and Europeanists. Pragmatic multilateralists typically formulate their ideas comprehensively, always for something and almost never against something. This *sowohl-als-auch* policy sees no contradiction between a growing regional and international role, or between national interests and international responsibilities. On this view, opinions differ over how the process of European integration should be extended. Pragmatic Multilateralists do not see the contradiction between enlarging and deepening European integration, whereas Europeanists clearly prefer deepening the European Union to enlarging it. In their view integration should be deepened independently of whether or not all member states are willing to proceed at the same speed.

The idea of a core Europe consisting of Germany, France and the Benelux states was put forward in an internal paper by Lamers and Schäuble of the ruling CDU Party. For Lamers and Schäuble only a further deepening of European integration would prevent Germany from finding itself in a middle position (*Mittellage*) between East and West in Europe and returning to the old policy characterized by the to-ing and fro-ing between divergent interests. It is this idea in particular that has evoked critical responses from both the left and right: from the left it is seen as a symptom of power politics, from the right it is the ultimate sell-out of national interests.

The leftist current: a global civilian power

The central point for internationalists, according to Hellmann, is that today's foreign policy has to be conducted against the background of an ever more complex and interdependent world.[24] Therefore, stable peace, a clean environment, human rights and the elimination of poverty in the third world should be Germany's priorities. Normalization along the line of the mainstream policy for them means militarization. Similarly, participation in Western institutions, such as the EU, NATO or G8, stands mostly in opposition to the internationalist values that are better represented by the UN. Yet, even among internationalists wholly pacifist programmes are rare, and very few of them are arguing against Germany's commitment to Western institutions, including NATO.[25]

Joschka Fischer, the new Green Foreign Minister, departs even less from the multilateral and pragmatist mainstream. He sees continuing the self-imposed restraints on Germany's power as inevitable, but thinks it is a mistake to avoid the concept of national interest. Rather, he claims that the most important German interests rest on the refusal to renationalize foreign policy and stay away from the *Sonderwegtradition*. Democracy, rule of law, social welfare and the market economy are fundamental values upon which German foreign policy should be based. These values may necessitate military operations, as for example in the former Yugoslavia. Moreover, the continuity of Western integration does not contradict these values. Further Europeanization is the prime interest for Germans: they should not consider other options. In Fischer's view Europe should play a more active role on the world political scape, but Germany itself is too vulnerable for such a global role. Germany's interests lie in Europe: it should deepen and enlarge European integration and support Russia on its way towards democracy and a market economy. The eastern enlargement of NATO supports these aims. At the same time, however, NATO should be transformed towards an all-European security system that entails the possibility of Russia's inclusion. [26]

Jürgen Habermas has participated in the discussion on Germany's normality by arguing against the tendency of regarding the Nazi past as a sidetrack of German history. For Habermas the 'dialectic of normalization' means that one should never forget how different the German past has been. The idea that Germans have become normal is, for Habermas, the second big lie (*Lebenslüge*) of the Federal Republic of Germany. In his view, however, one should also remember the positive elements of German history. Habermas calls for carrying on the legacy at a European level:

> We should push toward the political union of Europe but not as we have up to now administratively without regard to the people. We need public dialogue about the further development of the European Community – which must seek a decisive democratization of the Brussels institutions and an effective political meshing of the national public spheres in Europe.[27]

In Habermas's view, Germany should also develop its global role. It should participate in UN military operations whilst at the same time the UN should be transformed into a more active political organ. Habermas assumes that his European and internationalist views would constrast with an eastward-looking sovereignty-conscious militarized German foreign policy. Such views one can find in the texts of the Normalization Nationalists.

The rightist current: a central European great power

For the advocates of normalization on the right the point is that Germany should be like other European powers. It should be more self-confident of its national values. Due to its regained sovereignty and increased area and population, Germany can no longer act as a small state. Germany can no longer be a reluctant power or a *Zahlmeister* of European integration. Germany should be able to foster its own interests and carry global responsibility. Yet, Normalization Nationalists do not argue that Germany is a great power in the traditional sense, since all great powers are now 'postmodern' in the sense that they are bound to international commitments. In a similar vein, Germany is said to be no longer a classic nation-state but a post-classic nation-state.[28]

Normalization Nationalists actually deny that they are nationalists in any nineteenth-century sense of the word:

> The assumed nationalism of the moderate right accepts the process of integration which has been ongoing for a long time, both European integration and economic integration of the world. It is not offensive but defensive, it does not defend the absolute sovereignty of the nation but the national consciousness, it is exactly not 'nationalism'.

The concept of the nation-state should not be associated with the *Machtstaat* as it is not the yard stick of a modern nation-state.[29] Although the era of traditional power-seeking states is over, nation-states have not vanished from history. Neither should multi-culturalism be seen as an absolutely higher value. The idea of a world state is a Utopia and notably the multi-ethnic states in Europe have proved to be weak. Belonging to a nation is existential, and it is still a given characteristic of every state.

Although Normalization Nationalists do not want to be associated with the nineteenth-century nationalist thinkers, there are some striking similarities with von Treitschke's ideas. Von Treitschke, too, argued that the Germans will always be at risk of losing their state because they have too little political pride. The lack of political or national pride has been the central concern of the Normalization Nationalists, as well. In their view national unity gives ground for an enhanced self-consciousness. The loss of identity and self-confidence during the postwar era must be replaced by a normal sense of national pride.

This pride is to be based also on national history and not only on the economic success of postwar Germany. For Normalization Nationalists, German history is not that exceptional after all. Hans-Peter Schwarz asks:

Have not all the great countries in Europe taken a special path, so that the talk about a normal case is hardly possible? Should not British history be seen as a special case as well? Up until the 20th century, doesn't it also show remarkably many features of an authoritarian state? – And does not the Third Reich show not only continuities of negative tendencies of the past, but also monstrous characteristics that differ significantly from the earlier phases?[30]

From the point of view of Normalization Nationalists, history should not be taboo. For some the Third Reich was an exception, for others Germans in the 1930s did not differ radically from their enemies. Normalization of history means that the history of the Third Reich should be demystified. Normalization Nationalists do not deny the evils of the Third Reich; it does not constitute any nostalgic elements of national greatness, but neither should present day Germany be the ultimate mirror image of the Third Reich. Instead of the Third Reich, a more positive reference point in history is the Wilhelminian Second Reich, and especially the era of Bismarck.

Normalization Nationalists emphasize that enhanced national self-confidence is not opposed to values of democracy, freedom and peace.[31] The main target of criticism is the idea of European integration as a *Staatsräson* of Germany. Although Germany should not elevate its national identity to a mythical status, it must retain its sovereignty. The assumption is that co-operative international communities can only function between states.[32] Europe cannot function as a substitute for national identity. In Arnolds' view only the rational management of the German nation state can prevent a national outburst which would emerge in a united Europe. Against this background Chancellor Helmut Kohl was characterized as a European illusionist and EU Europe accused of failing the test of popular legitimacy.

Some of the Normalization Nationalists of the Right also advocate the renaissance of geopolitics. The geopolitical argument is that Germany cannot escape its position as one situated in the middle of Europe. It is less clear, however, where this argument will lead, but usually it supports the view that Germany should pay more attention to its interests in Mitteleuropa and recognize the importance of building a bridge between Russia and the West. Yet, Germany's true 'national interests' lie more in stabilizing than in exploiting its surroundings.

Current discourse and Germany's course

Has the quest for normalization really changed German foreign policy after unification? Opinions differ. Gordon argues that whilst the long-standing characteristics of German foreign policy will not disappear quickly, the process of normalization has already begun. Meiers in turn sees that Germany is still far from being a 'normal' international actor.[33] For Ingo Peters, the unavoidable conclusion is that there are no changes in the goals or strategies of Germany in Europe or in the world.[34] For Hartmut Mayer, Germany's interests are geopolitically determined and reflect the old German saying that one's shirt is closer than one's trousers.[35]

The continuity thesis is supported especially by Germany's commitment to deepening European integration. In the spring of 1998, Kohl's compromise on the election of the head of the European Central Bank sent signals to some observers that Germany was not normal enough to defend its national interests and fight openly on Europe's future.[36] Even more strikingly, the assertions of the new Chancellor and Foreign Minister not to countenance any experiments in German foreign policy seems to show that inherited discursive structures persist over generations as well as crossing party-political lines. In this sense, they can be seen as more significant determinants than purely material relationships of power.

The claim that Germany's role has adapted to become more assertive is often supported with reference to the unilateral recognition of Croatia and Bosnia in December 1991 and its defence of its closest neighbours in the negotiations over EU enlargement. What makes these arguments over the nature of Germany's foreign policy problematic is that any empirical evidence of what Germany is doing can be interpreted as supporting both Germany's reluctance and its assertiveness. In Thuman's view, for example, 'by recognising Croatia and Slovenia, German foreign policy was not assuming more responsibility for the Balkans. It simply used this highly symbolic action to escape further commitments in the peacekeeping effort. The apparent German ambition merely disguised the actual paralysis of German foreign policy.'[37] Similarly, the efforts at enlarging the EU can be seen not simply as an attempt at creating a German sphere of interest, but as a rejection of such aims in favour of multilateralism.[38]

Discourse analysis is not able to predict which course German foreign policy is taking, but it can point out that some positions are excluded and therefore very unlikely to emerge as signposts of foreign policy of the 'Berlin Republic'. Shared understandings range from European integration to growing global responsibility in promoting democracy and human rights. The mainstream will remain strong, although the new right has changed the position of the middle as the boundaries of the politically acceptable ways to talk about German foreign policy have been extended.[39] Yet, as Hellmann argues, the influence of the New Right has actually declined since 1994.[40] The statements of the new German foreign policy decision-makers have shown that the discursive field is quite consolidated. Moreover, public opinion has typically been more conservative than elite opinions. For example, the people have been critical towards German military contributions abroad.

On the level of discourse, the values of peace, democracy and human rights are undisputed aims of German foreign policy. Multilateralism remains the means and international acceptance the condition to achieve them. References to other states and their views of Germany are still needed in order to persuade the audience that Germany's foreign policy is not particularistic. Germans agree that they must not forget the lessons of the past. They have also started to use the concept of national interests. Of course, the discussants may differ in their views of what national interests are, what democracy, peace and human rights mean, what the expectations of others are or what the lessons of the past are. Nevertheless, there remains a broad area of discursive overlap. Most concretely, Germany's integration with the Western institutions such as the European Union and NATO is not challenged, although some normalization nationalists and internationalists alike have criticized the aims of deepening European integration or US dominance in NATO. None the less it seems, as Baring has put it, that 'multilateralism has become second nature to Germany'.[41] It is noticeable that foreign analysts are often more fond of the idea of Germany developing into a traditional great power than the Germans themselves.

Notes

1 E.g. Kohn, H., *The Mind of Germany* (London: Macmillan, 1960).
2 Ludwig, E., *Geschichte der Deutschen. Studien über Geist und Staat* (Zürich: Carl Posen, 1945).
3 See in particular Katzenstein, P., 'United Germany in an Integrated Europe', in Peter Katzenstein (ed.), *Tamed Power. Germany in Europe.* (Ithaca: Cornell University Press, 1997).
4 Mearsheimer, J., 'Back to the Future: Instability in Europe after the Cold

War', *International Security*, Vol. 15, No. 1 (1990) pp. 5–56.

5 See e.g. MacAdams, J. A., 'Germany after Unification. Normal at Last?', *World Politics*, Vol. 49, No. 2 (1997) pp. 282–308; Dorff, R., 'Normal Actor or Reluctant Power? The Future of German Security Policy', *European Security*, Vol. 6, No. 2 (1997) pp. 56–69; Wette, W., '*Sonderweg* or Normality. The Discussion of the International Position of the Federal Republic', *Debatte*, Vol. 4, No. 1 (1996) pp. 9–20; Gordon, P., 'Berlin's Difficulties. The Normalization of German Foreign Policy', *Orbis*, Vol. 38, No. 2 (1994) pp. 225–43; Bulmer, S. and Paterson, W., 'Germany in the European Union. Gentle Giant or Emergent Leader?', *International Affairs*, Vol. 72, No. 1 (1996) pp. 9–32; Janning, J., 'A German Europe – A European Germany', *ibid.*, pp. 33–41; Krippendorf, E., 'Germany as a World Power and as a European Power', in Heurlin, B. (ed.), *Germany in Europe in the Nineties* (London: Macmillan, 1996).

6 Michal, W., *Deutschland und der nächste Krieg* (Berlin: Rowohlt, 1995).

7 Berlin, I., *Vico and Herder. Two Studies in the History of Ideas* (London: Hogarth Press, 1976) p. 161.

8 Hellmann, G., 'The Sirens of Power and German Foreign Policy. Who is Listening?', *German Politics*, Vol. 6, No. 2 (1997) pp. 29–57; Hellmann, G., 'Goodbye Bismarck? The Foreign Policy of Contemporary Germany', *Mershon International Studies Review*, Vol. 40, No. 1 (1996) pp. 1–39.

9 Schöllgen, G., 'Der Blick von aussen ist fordernd und erwartungsvoll', *Frankfurter Allgemeine*, 13 August 1993.

10 See e.g. Korte, K.-R., 'Was Denken die Anderen über uns? Fremdbilder als notwendiges Korrektiv der deutschen Aussenpolitik', *Internationale Politik*, Vol. 52, No. 2 (1997) pp. 47–54; Hubel, H. and May, B., 'Ein 'normales' Deutschland? Die souveräne Bundesrepublik in der ausländischen Wahrnehmung', in *Arbeitspapiere zur Internationalen Politik*. (Forschungsinstitut der Deutschen Gesellschaft für auswärtige Politik, June 1995).

11 Walker, M., 'Overstretching Teutonia. Making the Best of the Fourth Reich', in *World Policy Journal*, Vol. 12, No. 1 (1995) pp. 1–18.

12 Wette, *op. cit.* (1996) p. 9. In Wilfried von Bredow's view, 'the word normalisation has the function of announcing in a rather solemn manner that one does not really know what foreign policy priorities are to be chosen'. Von Bredow, W., 'Dragged along by Globalization, Slowed down by History. The Framework, Objectives and Comprehension Problems of German Foreign Policy', *Debatte*, Vol. 5, No. 2 (1997) pp. 137–50.

13 See e.g. Schweigler, G., 'Normalität in Deutschland', *Europa-Archiv*, Vol. 44, No. 6 (1989) pp. 173–82.

14 MacAdams, *op. cit.* (1997) p. 282.

15 See Dahrendorf, R., *Gesellschaft und Demokratie in Deutschland* (München: Beck, 1965); and Wehler, H-U., *Das deutsche Kaiserreich 1871–1918* (Göttingen: Vandenhoeck & Ruprecht, 1980).

16 Stürmer, M., 'Deutsche Interessen', in Kaiser, K. and Maull, H., *Deutschlands neue Aussenpolitik. Band 1: Grundlagen.* (München: R. Oldenbourg, 1994).

17 Maull, H., 'Germany and Japan. The New Civilian Powers', *Foreign Affairs*, Vol. 69, No. 5 (1990/91) pp. 91–106.

18 Von Treitschke, H., *Politik. Vorlesungen gehalten an der Universität zu Berlin*, 5th edition (Leipzig: Hirzel, 1922).

19 Rosecrance, R., *The Rise of the Trading State: Commerce and Conquest in the Modern World* (New York: Basic Books, 1986).

20 Maull, *op.cit.* (1990/91); Maull, H., 'Zivilmacht Bundesrepublik Deutschland. Vierzehn Thesen für eine neue deutsche Aussenpolitik', *Europa-Archiv*, Vol. 47, No. 10 (1992) pp. 269–78. See also Tewes, H., 'The Emergence of a Civilian Power: Germany and Central Europe', *German Politics*, Vol. 6, No. 2 (1997) pp. 95–116; Tewes, H., 'Das Zivilmachtkonzept in der Theorie der Internationalen Beziehungen', *Zeitschrift für Internationale Beziehungen*, Vol. 4, No. 2 (1997) pp. 347–59.

21 Herzog, R. 'Grundkoordinaten deutscher Aussenpolitik' *Internationale Politik*, Vol. 50, No. 4 (1995) pp. 3–11.

22 Rühe, V., *Deutschlands Verantwortung. Perspektiven für das neue Europa* (Frankfurt am Main: Ullstein, 1994) p. 43.

23 Scharping, R., 'Selbstbewusst und zurückhaltend zugleich', *Frankfurter Allgemeine Zeitung*, 16 October 1997.

24 Hellmann, *op. cit.* (1996) p. 13.

25 See Volmer, L., *Die Grünen und die Aussenpolitik – ein schwieriges Verhältnis. Eine Ideen-Programm-und Ereignisgeschichte grüner Aussenpolitik* (Münster: Westfälisches Dampfboot, 1998).

26 Fischer, J., 'Les Certitudes Allemandes. Grundkonstanten bundesdeutscher Aussenpolitik', *Blätter für deutsche und internationale Politik* (1996); Fischer, J., 'Die Selbstbeschränkung der Macht muss fortbestehen', *Frankfurter Allgemeine Zeitung*, 10 August 1998.

27 Habermas, J., '1989 in the Shadow of 1945. The Normality of the Future Berliner Republic', in Habermas, *A Berlin Republic: Writings on Germany* (Oxford: Polity Press, 1997).

28 Hacke, C., 'Die neue Bedeutung des nationalen Interesses für die Aussenpolitik der Bundesrepublik Deutschland', *Aus der Politik und Zeitgeschichte,* 3 January 1997.

29 Mayer, T., 'Fragmente zur Bestimmung der deutschen National-staatlichkeit', in Zitelmann, R., Weissmann, K. and Grossheim, H. (eds.), *Westbindung. Chancen und Risiken für Deutschland* (Frankfurt am Main: Propyläen, 1993).

30 Schwarz, H-P., *Die Zentralmacht Europas. Deutschlands Rückkehr auf die Weltbühne* (Berlin: Siedler, 1994).

31 Mechterscheimer, A., 'Nation und Internationalismus. Über nationales Selbstbewusstsein als Bedingung des Friedens' and Inacker, M., 'Macht und Moralität', in Schwilk, H. and Schacht, U. (eds), *Die Selbstbewusste Nation* (Frankfurt am Main: Ullstein, 1994).

32 Arnold, H., *Deutschlands Grösse. Deutsche Aussenpolitik zwischen Macht und Mangel* (Munich: Hanser, 1995).

33 Meiers, F-J., 'Germany: The Reluctant Power', *Survival*, Vol. 37, No. 3 (1995) pp. 82–103.

34 Peters, I., 'Vom "Scheinzwerg" zum "Scheinriesen" – deutsche Aussenpolitik in der Analyse', *Zeitschrift für Internationale Beziehungen*, Vol. 4, No. 2 (1997) pp. 361–88.

35 Mayer, H., 'Early at the Beach and Claiming the Territory. The Evolution

of German Ideas on a New European Order', *International Affairs*, Vol. 73, No. 4 (1997) pp. 721–37.

36 Vinocur, J., 'A Tale of Two Germanys: Assertiveness vs. Reserve', *International Herald Tribune*, 11 May 1998.

37 Thuman, M., 'Between Ambition and Paralysis – Germany's Policy toward Yugoslavia 1991–93', *Nationalities Papers*, Vol. 25, No. 3 (1997) pp. 575–85.

38 Friis, L., 'Tyskland og EU's ostudvidelse. På vej mot tysk "normalitet"?' *Internasjonal Politikk*, Vol. 56, No. 1 (1998) pp. 31–49.

39 Heilbrunn, J., 'Germany's New Right', *Foreign Affairs*, Vol. 75, No. 6 (1996) pp. 80–98.

40 Hellmann, *op. cit.* (1997).

41 Baring, A., 'Wie neu ist unsere Lage? Deutschland als Regionalmacht', *Internationale Politik*, Vol. 50, No. 4 (1995) pp. 12–21.

8
Human Rights Universalism and Patriotism: Kant's Political Legacy to Our Time

Manfred Riedel

'Universalism' was once the paradigmatic doctrine of the Christian theology of the redemption of all, i.e. the assumption that divine mercy would save everyone after death, and a 'universalist' a believer in the redemption of all. Today the word describes the paradigm of discourse ethics, that is, the assumption that all human beings are capable of living by universal moral and legal norms through the fulfilment of obligations of rationality in a community of discourse. This is based on a principle of universalization, which is held to be pre-formulated in the moral law of practical reason: not in each of its formulations but in the idea of Kant's basic formula of the categorical imperative, to act only upon the maxim 'of which you can want at the same time that it become a general law',[1] a formula that is supposed to 'account for the impersonal and general character of valid moral laws'. Thus we encounter it in the version of Kant's principle of right: 'Any act which or according to the maxim of which the freedom of the will of each can exist together with everyone's freedom on the basis of a general law is *right*.'[2] As neo-Kantian interpreters argued at the beginning of the twentieth century in relation to Kant's *Metaphysics of Morals*, its content really consists in establishing one single law: live rationally, in accordance with the law; in short: universalistically.[3]

This does not fit well with the character of the Kantian moral law as a synthetic *a priori* principle since the universal law conversely implies the possibility of its realization under the condition of an individualized 'you' choosing maxims. Maxims refer to fundamental ways of human living (Kant speaks of 'way of life' and thereby means acting responsibly or arbitrarily, truthfully or deceitfully) which must be judged on the basis of their compatibility with the laws of morality; in addition to the free exercise of judgement this presupposes freedom in the idea of the first person, who demonstrates his consciousness of being obliged in resorting to the law as a 'fact' of 'reason'. And the judgement *sub specie universalitatis* shows (for instance, through a deceitful promise which is based on a unilateral reservation of the will) why the law *der Sache nach* contains a principle which only attains the character of *universality* according to the original meaning of *universalis* through the concretization by one's *own* (good) will.

Thus the interpretation of the principle of universalization of discourse ethics seems to be tailored to Kant's principle of right, which does not constitute a principle for an individualized 'you', for whom the consciousness of being obliged by itself determines the maxim to the law of one's own (good) will, but one for the 'general will' which reveals the totality of human rights in the idea of the *a priori* unified will of all as the capacity to oblige others. However, it only appears thus as Kant also employs the variant of a universal *law of right* which in its formulation is based on the categorical imperative: 'Act externally in such a way that the free employment of your will could coexist with the freedom of all on the basis of a universal law.'[4] As Kant recognized early, the character of this law is not exhausted by the knowledge of the idea of reason concerning the universal, legitimate will of all. Rather, it depends on an understanding of the kinds of means with which the resistance of others, against the law which, as experience shows, can never be discounted, can be met. Thus develops the question of whether under the conditions of the universal, legitimate will the employment of *force* is permitted which enforces observation of the law and secures the right of everyone.

The law *in abstracto*, argues Kant – and he argues it with respect to that original coercive force – which the law presupposes as a fundamental fact of human social existence, 'can be thought without the means whereby it can be actualized. But *in concreto* one must look to the security (*Sicherheit*), through which it can be actualised.' The problem of right then consists in making concrete the universality of the concept of right, which is equated in the Christian doctrine of natural law of the early modern age up to Leibniz with the love for divine justice (*iustitia universalis*), in Kant, as we will see with the respect for the right of humanity (*ius connatum*), according to conditions of rendering right (*Verrechtlichung*) the forms of public force, namely their 'separation' in a community. To put it into the language of formal logic: 'What is possible in universal and abstract notions, is not always possible *in concreto*, because the universal is undetermined with respect to many characteristics; therefore, that which does not contradict the universal may conflict with the individual or the species'.[5] In the transcendental logical language of the *Critique of Pure Reason* (1781) this is: morality (and that includes the right according to the outline of Kant's originally planned metaphysics of morals) 'can also state its principles altogether *in concreto*, together with the practical consequences, at least in possible experiences and thereby avoid the misunderstanding of abstraction' (B452/53).

Let us recall briefly the transcendental philosophical approach of the *Critique of Pure Reason*. All fundamental concepts, including practical ones, which as regards to content are related to the common fundamental concerns of being human and thus address the objects of pleasure and displeasure, 'accordingly at least indirectly' the objects of '*Lebensgefühl*' (B 829 Fn.), are formally characterized by analytical universality (*universalitas*). Their usage follows the logical principles of universal consistency and identity. 'Universality', however, is not a category of transcendental logic. To Kant the traditional ontological 'thinking in concepts' is no longer self-evident. Rather, categorization, scope and the validity claim of the embodiment of the universal and its relation with things (as articulated in the concept of mind [*Gedankending*], *ens universale*) have to be 'proved' by transcendental deduction, in our case by proof of the justified usage of the concept of the universal, which fulfils synthetic functions of agreement among diverse ideas of an intuition, together with the universal analytic function in a judgement; which leads on this side of the mere concept of mind (*Gedankending*) to the quantitative category of *totality* (*universitas*). Following the explanation of the tables of categories in the *Prolegomena* (§25) it is not a concept of quantity but of wholeness (*Ganzheit*), which must be visualized in the application to factually diverse ideas, together with the categories of *unity* (measurement) and *multiplicity* (size), be it through the schematism of the imagination in the legislation of reason for the realm of nature (as *universitas rerum*) or in the typification of the law of morals or practcal reason for the realm of freedom (as *universitas personarum*). The problem of judgement using the category is its representation in the intuition which creates its object. For it only thereby attains objective reality or the status of meaningful reasoned knowledge of concepts, which the concept of universality in the sense of discursive universality (unity in many) does not possess. Synthetic unity in the *comprehensive* sense is only a characteristic of the category of totality, which *unifies a lot in one* and achieves concrete knowledge through intuition.

Kant used this categorial *manual* to put the basic formula of the Categorical Imperative as well as of the law of right into more concrete terms. And in both directions it becomes clear how the notion of the universality of law develops from the category of the unity of will to the category of multiplicity (of matter as purposes: persons or things respectively) and further to the category of *Allheit* or totality (*universitas peronarum et rerum*), whereby the determination of the universal notion of right arises from the *a priori* unified will of all. Thereby the category of *Allheit* in a practically legally fulfilled sense of *wholeness* gains a function of orientation from the outset, not least in the portrayal of the *evolution of a state* of a people on the basis of the concept of reason of the original contract by which all (*omnes et singuli*) of the people 'give up their external freedom, in order to take it up again at once as members of a common body, i.e. of the people understood as the state (*universi*)'.[6] The claim to the universality of the law remains empty as long as it is not put into more concrete terms by public law in a state, which presupposes a publicly declared, *power-holding* will, which 'constitutes a *Universitatem*' 'out of all the individuals', in other words: the whole of a *civil society* (*Gesellschaftsbund*) in the sense of a politically constituted community.[7]

Therefore, it is factually justifiable to remark, as H. Heimsoeth does, that all the categories of quantity have meaning in the *conception* (*Entwurf*/sketch) of practical reason. 'Unity' here unambiguously is to be thought of as 'oneness' (individual) and concretely to be imagined as an individual person ('self', 'personality'), who acts through his freedom and is, as a part of a whole, always also 'purpose in itself', in all the entanglements of the many individuals' action. Heimsoeth continues: 'The kingdom of ends is *Allheits-Zusammenhang* of this indeterminable multiplicity or mass of all individuals with mutual interconnection under the one law of morals, which is, however, rooted at the same time in each individual person as an independent-autonomous "intelligence" as demanding and universal.'[8]

What this means for our topic will have to be discussed in what follows. So far we emphasize that to see the core of the Categorical Imperative in the principle of the generalization of norms for behaviour leads to an abstract conception of 'universality', which is exactly what Kant overcomes. And it is equally misleading to understand the principle (the 'principle of universalization') in an application of discourse theory as a procedure of reaching a universal consensus and to define it in such a way that it excludes those norms as morally

invalid which cannot find the qualified agreement of everyone potentially concerned. By serving as a principle which enables consensus by
bridging and selecting norms according to whether they can
command a general consensus, the principle not only distances from
the conception of a single individual; it also skips the act of the choice
of maxims, which practically cannot be circumvented and its relation
to basic ways of human forms of living, about which the *Groundwork
of a Metaphysics of Morals* instructs to communicate (*Verrtindigen*) on.

If morality can give its principles, as Kant assumes, altogether *in
concreto*, together with the practical consequences, in possible experiences and thereby avoid the misunderstanding of abstraction, then
the task of communication focuses on the basic ways and conditions
of human coexistence, which is necessary for concretization. This task
is made more difficult, if not impossible, by emphasizing the principle of universalization. Preferring it methodically leads to a
confrontation of the modern 'universalism' of a *declared* philosophy
of modernity with the personalism of the supposed conventional
ethics on the one hand, and the 'nationalism' of the supposed
conventional politics (which falls back into the outdated traditions of
'nationalism') on the other hand, as happened in the debate about
German unification and happens to this day in the reverberations
around the pros and cons of the supposedly conventional patriotism
and the 'enlightened' cosmopolitanism.[9]

The debate refers to Kant's human rights universalism, his plea for
a cosmopolitan 'open' republic; this is in some points legitimate but
nevertheless mainly wrong, it seems to me. For the Kantian 'universalism' does not exclude patriotism; nor does it reduce it to the
constitution. Rather, Kant's thinking paves the way from the principle
of universal *human rights* via the right of the citizen to *ius
cosmopoliticum*, the *cosmopolitan right* on the basis of a universal
community of all peoples on earth, which in contrast to the vulgar
Enlightenment retains the equality of patriotism and cosmopolitanism.

I want to rethink this paving of the way for a bit (with reference to
the question under discussion). In order to explain my question in
relation to the contemporary debate I will first mention the critique of
the universalism in the French declaration of human rights by the
Kantian of the postmodern philosophers, Lyotard, who places Kant
'between' modernity and postmodernity, so in a (transitional period)
interregnum like ours, on which rests the relevance of Kant's philosophy for us today.

II

According to Lyotard the declaration of the French National Assembly from 27 August 1789 consists of a complex of legal norms of different *degrees*, which resemble the system of rules of the Kantian Critique of Reason in so far as the constitutional text, which was enacted through the normative act of the Assembly, starts from the idea of natural, inalienable and sacred human rights, in order to pass to the idea of the highest creature, under whose auspices they are recognized as valid for all human beings and accepted everywhere and forever; ideas, which do not relate to an object of possible experience, which therefore cannot be named either. The world of names and with it history only return at the end of the text, with the signatures of the representatives of the Assembly, which represents a people with the proper name 'The French'. The return shows the historically heterogeneous experience between the universal and the national, a heterogenity which in a different way also characterizes the *Communist Manifesto* of Marx and Engels, which was only able to legitimize its claim to universality in terms of internationalism. In the tradition of the modern movement of workers this meant a return to the history of national communities.

The transition, as Lyotard describes this ambivalence, is being pushed by the imperialist principle of legitimation, which pushes towards generalization, whilst the widening of the space of legitimation to the whole of humankind restricts itself in the same movement in favour of the nation, which it claims to represent. Lyotard speaks of an 'impossible transition' in which the contradiction at the foundation of the modern revolutionary movement originates: 'From now on one will no longer know whether the law, which has been declared in this way, is of French or human nature, whether the war fought in the name of human rights aims at conquest or emancipation, whether the violence committed in the name of freedom is of repressive or educational (progressive) nature.'[10] This dialectic which was not envisaged by Kant cannot be resolved, and Lyotard presents a number of impressive examples of how, starting with the radical (*Jacobin*) phase of the French Revolution, the emancipatory, sympathetic feelings of *emotiveness* (what Marx called 'revolutionary enthusiasm') turns into fanatic nationalism time and again, starting with Robespierre, to whom the selfish preservation of his supporters (of the 'patriots') meant the preservation of the human species.[11] By 'hallucinating' humankind in the nation the revolutionary succumbs to the 'transcendental appearance'. Lyotard, following Kant, counters his fanatism with 'real enthusiasm', which 'always aims only for the *ideal* and therefore the purely moral, such as the concept of right, and which cannot be based on selfishness'.[12]

This is Kant's view of the enthusiastic participation of the European peoples in the truth of the ideas of 1789 in the *Contest of the Faculties* (1798), whereby each people has the right of non-intervention into its domestic affairs and of political self-determination, namely to enter by the acceptance of a 'republican' constitution into conditions whereby the relapse into belligerent barbarism 'is avoided and thus the progress to the better in all its fragility is ensured negatively for the human species'.[13] What is interesting here is Kant's interpretation of enthusiasm as a sign of the existence of morally based emotions, which are potentially universal and patriotic at the same time, that is, which are related to one's own people, where they are being articulated publicly (in danger of prosecution by the police). Lyotard does not put it that way because he believes that there is no transition but an *Übergehen*, a 'transition' merging into itself, which does not progress (*auf der Stelle tritt*), the high-flying state of mind of the spectators of the revolutionary spectacle, which may well turn into the contrary, as the change of atmosphere with respect to revolutionary events proves to this day. Lyotard explains this with respect to Kant's interpretation of the really inconsequential emotional reaction to the events at the time by saying that his ethic (in contrast to the Christian ethic of love as a basis of human coexistence and its continuing effect in the republican-communist idea of 'universal brotherhood') requires the 'freeing from all motivating emotiveness and allowing only that "apathic emotiveness" which the obligation of the law of morals of practical reason accompanies: respect'.[14]

By distinguishing the fanatic from the enthusiast Lyotard touched on a central question, which occupied Kant on the occasion of the American War of Independence and the Declarations of Human Rights which legitimized it, and even earlier (in view of the preceding history in Western European publications in journalism and philosophy).[15] Nevertheless his argument misses the centre of the Kantian ethic because it construes a difference between the Christian precept of love and the moral precept of obligation, which Kant does not establish in this way. *The Critique of Pure Reason* develops the compatibility of the respect for the law of morals with the love of God and one's neighbour, provided that its core is seen in active love of humans and in the demand, which supplements the precept, to strive permanently for the fulfilment of the laws.[16] The *Metaphysics of Morals* presupposes *apathy* (seen as strength) for virtue. However, it builds a bridge with respect to the enactment of duties towards other human beings *from respect* (in the case of 'owing obligation', which is based on a mutuality of obligations) *to love* (in the case of 'owed obligation', which does not impose obligations on the other). *Love* and *respect* 'are emotions, which accompany the performance of these obligations. They can be evaluated separately (each on its own) and also exist in that way ... They are, however, fundamentally linked at any time in one obligation; only such that now the one obligation, now the other principle makes up the subject to which the other is related as an accessory'.[17]

Kant looked for the possibility of this link early. It seems relevant to the question of human rights in so far as, according to Kant, we owe respect to every human being 'on the basis of the right of humankind in our own person'. The respect of the law is a consequence of the principles which oblige us universally,[18] whereas we are not entitled to the same regarding love. From there Kant then transposes respect to the highest principle of the law of morals, whose universal claim transforms love into universal justice in the 'respect for the right of human beings'. Nevertheless there is a 'transition'. For both, argues the late Kant, *love* as well as *respect for human rights*, is an obligation, but the former only a *conditional duty of virtue* ('on the basis of the purpose of humankind'), the latter an 'unconditional, absolutely demanding obligation', a *duty of right* in the narrow sense of the Kantian law of right.

I will come back to these connections below. In the next step of our train of thought I will concentrate on clarifying the relationship of human rights universalism to patriotism, with relevant reflections on the *national hysteria* of peoples in the lectures on *Anthropology*.

III

In the book version of *Anthropology from a Pragmatic Point of View* (1798) the *Characteristic of the People* finishes with the sentence: 'We can say as much that probably the mixing of the tribes (during great conquests), which gradually extinguishes the characters, despite all supposed philanthropy is not beneficial to humankind'.[19] No doubt: Kant is at odds with the Enlightenment idea of universal brotherhood.

Thus he virtually declares it an 'intention of Providence' that peoples do not merge but keep a distance because of repelling forces. And according to these circumstances, that is, if everything continues to be merely up to nature, he holds national sentiment/feeling (*Gefühl*) as well as national pride to be necessary. They are natural factors which separate and which are reinforced by artificial ones such as religious zeal, military spirit and nationalism (if 'a people loves its own country over others') and can be utilized in the struggle for power in foreign policy. Kant neither judges the separation nor the employed means as positive, as some have argued.[20] And even though he speaks of a '*mechanism* in the functioning of the world', which 'links and separates us by instinct', he does not see the process of separation as a work of nature but a work of human *national hysteria*, which governments 'like to see'. In short: Kant does not justify the *status quo* of the natural world view but the *practical possibility* to leave it, in order to take up the morally based position of freedom to the world with respect to ourselves and our history. It is the method of the free choice of positions in morals and their use through judgement, the transition of the *statio moralis per instinctum* to the *statio moralis per intellectum*, which makes Kant say: 'On the other hand reason gives us the law which directs our animality because instincts are blind but must be replaced by maxims of reason ... Therefore this *national hysteria* must be extinguished which must give way to patriotism and cosmopolitanism'.[21] The reflection is marked: *On German National Spirit*. This may refer to F.C. Moser's apology of imperial patriotism, which, following the Western European model, is meant to reach 'across all affairs, needs, rights and conditions of our whole people and state', whereby, according to Kant, the originally cosmopolitan spirit of the country of the European middle has been weakened.[22] A more probable background seems to me to be the dispute about a similar question at the outbreak of the American War of Independence related by Jachmann. Kant defends the Americans' right to a revolution at a reception and criticizes bitterly the behaviour of the English, whereupon someone makes it known that he is English and declares himself and his nation to be insulted and demands satisfaction; as a result Kant continues the conversation as if it were meant to demonstrate the practical possibility of the choice of the morally founded reasonable position in this dispute *ad personam* and begins 'to describe his political principles and opinions and the point of view from which every human being as a citizen of the world must judge such events in the world regardless of his patriotism with such fantastic eloquence, that Green – that was the Englishman – full of astonishment extended his hand in friendship'.[23]

The report extends far beyond the current occasion of the American

Revolution. It refers to the debate of the German and European Enlightenment in relation to this disputed question, which Kant incorporates into his lectures on practical philosophy and which he poses to reason for a decision by justifying the choice of an ethically necessary position through the exposition of the principles of the law of morals. The principle to act only in accordance with such a maxim, which could at the same time serve as a general law, is the highest rule of obligation (of oneself and others), which is valid for the theory of virtues as well as of rights.[24] Everything which is demanded or prohibited according to the principle of right is also demanded or prohibited according to the notion of virtue, which is the obligation of oneself on the basis of the law of morals and of the idea of the good which is defined in it. Duties of right and of virtue are different only in form, not in substance. Consequently, the compatibility of patriotism with cosmopolitanism can be justified morally, even more: both positions allow for a double justification: first as a *duty of right* and then of *virtue*.

Let us remember the preliminary reflections about the practical-philosophical transformation of the universal love of justice by the respect for the universal human right, of which Kant claims in the *Metaphysics of Morals* that it is 'only one' – the freedom in the sense of independence from coercive will of others as a principle of the right of human beings which everyone is entitled to from birth.[25] This respect is articulated in history in the declarations of human rights by the states of the North American Union and the French National Assembly. Kant rejects their negative interpretation of freedom ('To be free means to be able to do anything which does not harm others') as well as the restricted interpretation of the resulting duty of right ('the law may only prohibit harmful acts by society'),[26] because it is possible to prove the opposite for both sentences, whilst he (indirectly) criticizes the laying-down of the pursuit of happiness in the American Constitution, only to take its underlying principle of the separation of powers for his own sketch of a state according to the idea of an *association of civil society*. The 'definition of freedom in the presentation and determination of human rights by the national assembly in Paris' obliges practical acts according to a public law, without determining the law itself as a basis for obligation of the right of human beings within a community, which has to be sanctioned by use of publicly recognized authority. This means at the same time that the Preamble to the French Constitution, as well as the Introduction to the General Law of the Land for the Prussian States (1794), which also bases the general rights of the human being in the 'natural freedom to search for and pursue one's own welfare, without harming the rights of others' (§83), contains no principle for the limitation of the state's power.

The question really is this, Kant responds to an enquiry in the spring of 1789 about the principles of legislation for a community in the spirit of Montesquieu, on how laws should be enacted in a presupposed civil society.[27] The answer directs our attention to the divergence from Rousseau at the starting point of Kant's way back to practical philosophy, the opponent of that teacher of the separation of powers who inspired the founding fathers of the American Constitution and Kant himself, when he starts at the beginning of the 1770s to distinguish the patriotic and the despotic state. A ruler governs 'despotically' if he treats a state as his inheritance (*patrimonium*), 'patriotically', if he treats it as his fatherland, which belongs to him together with all the citizens, that is as a country in which (according to the author of the *Contrat social*) all humans are equal and everyone 'also reaches the dignity of every one else, according to the equality of merits which he can *obtain*'.[28] These are distinctions which Kant introduces in the middle of his intellectual development as an innovation, in order thereby to 'improve' the common distinction between 'despotic' and 'moderate' rule (*imperium temperatum*) using Montesquieu's (and Locke's) ideas.[29] In the light of the critical question about legislation for a presupposed civil society they are finally (in the *Metaphysics of Morals*) reduced to a principle, namely 'to realize the natural right of human beings, which is a mere idea in the *statu naturali* (before the civil association), that is, to bring it under general public norms which are accompanied by appropriate *coercion*, according to which the right of each can be secured or provided'.[30]

Kant argues in the preliminary works on the *Common Saying* (1793) in relation to a critique of the justification of monarchic-corporate rule according to the principle of the welfare of the state ('happiness') using the Prussian Law of the Land which *cum grano salis* is also valid for the American and French Constitution, that the right of human beings as a coercive right must not be based only on a notion of duty which may be expected of someone: which would be nothing but an *duty of virtue*, which cannot be enforced by any law. Rather it must be a *duty of right*, which 'is in accordance with public laws of a will which has command over all (who are in a certain community with each other)'.[31] That community is the civil society, according to its form, which is based on the *a priori* unified will of all (*universi*) according to the principle of contract, which is equivalent with the *community* (*res publica*) 'in the internal relationship' and with the *state* externally and which possesses public power (*vis publica*). 'State' (*civitas*), this name comprises both relationships, it comprehends 'people and sovereign' at the same time.[32] And the universal right of humankind in its concretization as an innate human right, the '*freedom* of each member of the society, as *humans*', according to section (II) on constitutional law of the *Common Saying* forms its foundation. This principle of a human right and the principles of legal equality and independence derived from it are the basis of Kant's so called 'civil society' and as such *conditions* 'according to which the establishment of a state in accordance with pure principles of reason is only possible at all'.[33]

A passage in the *Common Saying* explains the basic position of the innate human right to freedom with the formula: 'Against hereditary subservience',[34] that is the *patrimonial* state, the *text* with the distinction between 'paternal' and 'patriotic rule' (*imperium non paternale, sed patrioticum*), which 'can be thought only for people who are capable of the rights in relation to the goodwill of the ruler'.[35] On the part of the ruler the duty of virtue here plays a part, which may be 'expected' of him by the subjects: 'Patriotic is that way of thinking where everyone sees in the state (the head of it not excluded) the community as the *maternal bosom*, or the country as paternal soil, out of and on which he himself arises, and to which he must leave as a dear pledge anyway'.[36] These are subjective considerations of the poltically reflecting power of judgement, which guide the sense of duty of the ruler, so that he renews and protects the law of the land (as Kant pictured Friedrich II) through laws of a common will, instead of considering himself to have the authority to 'subject' the land 'for usage to his unrestrained will'. Its counterpart is the justification based on public law of the difference between despotic and patriotic rule according to the 'state's principle of separation of the executing (the government) from the legislating power' in *Perpetual Peace* (1795) and in *Metaphysical Elements of Right* (1797).

As has been said, Kant mainly takes Montesquieu as a point of reference, who, referring to the English constitution, showed that there can be no freedom for the citizens without separation of the legislative, executive and judicative powers.[37] What matters to Kant is not only the functional distinction and balance but its 'organic' structure within the *a priori* unified will of all – in that totality (*universitas*) of the 'civil society', which is represented for the 'community' in the relation of the legislatve power (by the people as sovereign) to government and jurisdiction. They are counter-thoughts to Hobbes' justification of the despotic practice of government following Rousseau's ideal theorem of the 'association of citizens',[38] where Kant refers, in a manner different from Rousseau, to the structure of the universal in the premise (*Obersatz*) of a conclusion of practical reasoning, which cannot at the same time be the principle of subsumption for the specific in the *Untersatz*.[39] A *government* which enacts laws at the same time, argues Kant in favour of the distinction familiar to us, 'would have to be called *despotic* in contradiction to *patriotic*, which means however not paternal but patriotic (*regimen civitatis et patriae*)'.[40] Now Kant employs the principle of legal independence, derived from the principle of human rights, for his justification, in so far as the state which is ruled in a patriotic way 'treats its subjects as members of a family so to speak but at the same time as citizens, that is, according to laws of their own independence, each possesses himself and does not depend on the absolute will of an other next to or above him'. This implies the independence of the administration of justice for the judicial power, for the legislating and governing power the separation and finally the duty of right of the governor to *subordinate himself* to the will of the legislator: 'The governor of the people (the legislator) thus cannot at the same time be the *ruler*, for he stands below the law and is obliged by it, consequently by *another*, the sovereign'.[41] Whoever may represent him, whether the people itself or the monarch, the ruler can never be governor, legislator and judge in one person. Nevertheless this doctrine (*Lehrstück*) ends with the sentence that the 'welfare of the state' (*salus republicae*) consists in the *unification* of the three powers, whereby Kant however does not mean the welfare or happiness of the citizen but the preservation of the juridical condition – the 'condition of the greatest agreement of the constitution with the principles of right, for which to strive reason obliges us *through a categorical imperative*'.[42]

IV

'State' means the 'real modification' of a 'state' (*status*), the *position* which someone occupies in relation to others, from whence derive the 'laws of his circumstances'. The position determined in this way is equivalent to the 'place' (*positus*) in the sense of a *station*, the common place which everyone occupies in relation to everyone else. The *place* or station, Kant argues in the preliminary notes (*Vorarbeiten*) to international law, 'must as such involve principles which apply to every condition'.[43] We know that these are the universal principles of human rights, the principle of the legitimately restricted freedom as the only innate right with the principles of equality and independence of all following from it, which are at the basis of the 'possible forms of a legal condition' and which hang together internally in such a way that the whole construction of the legal order would collapse if 'only one principle restricting external freedom was missing'.[44] To avoid this case it is necessary to restrict the notion of human rights not only to the constitution of one people but to extend it to the relation of peoples and states.[45] Without the extension the continuous relapse into the state of nature of war between the states would remain, so that the foundation of a civil society would be in vain. Therefore the duty of right demands to leave the inter-state state of nature of war and to search for analogous relations between peoples for the purpose of the permanent preservation of peace.[46]

International law (*Völkerrecht*), which, according to Kant, should be called 'law of the states' (*ius publicum civitatum*) and comprises as such not merely the relation of one state against the other as a whole but also of individual persons of one state against individuals of the other as well as against the whole other state. After all Kant reserves the concept of people for the members of the state, the multitude of human beings who as 'born on the land are imagined by analogy to the procreation from a common line of parents (*congeniti*), although they are not' (§53). As we derive from the meta-theoretical reflection, these are also interpretations of the politically reflecting faculty of judgement which expects a multiplicity of fatherlands for the future, without yet including them into the narrow boundaries of the revolutionary concept of the national state (*Staatsnation*) (or even the romantic notion of spirit of the nation (*Volksgeist*)).

One can even interpret it this way because natural conditions of birth and descent are pre-factual conditions of the legal-practical knowledge of reason without the recognition of which the philosophical 'knowledge based on concepts of reason' (according to the guiding idea (*Leitfaden*) of the idea of the universal human right) would ossify into ideology. However, one can oppose the idea of motherland to that of fatherland which has been derived from this standpoint by seeing the members of the people or nation 'as born from a common mother (the republic)', which 'make up a familiy so to speak (*gens, natio*)' (§53), without moving the perspectives of reflection. On the contrary: they supplement each other. For what The Doctrine of Rights calls 'the government of the fatherland (*regimen*)

civitatis et patriae)' is called 'republican form of government' in
Perpetual Peace. And it is based on the same priciple of intrastate separation of the executive from the legislative power, which guarantees
the starting-point for the, in practice, necessary legalisation
(*Verrechtlichung*) of the forms of interstate violence in contrast to the
uncontrollable tendencies of the absolutist power of the state to
submit other states in war with the aim of dominance of the world in
the analogous idea of the *association for peace (foedus pacificum)*.

Kant himself negatively speaks of the 'surrogate of the association of
civil society', which seems to point towards a positive relationship
between the idea of peace and the enlightenment dream of a world
state.[47] This only appears so. In truth Kant not only rejects the dreams
of hegemony of a universal monarchy and its (futile) prevention
(*Bannung*) through the diplomatic quest for a European balance of
power but also the cosmopolitan dreamings of a universal republic. In
The Doctrine of Rights the 'league of nations according to the idea of
a original social contract' is mentioned, which 'need not contain a
sovereign power (as in a civil constitution) but only a co-operative
(federation)'. This is the '*union* of several states', namely the European
states which are meant to form a *permanent congress of states* following
on from the *ius publicum europaeum* (Kant points to the courts of
appeal of the general states of The Hague established after the peace of
Westphalia which 'imagined Europe as a single federal state'), in order
to realize the idea of a public law of the peoples in a civil way by deciding their disputes in legal processes.[48]

If the way to a universal order of right proceeds in these stages and
each of them involves the principles of the human right, then he
cannot move in one leap from the declaration of universal human
rights to the absolute rule of reason in the name of a universal republic. According to Kant's tripartite division of possible forms of legal
states it leads from the replacement of the patrimonial goverment by
the patriotic (that is originally republican) via the *civic association* realized in the 'community' and then on to the voluntary federation in an
association of peoples encompassing the whole globe.[49] The transition
from one stage to the next is equivalent to the progressive realization
of the idea of reason concerning right. In its light the patriotically
minded citizen of the state appears in the full *splendour* of the citizen
of the world who knows himself to be destined to solidary unity with
the whole of humankind: 'To think of oneself as a part of the
cosmopolitan society that has been agreed upon according to the law
of the citizen of the state is the most *elevated* idea which a human

being can have of its destiny, and one which cannot be thought without enthusiasm.'[50]

The passage must be read in the context of Kant's analysis of the French Revolution. Thus looking back on our reasoning it offers us the opportunity to answer conclusively the question raised as to the compatibility of human rights universalism with patriotism. Kant's reflections always revolve around the delimitation of enthusiasm from political fanaticism on the one hand, and cosmopolitan fantasies on the other. If the enthusiastic feeling, as Kant presupposes, is a consequence of the respect for the law in which morally legislating reason attains effective power in the codification of human rights, it need not *disappear* in the *flight of fancy of utopian rapture*. The participation in the foundation of the civil association through the contemporary declarations of human rights is not an imagined elevation for the idea of humankind, which does not make any progress in its emotional exuberance (as Lyotard pretends about Kant's interpretation of enthusiasm) but a descent – the movement of 'transition', which finally finds support in the stage which is given naturally in the sense of a common *residence* of the peoples on the globe inhabited by them.

In *Perpetual Peace* as well as in the *Rechtslehre* Kant emphasizes that the idea of cosmopolitanism is not a question of philanthropy but a legal principle.[51] Nature – and we, says Kant, must use this word in accordance with its 'formal meaning' because it means the 'first, inner principle of all that which belongs to the existence of a thing'[52] – has 'included' all peoples 'together (by force of the spheric form of their abode as *globus terraqueus*) into certain boundaries', without excluding them within these boundaries from any one part of the whole.[53] On the contrary: because of the limited surface of the sphere one cannot disperse as one likes, so that they necessarily come into a community with each other. It is again a basic condition of human existence which Kant uses for the understanding of the factual content of the cosmopolitan law, which rests in its core on the innate right of human beings as *residents of the globe* (Kant also speaks of the 'citizens of the globe'). Owing to the 'naturally determined size and shape of the inhabitable earth' each human being has an 'innate right to each place on the same ... that is he is in potential but only *disjunctively general* possession of the whole of the earth'.[54] By virtue of their common descent and belonging to the earth all human beings (*singuli*) are entitled 'to be where nature, or coincidence (without their will) has put them'.[55] And they have the right to exchange the traditional place where they are for other places. For in so far as they are on earth *at the same time* (*universi*, as members of the whole of humankind), they must *'therefore* also be in collective-universal possession of the whole surface of the earth, that is in possession which arises from the unified will of all'.[56] They have the right of the original collectivity of the earth not as a result of the nature of the earth, but by virtue of the innate human right to freedom, which allows everyone to enter into physically possible interaction and relation. And thereby they all become obliged by 'certain general laws of their possible contact' (§62).

As a result of the agreement about the possible community among humans being a 'necessary consequence of their existence on earth',[57] the cosmopolitan law is restricted to the conditions of general freedom of movement and hospitality. Kant interprets this not as a *right of hospitality but of visiting*, which 'all human beings are entitled to, to offer themselves *as community* by virtue of the right of common ownership of the surface of the earth'. This in turn obliges them through the duties of virtue of mutual toleration and peacefulness to the duty of right to abolish violations of human rights by 'inhospitable behaviour' principally of the 'civilized' (European) peoples with respect to the so-called primitive peoples (their colonization, war, extermination). Since it has come that far with the thorough and dominating community amongst the people of the earth, Kant remarks, that 'the violation of rights in *one* place on the earth will be felt *everywhere*: so the idea of the cosmopolitan law is not a fantastic and eccentric idea about the law (*Recht*) but a necessary supplement of the unwritten code of constitutional as well as international law about public human rights as such'.[58]

The performance of the duties of right as well as virtue are based on the compliance with the Categorical Imperative, thus the respect for the law (*Gesetz*) which comprises the respect for the right of humankind in one's own person and the right of human beings. Nevertheless it is a misunderstanding to think that Kant's understanding of duty excludes love. Respect does remain the first thing because without it there can be no true love either. But if it is compliance with duties, that is the subjective reason for the act, that matters , according to which it is most likely what someone *will do* (not only what he *ought to do*), then 'love as the free inclusion of the will of another under one's maxims' is 'an indispensible supplement of the imperfection of human nature'.[59] Via this 'piece' of applied ethics Kant derives the class of the 'duty of love towards other human beings' in the

Metaphysical Foundations of the Doctrine of Virtue (*Tugendlehre*). 'Love' here is not a feeling of affection but the moral demand of *goodwill*, from which follows the *good acting* and which rests on the principle of executing all duties of virtue: 'Act according to the maxim of *ends*, which can be a general law for everyone to have.'[60]

It follows from Kant's lectures on *ethics* that it is the *ethical principle* of *philanthropy*, of the concretization of the formally restricting prohibition to use neither oneself nor others as means, to the material obligatory commandment to turn humans in general into ends: 'Act in such a way towards other human beings that you *can want* that the maxim of your action becomes a general law.'[61] The standpoint of that law which does not concern general freedom but the relationship of the individual to the general will with view to the general purpose of all human beings (the 'principle of goodwill for the general purpose of happiness') makes it possible to see love towards others in its totality. Such a reflection *sub specie universalitatis* does not generalize, as this basic moral phenomenon shows. Rather it is held to 'reconcile' the idiosyncrasy of the phenomenon with the generality of the law of morals and accordingly to present the law *in concreto* together with its consequences of experience. The 'general love towards others', the universal love of humans, rests, as Kant formulates (this can easily be misunderstand and has been misunderstood time and again since Hegel), 'on the fact that our purposes agree with the purposes of other human beings in their kind, so that they can coexist according to the general rule of duty'.[62]

The 'general' is the 'common, shared love', which exists – according to the principle of 'agreement' which it is based on, which formulates not a principle of consensus but of harmony – 'towards any other in principle' (a), towards 'certain kinds of persons' (b) and towards the whole of humankind (c). To Kant patriotism and cosmopolitanism are amongst these phenomena. Instead of conflicting they agree with each other, and not because of a postponed, retarded (*erst nach*) 'justifying' principle of *universalization* but because the 'calling to love others of common descent' is based *in both*. This is originally also true for patriotism which may be represented adequately neither in the character of the form of government nor in the 'love for the constitution', especially since forms of government and constitution are not something that is reserved for an individual people. This, however, presupposes the 'actual love of the fatherland', of which we may speak according to Kant only if 'it is directed towards a unified society of a people, which we regard as a gens and us as its member'.[63] In the other case the love is directed towards the 'general *descent* of the world' and is then called 'world patriotism' in a derived sense, Kant's *synonym for cosmopolitanism*, which we can trace back to the late (Roman) Stoics. Kant uses this expression in order to underline against the abstractly universalist position of the vulgar enlightenment that human beings according to the idea of the cosmopolitan law deserve both: fatherland and world. From a critical position the enlightenment idea to regard the world as fatherland, proves to be ideology. It contradicts the *'obligatory global and local patriotism'*. For the human being as citizen of the world and earth, the true 'cosmopolitan', in his affection for his country, must 'have the inclination to support the welfare of the whole world'.[64] This is the conclusion in Kant's last lecture on *ethics*. It sounds like a *warning* to his time which began to break off this relationship and thereby ended up in extremes (*verstieg sich*), nationalistically and universalistically. *It is a legacy for our time.*

Notes

1 Kant, I., 'Grundlegung zur Metaphysik der Sitten', in *Kants gesammelte Schriften*. Edited by The Royal Prussian Academy of Science (Königl. Preuß. Akademie der Wissenschaften, Berlin, 1902–68), Vol. 4, p. 421. See Habermas, J., 'Diskursethik – Notizen zu einem Begründungsprogramm' in Habermas, J., *Moralbewußtsein und kommunikatives Handeln*. (Frankfurt am Main, 1983) p. 73.
2 Kant, I., *Metaphysische Anfangsgründe der Rechtslehre*, Einleitung, §C, Akad. VI (Königl. Preuss. Akademie der Wissenschaft) p. 230.
3 See Paulsen, F., *Immanuel Kant. Sein Leben und seine Lehre.* (Stuttgart, 1920) p. 290.
4 Kant, I., *Metaphysische Anfangsgründe der Rechtslehre*, Einleitung, § C, Akad. VI, p. 231.
5 Refl. 6595, Akad. XIX, p. 100.
6 Compare Kant, I., *Grundlegung zur Metaphysik der Sitten*, Akad IV, p. 436 to Kant, I., *Metaphysische Anfangsgründe der Rechtslehre*, Akad. VI, p. 315; also Kant, I., *Vorarbeiten zur Rechtslehre*, Akad. XXIII, pp. 218, 239, 302; Brief an Heinrich Jung-Stilling vom 1. März, Akad. XI, p. 10.
7 Kant, I., *Vorarbeiten zur Rechtslehre*, Akad. XXIII, p. 346.
8 'Christa Wolffs Ontologie und die Prinzipienforschung I. Kants', in Heimsoeth, H., *Studien zur Philosophie Immanuel Kants* (Köln, 1956) p. 51.
9 See Braitling, P. and Reese-Schäfer, W. (eds.), *Universalismus, Nationalismus und die neue Einheit der Deutschen* (Frankfurt am Main, 1991).
10 Lyotard, F., *Le Différend* (Paris, 1983). German edition: *Der Widerstreit*, (München, 1987) p. 244.
11 Speech at the Convention of 8 May 1793, in Kessel, P., *Les Gauchistes de 89* (Paris, 1969) p. 203.
12 *Streit der Fakultäten*, 2. Abschnitt, 6, Akad. VII, p. 86.

13 *Idem.*
14 Lyotard, F., *op. cit.* (1987) p. 275.
15 Compare Kant, I., *Beobachtungen über das Gefühl des Schönen und Erhabenen* (1764) to Kant, I., *Versuch über die Krankheiten des Kopfes* (1764), Akad. II, pp. 251 and 266; *Praktische Philosophie Herder*, Akad. XXVII, 1, 21f and 62ff.
16 Kant, I., *Kritik der praktischen Vernunft*, I, 1. Buch, 3. Hauptstück, Akad. V, 83f.
17 *Metaphysische Anfangsgründe der Tugendlehre*, II, 1. Hauptstück, 1. Abschnitt, § 23, Akad. VI, p. 499.
18 *Moralphilosophie Collins* (1784/85), Akad. XXVII 1, p. 415, which already start deriving acts of love (of 'benevolence' and 'goodwill') from a 'right of others' (p. 416).
19 Akad. VII, 320.
20 Refl. 1353 (around 1773–5), Akad. XV, 590f.
21 Refl. 1444, Akad. XV 2, 630.
22 Kant, I., *Der deutsche Nationalgeist*, in: Moser, F.C. *Patriotische Briefe* (1767). The *Abhandlung* is now reprinted in Batscha, Z. and Garber, J. (eds.), *Von der ständischen zur bürgerlichen Gesellschaft* (Frankfurt am Main, 1981) pp. 246–54.
23 *Immanuel Kant nach Darstellungen der Zeitgenossen Jachmann, Borowski, Wasianski* (Halle, 1902). See also Refl. 1444 (around 1775), Akad. XV, p. 630.
24 Kant, I., *Metaphysische Anfangsgründe der Rechtslehre* (1797), *Einleitung in die Metaphysik der Sitten*, Akad. VI, p. 226.
25 Kant, *ibid.* p. 237.
26 Refl. 8078 (end of 1789), Akad. XIX, p. 612.
27 'Brief an Heinrich Jung-Stilling vom März 1789', Akad. XXIII, p. 495. *Beobachtungen über das Schöne und Erhabene*, Akad. XX, 166f., *Logik Blomberg* and *Philippi*, Akad. XXIV, 1, pp. 300 and 495; Refl. 7538 and 7653, Akad. XIX, pp. 449 and 477.
28 Refl. 7771 (1772–5), Akad. XIX, p. 511. See Rousseau, J-J., *Emile* (1762), L.V.
29 See *Naturrecht Feyerabend, nach Archenwalls Juris Naturalis Pars Posterior* (1763), Lib. II, Tit. III; § 37: 'The Imperium superioris in subitum is either despoticum or patrioticum. Despoticum if it *extends to* all acts and times: We prefer to call the latter patrioticum' (Akad. XXVI), 2, 2, 1378).
30 Entwurf des Briefes an Heinrich Jung-Stilling vom März 1789, Akad. XI, p. 10.
31 *Vorarbeiten zum Gemeinspruch: Das Mag in der Theorie richtig sein, taugt aber nicht für die Praxis*, Akad. XXIII, p. 130.
32 See Refl. 7644 and 8023, Akad. XIX, pp. 476 and 585.
33 Kant, I., *Über den Gemienspruch* etc., Akad. VIII, p. 290.
34 Kant, I., *Vorarbeiten zum Gemeinspruch*, Akad. XXIIII, p. 136.
35 Kant, I., *Über den Gemienspruch* etc., Akad. VIII, 290f.
36 *Idem.*
37 Montesquieu, *De l'esprit des lois*, L. XI, Ch. VI, (Paris: G. True, 1748) pp. 163–74.
38 Refl. 6593 (1764–68), Akad. XIX, 99f.
39 See Kant, I., *Zum ewigen Frieden*, Akad. VIII, p. 352; Kant, I., *Metaphysische Anfangsgründe der rechtslehre*, §45, Akad. VI, p. 313. See on the other hand

the derivation of the *Trias politica* from the *theological doctrine of trinity* in: *Vorlesung über Rationaltheologie (Religionslehre Pölitz)*, Akad. XXVIII, p. 1074.

40 Kant, I., *Rechtslehre*, 2. Teil. 1. Abschnitt, §49, Akad. VI, 316f.
41 *Ibid.*, p. 317.
42 *Ibid.*, p. 318.
43 Refl. 8061 (1783–84), Akad. XIX, p. 598.
44 Kant, I., *Rechtslehre*, §43, Akad. VI, p. 311.
45 Kant, I., *Vorarbeiten zum ewigen Frieden*, Akad. XXIII, p. 175.
46 See Kant, I., *Rechtslehre*, §44 and 61, Akad. VI, pp. 312 and 61. Kant, I., *Zum ewigen Frieden*, Akad. VIII, 355f.
47 Kant, I., *Zum ewigen Frieden*, 2. *Definitivartikel*, Akad. VIII, 356f.
48 Kant, I., *Rechtslehre*, §61, Akad. VI, 350f.
49 Kant, I., *Über den Gemeinspruch*, Akad. VIII, 312f; Kant, I., *Zum ewigen frieden*. p. 349; *Religion innerhalb der Grenzen der bloßen Vernunft*, Akad. VI, p. 34.
50 Refl. 8077 (1796–8), Akad. XIX, p. 609.
51 Compare Kant, I., *Zum ewigen Frieden*, Akad. VIII, p. 358 to Kant, I., *Rechtslehre*, §61, Akad. VI, 352f.
52 See Kant, I. *Metaphysische Anfangsgründe der Naturwissenschaft*, Akad. VI, p. 467.
53 Kant, I., *Rechtslehre*, §62, Akad. VI, p. 352. See also §13, p. 262.
54 Kant, I., *Vorarbeiten zur Rechtslehre*, Akad. XXIII, p. 320.
55 Kant, I., *Rechtslehre*, §13, Akad. VI, p. 262.
56 Kant, I., *Vorarbeiten zur Rechtslehre*, Akad. XXIII, p. 322.
57 Kant, I., *Rechtslehre*, §13, Akad. VI, p. 262. See on this Lehmann, G., 'Kants Besitzlehre', in: Lehmann, G., *Beiträge zur Geschichtslehre und Interpretation der Philosophie Kants*, p. 210.
58 Kant, I., *Zum Ewigen Frieden*, 3. *Definitivartikel*, Akad. VIII, pp. 357–360.
59 Kant, I., *Das Ende aller Dinge*, Akad. VIII, (1797) 337f.
60 Kant, I., *Tugendlehre*, Einleitung IX; Akad. VI, p. 395.
61 Kant, I., *Metaphysik der Sitten Vigilantius*, Akad. XXVII 2, 1, p. 541.
62 *Ibid.*, p. 673. The systematic weight of Kant's derivation of the duty of love from the Categorical Imperative has been remarked most recently by H. Schmitz, who however does not seem to recognize the specifically moral dimension of the principle of harmony. See Schmitz, H., *Was wollte Kant?* (Bonn, 1989) 147f.
63 Kant, I., *Metaphysik der Sitten Vigilantius*, Akad. XXVII 2, 1, p. 673.
64 *Ibid.*, p. 647.

9
Jürgen Habermas and Manfred Riedel: Moving beyond Nationalism

Georg Cavallar

1. Introduction

Ever since German reunification, nationalism, patriotism and the problem of German identity have been topics for discussion.[1] Most of the essays and books analysed in this volume were written around 1993. Some hailed reunification as Germany's chance to regain the political position in (Central) Europe it was entitled to because of its economic success. Others saw this very possibility as a threat, and wanted to continue a tradition started by a politically moderate *Bonner Bundesrepublik* with citizens endorsing feelings of constitutional patriotism rather than those of (even diluted) nationalism. Whereas the first group favoured the concept of a pre-political, national 'community of fate' (*Schicksalsgemeinschaft*), the latter saw a community of citizens constituting themselves as a political body as the proper goal. This went together with an endorsement of Western liberal principles and usually a cosmopolitan attitude. There are, of course, no clear-cut 'camps', although polemics on both sides create this illusion. Some authors cannot be assigned to either 'camp'; Manfred Riedel is a case in point.

The attempt to combine cosmopolitanism, republicanism and some sort of national feelings has had a long tradition in Germany. In 1907, the German historian Friedrich Meinecke argued in *Weltbürgertum und Nationalstaat* (*Cosmopolitanism and the National State*) that the two concepts are not mutually exclusive. He pointed out that German national feeling had always been linked to the cosmopolitan ideal of a humanity beyond nationality.[2] Today, Meinecke's thesis is hardly convincing. In fact, his book is a defence of nineteenth-century German nationalism which was endorsed by various authors and reached an ignominious climax before and during World War I.

However, Meinecke's book was successful because it suggested that nationalism is intellectually sound: it is not the uninformed response of the manipulated masses, but the refined theory of intellectuals moving in academic circles.

My essay starts with an analysis and evaluation of Habermas's theory of constitutional patriotism. I will argue that his constitutional patriotism is, in fact, procedural patriotism, *Verfahrenspatriotismus* (2). The next section focuses on Riedel's interpretation of Kant's patriotism and cosmopolitanism (3). Both Habermas and Riedel draw upon Kant. The following two sections continue with an extended analysis of Kant's position: Kant on the German national spirit and national illusion (4), and Kant on cosmopolitan enthusiasm (5). I will argue that Habermas rather than Riedel builds upon the Kantian tradition.

Habermas's theory of constitutional patriotism

The term 'constitutional patriotism' (*Verfassungspatriotismus*) was coined by Dolf Sternberger and subsequently adopted by Jürgen Habermas.[3] It refers to the broad consent of citizens and their loyalty towards the constitution rather than the state, the nation or the administration. Habermas calls this patriotism 'abstract', because the focus is on abstract (democratic) procedures and (juridical) principles. Constitutional patriotism presupposes an historical development where culture and state politics have drifted apart, where various forms of living (*Lebensformen*) coexist and where collective identity is post-traditional.[4]

For Habermas, constitutional patriotism is the proper attitude of a citizen who lives in a democratic state governed by just laws (*Rechtsstaat*). Habermas's goal in *Faktizität und Geltung* is to show that *Rechtsstaat* and 'radical democracy' are mutually dependent.[5] This doctrine is the normative background for Habermas's theory of constitutional patriotism. The theory gets a specific Habermasian touch with the concept of popular sovereignty. Habermas sees popular sovereignty not as a 'principle' but as a procedure or process. His constitutional patriotism is, in fact, procedural patriotism, *Verfahrenspatriotismus*. Drawing on Rousseau and Kant, Habermas argues that popular sovereignty must be seen as the process of democratic self-legislation. Consent is based on the coherence of certain procedural practices consented to by the citizenry. Each citizen is respected as a unique individual, as a member of an ethnic or cultural group and finally as a citizen, a member of a political body.[6]

Habermas's arguments in favour of constitutional patriotism proceed on two distinct levels: the first is moral and universal; the second pragmatic and rooted in reflections on historical developments.

Principles, Habermas argues, have to be universal; otherwise they would not be legitimate. Particular ways of living are only acceptable and justified if they have a universal core.[7] National identity is particular and therefore *de jure*, logically and morally incompatible with universal principles.

Habermas points out that historically, (particular) nationalism and (universal) republicanism developed simultaneously, following the French Revolution. However, this does not imply that they are logically linked (which was, incidentally, Meinecke's implicit contention). From the very start, the national state of the nineteenth century was ambivalent. Whereas republicanism implied universalism, 'national freedom' towards foreign enemies was particular. The German *Sonderweg* meant extreme nationalism at the expense of republicanism.[8] Habermas seems to believe that this historical development was not 'inevitable', and if it was, we are now in a position to take another course. In his post-unification writings, Habermas is increasingly worried about particularist tendencies in contemporary Germany, and the re-emergence of nationalism.

Habermas adds an interesting logical argument. Procedural justice implies the idea of equality and mutual recognition, and this leaves room for the recognition of the particular and the individual. According to this argument, any given particular presupposes moral universalism for its justification. For Habermas, critics of universalist moral theories confuse two distinct categories.[9] If I understand Habermas properly, I think we can illustrate this argument with an historical example. When the National Socialists defended the rights of the German nation, they referred to a universal concept: that entities such as nations are the bearers of certain rights which must not be violated (e.g. by the Treaty of Versailles). They defended their particularist claim with a universalist argument.

Habermas's pragmatic argument takes three current developments in contemporary Europe as its starting point. National conflicts, European integration and a new mass migration from East and South point towards an endorsement of universal democratic and juridical principles.[10] European integration and the dawning of a multicultural society in Germany due to immigration are developments which are *de facto* in real life incompatible with a traditional concept of national identity. Both developments cannot be reversed.

Helmut Wagner has denounced Habermas's constitutional patriotism as 'ideology'.[11] This word has usually extremely negative connotations in German-speaking countries. Wagner argues that Habermas's radical attack on nationhood is mistaken. Siding with Habermas, I want to point out that Wagner's reasoning is unfounded.

Wagner claims that Habermas has three arguments against nationhood. First, nations are said to be historically outdated. Wagner believes that any nation is indispensable because it alone guarantees freedom and the rule of law. However, this is a juridical argument. It is rooted in the natural right theory that the state of nature among individuals has to be overcome. The logic of the argument implies that the establishment of a juridical condition does not stop at the state or national level. It is more coherent to assume that a full juridical condition (and thus security) is only attained on a global, worldwide level. Habermas wants nothing less, but also nothing more than this: a peaceful cosmopolitan condition, which is also Kant's ideal.[12]

According to Wagner's second argument, Habermas's praise of the USA and France as multicultural societies is mistaken. The US, Wagner argues, has created its own identity with the help of a common language and the 'American way of life'. I think Wagner underestimates the dialectical quality included in the process of creating this identity. The US Constitution which embodies universal principles, played an integral part in the formation of this identity.

Habermas himself mentions a line of reasoning related to Wagner's second argument. Communitarians have pointed out that universal principles require a concrete national or cultural foundation. Charles Taylor claims that 'patriotism is a common identification with a historical community founded on certain values'.[13] Habermas concedes that *some* form of groundwork or base is necessary. However, (some) communitarians are wrong in assuming that *only* the national base is sufficient. Multicultural societies like the USA or Switzerland suggest that the liberal political culture of constitutional patriotism can also serve as an adequate basis. This particular underpinning does not do away with universal concepts like human rights.[14]

Habermas points out that universal moral principles must rely upon forms of living that correspond with or approach these principles. These *'entgegenkommende Lebensformen'* are, above all, Western liberal traditions.[15] Habermas distinguishes between moral and ethical-political problems. 'Ethical' refers to 'ethos' in the original sense – the disposition, character or fundamental values peculiar to a specific people or culture. The moral level is the more abstract one: decisions must be based on reasons that can be shared by everyone in a projected republic of world citizens. The ethical-political perspective is contingent upon the form of living of a certain, single political community.[16]

These arguments seem to suggest that Habermas argues like, or has turned into, a communitarian. However, this is mistaken. Habermas's supposedly 'communitarian' line of reasoning should be seen as an attempt to relate universal principles to a concrete historical situation. Habermas is communitarian on the level of application, not on the level of principles. In this regard, Habermas is in the Kantian tradition. Kant tried to bridge the gap between universal principles and a certain historical situation with the theory of permissive laws of reason (VIII, 347, 16–348).[17] Wagner, however, wants to debunk Habermas as a stubborn Marxist who tends to justify violence. Wagner misunderstands Habermas's ideal: it is certainly not the ideal of a (violently) 'unified world', where freedom is abolished in the name of abstract reason.[18] This is not the intention or the logical consequence of Habermas' theory. Wagner's third argument is distorted intellectual history: Rousseau and Marx are turned into totalitarian monsters, and Habermas is seen as their modern, seemingly innocuous child. Thus he misses Habermas's central argument. Constitutional, consensual patriotism is the missing link between abstract, universal principles of right and certain forms of living.

Habermas can demonstrate that different national cultures can harmonize with universal principles, as long as the latter takes precedence or primacy over the former because these cultures share political-juridical standards. A formal 'umbrella' of shared political culture leaves plenty of room for various (national) ways of living. Habermas's concept of constitutional patriotism is, above all, a 'reordering of priorities in which national identity is displaced from its previously central position'.[19] This does not imply, however, that Habermas envisages only one form of identity. The identity of a certain group is always something particular, but has to correspond with moral standards, and it can be formed by our way of thinking and acting. 'We cannot choose our traditions, but we can know that it's up to us *how* we are going to continue them.'[20]

Manfred Riedel's interpretation of Kant's patriotism

Kant's theory is important for various reasons. His theory is the philo-sophical background in the debate on constitutional patriotism. All the contemporary authors involved appreciate Kant. Habermas's theory is 'highly Kantian in nature', and Riedel draws heavily upon Kant, whereas Wagner sees the Kantian federation of states as a desirable goal. Quoting Kant seems to be the proper thing to do for everybody at the moment.

We cannot be certain that Riedel's essay was intended as an answer to Habermas's theory. In an interview with Habermas in 1988, Jean-Marc Ferry suggested that discursive theory renews Kantian universalism, which might be seen as the formal framework for Habermas's constitutional patriotism. In his reply, Habermas did not contradict this statement.[21] Manfred Riedel does not mention Habermas in his essay; however, it is obvious that he is attacking Ferry's contention in the interview. Riedel's main theses in the essay are: 1. both concepts are compatible with each other, as 'Kantian "universalism" does not exclude patriotism' (Riedel 1993: 6; 5); 2. Kantian patriotism goes beyond mere allegiance to the constitution (Riedel 1993: 21); 3. Kant has allegedly criticized cosmopolitan dreamings (*'Träumereien'*) of a universal republic (Riedel 1993: 17; 15), and 'cosmopolitan fantasies' (*'Phantasterei'*; Riedel 1993: 18; 16). Riedel wants to convince us that Kantian cosmopolitanism is more down-to-earth than that of the 'vulgar' Enlightenment. The Enlightenment idea of the world as a fatherland is, according to Riedel's Kant, uncritical ideology.

I will argue that Riedel's three theses are either imprecise, misleading or simply wrong.

My first argument is that Kantian patriotism should be described as constitutional patriotism or 'cosmopolitan patriotism' (this term is my invention, it seems to be a contradiction in terms), and that we find hardly anything in his concept of patriotism that goes beyond the two elements, juridical and cosmopolitan.

We have to keep various meanings of patriotism separate. The modern (and our current) understanding of patriotism identifies it as a mild (and acceptable or palatable) form of nationalism;[22] secondly, many German-speaking authors in the eighteenth century favoured what has been termed *Reichspatriotismus* (imperial patriotism), loyalty to the Holy Roman Empire; thirdly, the often tiny political units scattered across the territory of the Empire prior to 1806 developed so-called *Lokalpatriotismus* (local patriotism). To complicate matters even further, some have referred to *Verwaltungspatriotismus* (administrative patriotism) in Germany.[23]

In the eighteenth century, the Holy Roman Empire had virtually disappeared as a political power in Europe, and had been replaced by the dualism of Prussia and the Habsburg territories. Towards the end of the century, authors like Friedrich Carl von Moser romanticized the Empire. They cherished its liberal constitution which guaranteed peace and freedom for all.[24] For a long time, Kant followed Saint-Pierre's and Rousseau's respect for the Empire and saw it as a focal point of a possible European federation of states (cf. XV, 591). Two things should be kept in mind here: Kant appreciated the Empire because of its juridical, legal qualities (federal constitution, peaceful settlement of disputes); secondly, the empire was seen as a suitable starting point to go beyond itself, to expand into a federation of states. These two features, the juridical and the cosmopolitan, are typical of Kantian thought. By 1795, Kant had ceased referring to the Empire: apparently he had realized and accepted that it had stopped functioning as a political body with any influence.

We can find some traits of provincial or local patriotism in Kant. As we all know, he cherished his home town of Königsberg, but again we find a cosmopolitan argument. According to Kant, a town such as Königsberg helps us to broaden our knowledge of distant countries, foreigners, humans in general and the whole world (cf. VII, 120f. note).

I think that Kant's position amounts to constitutional patriotism. The term is the best 'label' for his position. We can approach it from an historical and a systematical perspective.

For most authors of the eighteenth century, patriotism and republicanism went hand in hand. The *Dictionary of the Constitution*, published during the French Revolution, defined patriotism as 'l'attachement à un pays où règnent les loix de la justice et de l'humanité' and 'l'amour générale de l'humanité'.[25] Lessing, Albrecht, Rebmann, Iselin, Bergk, Krug and Forster were among German-speaking authors who linked patriotism with mutual rights, the principle of justice, the constitution or plain humanity. They thought that patriotic sentiments can only prosper in a republic, and that this 'true' patriotism is compatible with cosmopolitanism. During the wars with revolutionary (later Napoleonic) France, our modern concept of patriotism evolved: as a form of nationalism, and opposed to cosmopolitanism.[26]

We have to keep this eighteenth-century understanding of patriotism in mind to understand Kant properly when he uses the term. In this respect, Riedel's analysis is misleading. He confuses our modern concept with that of the eighteenth century. For the Enlightenment authors mentioned above as well as for Kant, patriotism has no ethnic connotations at all. In fact, Kant's position is almost identical with that of his contemporaries.

Next, I will look at some Kantian passages which clearly demonstrate the dominant legal or constitutional element in Kant's concept of patriotism. In a key passage from *Theory and Practice*, Kant contrasts a 'paternal government', where the subjects are seen and treated as 'immature children' who have no rights, with a 'patriotic government', which is the opposite of this despotism. The 'patriotic government' is identical with republicanism. 'A patriotic mode of thinking [*Denkungsart*] is one where everyone in the state ... regards the commonwealth [*das gemeine Wesen*] as a maternal womb ... Each regards oneself as authorised to protect the rights of the commonwealth by laws of the general will' (VIII, 291; 74). The true juridical duty, or *Rechtspflicht*, of the patriot is restricted to the protection of the political body and its just constitution. If patriotism and republicanism are both the opposite of despotism (see also VIII, 352, 13–18), then they must be identical (granted that *tertium non est datur*). Other passages support this thesis (cf. XIX, 511, 21–6; VI, 316, 34–317, 8), and they are quoted by Riedel (cf. Riedel 1993: 12f.; 14f.). My analysis is supported by the fact that Kant's concept of *Volk* (populus) is neither ethnic nor sociological, but juridical. Anyone who agrees to the original contract is, by this mere act of will, a member of the 'Staatsvolk'.[27]

Kant on the German national spirit and national illusion

Riedel claims that 'Kant fights the Enlightenment idea of universal brotherhood (*Menschheitsverbrüderung*)' (Riedel 1993: 9, 8). He supports this thesis with a quotation from Kant's *Anthropology*, where Kant states that the 'mixing of the tribes' is not 'beneficial to humankind' (VII, 320, 12–15), because it destroys the national character. In the original text, Kant uses the word *Stämme*, which is a translation of the Latin word *gentes*.[28] What I want to criticize here is Riedel's implication that a mixing of tribes is identical with universal brotherhood. I think it is completely consistent to reject the first (the mixing of tribes) and appreciate the second (universal brotherhood). Not only Kant's concept of patriotism, but also his notion of cosmopolitanism is highly legalistic. Kant does not defend a form of cosmopolitanism that sets up the ideal of, for instance, only one way of life for the whole world.[29] Kant's approach is – like that of Habermas – more moderate. He accepts that there are cultural, national and religious differences among states, but claims that these should not prevent people from establishing a juridical condition (*Rechtszustand*) with shared legal principles (as developed in *Perpetual Peace*). This is possible because we all share the same (practical) reason.

Riedel also draws upon unpublished reflection 1353 (around 1773–75) to support his thesis that 'Kant fights the enlightenment idea of universal brotherhood'. The reflection argues on two distinct levels, one being that of instinct and the mechanism of nature, the other being that of reason (cf. XV, 590, 25–8; VII, 119, 9–27). I think we should see this reflection within the context of Kant's published work on anthropology (1798), which provides the systematic framework.

On the natural level, Kant readily admits that there are different nations (or *Stämme*, that is *gentes*) in the world, who define themselves as originating from 'common descent' (VII, 311, 8f.). Kant also concedes that there is something like the 'spirit of a nation' (*'Geiste der Nation'*, cf. VII, 319, 10; *'Nationalgeist'*, cf. XV, 590, 15). Germans, for instance – and Kant sees himself as a Geman (VII, 311, 34) – seem to like hierarchies (cf. VII, 319, 1–20). These are empirical considerations and highly problematical. It is difficult to decide which aspects of character are innate, or natural, and which are artificial and acquired (cf. VII, 319, 27–31). In addition, we never know if our generalizations are justified. Finally, Kant acknowledges that, genetically, heterogeneity of individuals and nations is acceptable. We need variation to avoid infertility (cf. VII, 321, 1–9) and perhaps stupidity.

Kant's reflections on natural dispositions are embedded in his philosophy of history. This philosophy postulates an intention (*Absicht*) of nature or Providence (XV, 590, 16; VIII, 360, 12–362, 39) which uses our natural dispositions to promote moral ends. Our natural condition is discord and conflict, for instance among nations; our moral and juridical duty is to establish concord and harmony with the help of our reason; nature uses discord and conflict as a means to moral ends like harmony and peace (VII, 322, 5–12).

Reflection 1353 fits into this systematic framework. Our vocation (*Bestimmung*) as 'citizens of the world' (VII, 120, 5) is to establish a cosmopolitan society, and this is also the purpose or end of nature/Providence (cf. VII, 331, 23–30). Nature uses national pride and national hatred to keep nations and states separated (XV, 590, 18f.). This is exactly in accordance with practical reason, as the 'idea of international right presupposes the separate existence of many independent adjoining states' (VIII, 367, 8f., Reiss 1991: 113).

In reflection 1353, Kant polemicizes against national illusion

(*Nationalwahn*). According to Kant, illusion is the deception that the mere representation (*Vorstellung*) of a thing is identical with the thing itself (VI, 168, 20f.; cf. VII, 275, 20–2). I believe this is an apt description of nationalism itself. It is based on the fiction that we can distinctly assign citizens to a certain nation, that territories have been peopled by a homogeneous group, that nationalities can be defined and distinguished from others by certain criteria. The fictional element is also dominant in all attempts to specify these criteria – they may be language, history, common descent, collective features or characteristics, the identity of political life, shared culture and religious convictions, or all of the above together.[30] Kant emphasizes language and religion (VIII, 367, 22; Reiss 1991: 113f.). A strong subjective element is included: a nation understands itself *as* a nation, has self-consciousness and the will to constitute itself as a (national) unit.[31] Kant is wrong in assuming that nationalism can neatly be subsumed under the heading of instincts. If illusion is a defect of our faculty of judgement, national illusion seems to combine natural and intellectual elements. However, Kant is right to insist that national illusion must be 'extinguished' or 'wiped out' (*auszurotten*) and replaced by 'maxims of reason': (constitutional) patriotism and cosmopolitanism (refl. 1353, XV, 590, 28–591, 2; cf. Riedel 1993: 10, 9).

Cosmopolitan enthusiasm

The eighteenth century is usually seen as an age of cosmopolitan thinking.[32] Riedel claims that the Enlightenment idea of the world as a fatherland is uncritical ideology (Riedel 1993: 22), and he thinks that this is also Kant's belief. I will now turn to the passage in Kant's *Lectures on Moral Philosophy* quoted by Riedel to support his thesis. My interpretation is different. Paragraph 116 focuses on love for others. Kant makes the following distinction: we can love (1) any other person, (2) certain kinds of people, (3) all of humankind (*Menschengeschlecht*; cf. XXVII, 2, 1, 673, 5–7; Riedel 1993: 21, 18). On two pages, Kant polemicizes against any form of exclusive love. Members of sects are a case in point. Their love and affection is limited to members of their own group, their *esprit de corps* causes indifference towards humankind and diverts their attention from objective and universal moral principles (cf. XXVII, 2, 1, 674, 7–19; cf. *ibid.*, 673, 13–25). The same applies to any form of exclusive patriotism and nationalism. They replace universalism by relativism and the conviction that nations are *not* (morally or juridically) equal.[33] Only constitutional patriotism is by definition all-inclusive and comprehensive, because it is based on the universal principle of right. Only constitutional patriotism doesn't contradict cosmopolitanism. The true cosmopolitan, 'in his affection for his country, must have the inclination [*Neigung*] to promote the welfare of the whole world' (XXVII, 2, 1, 673, 38–674, 2; cf. IX, 499, 19–25).

The quotations shows that Kant did not object to love for one's own country. However, they are subordinated to and limited by 'general love for humans' (*allgemeine Menschenliebe*; XXVII, 2, 1, 19). Like Habermas, Kant advocates a proper reordering of priorities. Riedel provides a good example of a true cosmopolitan: Kant himself (cf. Riedel 1993: 10f.). We are all familiar with the episode when Kant defended the American revolutionaries against his later friend Green.[34] The cosmopolitan tries to overcome affection or prejudice in favour of a particular country or nation (for example, his/her own) and tries to find an impartial and rationally justified perspective. His/her thinking is 'enlarged' (*erweitert*; cf. V, 295, 9f.). The cosmopolitan's major question regarding history or current political affairs is: what did/do people or nations contribute to a realization of the ideals of reason (republicanism, world federation etc.)? (cf. VIII, 29, 27–30, 10, Reiss 1991: 52; refl. 1442, XV, 630, 2–5; refl. 1436, XV, 627, 12–20). Kant supported the American and French revolutionaries because they tried to put the idea of a just constitution into practice, and disliked the British because they aimed at thwarting this endeavour. Their wars ruined their cosmopolitan 'reputation' (*Andenken*; refl. 1444, XV, 630).

When Riedel denounces the cosmopolitan idea of the world as a fatherland as 'ideology', we have to be careful: What is cosmopolitanism? If there are several types, which one is 'critical', i.e. can be justified rationally? I have already pointed out that Kant endorses a purely juridical concept. He does not think that our proper task is to abolish national features or distinctions, or that any trends towards levelling differences have moral significance.

'Cosmopolitan' is the key concept in Kantian thinking on an international level, and the sphere that goes beyond the 'Westphalian model' of sovereign states. Cosmopolitan right (*Weltbürgerrecht*; cf. VIII, 357–60; VI, 352f.)[35] sees individuals, not states as the primary juridical units. Sometimes Kant calls a federation of states a 'cosmopolitan society' (VII, 331, 23f.; cf. 333, 9f.), which is the vocation of humankind and a possible purpose of nature.

Apart from the juridical context, Kant uses the notion of 'cosmopolitan' to describe a certain mode of thinking (*Denkungsart*), or mentality (*Gesinnung*; IX, 499, 19f.) of individuals. I have already pointed out that Kant should be seen as a representative eighteenth-century example. The cosmopolitan patriot works in one's own political community to promote the highest political good, i.e. perpetual peace. Benjamin Ferencz coined the injunction and catchy slogan: 'Think globally – act locally.'[36] This might be an appropriate description of the Kantian position.

I want to conclude with some reflections on cosmopolitan enthusiasm. Riedel claims that Kant has criticized cosmopolitan 'dreamings' (*Träumereien*; Riedel 1993: 17; 15) and 'fantasies' (*Phantasterei*; Riedel 1993: 18; 16). The way we distinguish among forms of cosmopolitanism, we should also keep dreaming, fantasies, fanaticism and enthusiasm apart. Anyone familiar with Kantian thought will agree that Kant fights against associating ideas of practical reason with negative connotations such as 'utopian', 'fantastic', 'unrealistic' or 'a pipe dream'. Kant claims emphatically that we should give the 'phantastic' or enthusiastic people credit for all the important achievements in history (cf. II, 267, 10f.). Moral enthusiasts are, for instance, Plato, Saint-Pierre and Rousseau (cf. XV, 210, 26f.; 406f.). Riedel's charge and debunking is too sweeping.

Concluding remarks

Habermas's theory of procedural democracy and thus of constitutional patriotism is not flawless. One major problem is Alexis de Tocqueville's contention that popular sovereignty can lead to the tyranny of the majority. Habermas's claim that this argument reflects the fear of the bourgeios that he might be overcome by the *citoyen* is not convincing. It does not solve the systematic problem behind Tocqueville's contention, the tension between the normative *volonté générale* and the factual *volonté de tous*.[37]

However, his analysis is more convincing and coherent than those of Riedel or Wagner. Wagner tends to get too polemical and constructs antinomies that cannot do justice to Habermas's complex approach. Riedel is somewhere between Wagner and Habermas. His interpretation of the Kantian position is mistaken. Although Habermas does not offer a detailed analysis of Kant's writings and refers to Kant only casually, he is closer to Kant.

Patriotism in our modern sense is incompatible with the universal principle of right. In addition, constitutional patriotism is the more prudent choice. There are pragmatic considerations in favour of constitutional patriotism. Kant points out that one of the reasons for the decline and fall of the Greek *polis* was that the Greeks tended to see any foreigners (*extraneos*) as barbarians and enemies (*hostes*; cf. XXVII, 2, 1, 674, 2–7). Similarly, we might argue that any form of ethnic patriotism is sheer nonsense in a country with a low birthrate, an ageing population and an economy that consequently depends on a certain number of immigrants from abroad. Trends of economic globalization, the rise of an 'international public opinion' or a 'global civil society' and the decline of the classic nation-state also point towards constitutional or cosmopolitan patriotism.[38] Other truly global challenges are ecological problems and the number of refugees all over the world. Both phenomena are without precedent in human history, and again, the traditional nation-states seem unable to cope with these challenges.[39]

I have argued before that any form of cosmopolitanism is based on the belief that we all share the same (practical) reason, that we can't do without universal concepts like human rights, human dignity or freedom. Nationalism is exclusive and usually sides with relativism. I cannot go into the debate between universalist and relativist positions in ethics.[40] I only want to express my personal conviction that a universalist position seems to be more plausible, and I want to side with Hegel who writes: 'Der Mensch ist an sich vernünftig; darin liegt die Möglichkeit der Gleichheit des Rechts aller Menschen – die Nichtigkeit einer starren Unterscheidung in berechtigte und rechtlose Menschengattungen.[41]

Notes

1 See above, pp. 41–63.
2 See Meinecke, F., *Weltbürgertum und Nationalstaat. Werke, Vol. 5*, edited by Herzfeld, H. (München, 1962) pp. 9–26 (English edition: Princeton, NJ.: Princeton University Press 1970).
3 See Sternberger, D., *Verfassungspatriotismus* (Frankfurt am Main, 1990) 13f.; Vollrath, E., 'Verfassungspatriotismus als politisches Konzept', in Birtsch, G. and Schröder, M. (eds.), *Patriotismus in Deutschland* (Trier, 1993) 29f.
4 Habermas, J., 'Geschichtsbewußtsein und posttraditionale Identität. Die Westorientierung der Bundesrepublik', in *Eine Art Schadensabwicklung. Kleine Politische Schriften VI* (Frankfurt am Main: Suhrkamp, 1987) p. 173. Habermas's concept of constitutional patriotism is developed more thoroughly in Williams, Bishop and Wight, *op. cit.*, pp. 46–53.
5 Habermas, J., *Faktizität und Geltung. Beiträge zur Diskurstheorie des Rechts*

und des demokratischen Rechtsstaates (Frankfurt am Main: Suhrkamp, 1992) p. 13; cf. 527.

6   Habermas, J., *Staatsbürgerschaft und nationale Identität. Überlegungen zur europäischen Zukunft* (St Gallen: Erker,1991), 10f. A more extensive analysis is: Habermas, J., 'Volkssouveränität als Verfahren', in *Die Moderne – ein unvollendetes Projekt* (Leipzig, 1990) 180ff.

7   Habermas, J., 'Über Moral, Recht, zivilen Ungehorsam und Moderne', in *op. cit.* (1987) p. 64.

8   Habermas, J., 'Die Stunde der nationalen Empfindung. Republikanische Gesinnung oder Nationalbewußtsein?', in *Die nachholende Revolution. Kleine Politische Schriften VIII* (Frankfurt am Main: Suhrkamp, 1990) 158f.

9   Habermas, J., *Die Normalität der Berliner Republik. Kleine Politische Schriften VIII* (Frankfurt am Main: Suhrkamp, 1995) p. 83.

10 Habermas, *op. cit.* (1991), p. 5. See Nochmals, 'Zur Identität der Deutschen. Ein einig Volk von aufgebrachten Wirtschaftsbürgern?', in Habermas, *op. cit.* (1990), in particular 217f. Habermas's position within the context of the German debate on immigration policy is developed in Habermas, J., 'Die Asyldebatte', in *Vergangenheit als Zukunft. Das alte Deutschland im neuen Europa? Ein Gespräch mit Michael Haller* (München: Piper, 1993) pp. 159–86.

11 Wagner, H., 'Verfassungspatriotismus' als negativer Nationalismus', *Aussenpolitik. Zeitschrift für internationale Fragen*, Vol. 44 (1993) p. 243.

12 Habermas, J., 'Der Golf-Krieg als Katalysator einer neuen deutschen Normalität?', in: Habermas, *op. cit.* (1993) p. 32.

13 Taylor, C., 'The Liberal-Communitarian Debate', in Rosenblum, N. L. (ed.), *Liberalism and the Moral Life* (Cambridge, Mass.: Harvard University Press, 1989) p. 178; quoted in: Habermas, *op. cit.* (1991) p. 15.

14 *Idem.*, 15f.

15 Habermas, J., 'Moralität und Sittlichkeit. Treffen Hegels Einwände gegen Kant auch auf die Diskursethik zu?', in Kuhlmann, W. (ed.), *Moralität und Sittlichkeit. Das Problem Hegels und die Diskursethik* (Frankfurt am Main: Suhrkamp, 1986), 28f.

16 Habermas, *op. cit.* (1992) p. 139.

17 I have used the Akademie edition: Kant, I., *Kants Gesammelte Schriften*. Ed. Prussian (later: German) Academy of Science (Berlin, Leipzig: de Gruyter), 1900ff. to quote from Kant's works. This edition is referred to with Roman (volume) and Arabic numbers (pages and sometimes lines) in the text. Occasionally I changed the translation to ensure the consistency of the central terms. The page number of the Reiss edition follows the page number of the Academy Edition: Kant, I., *Political Writings*. Ed. Hans Reiss. Translated by H. B. Nisbet. Second, enlarged edition (Cambridge: Cambridge University Press, 1991).

18 Wagner, *op. cit.* (1993) 250f.

19 Williams, Bishop and Wight, *op. cit.*, p. 53.

20 Habermas, J., 'Grenzen des Neohistorismus', in Habermas, *op. cit.* (1990) p. 155. Translation by the author.

21 *Ibid.*, p. 154.

22 See 'Patriotismus' in Ritter, J. and Gründer, K. (eds.), *Historisches Wörterbuch der Philosophie*, Vol. 7 (Basel: Schwabe & Co., 1989) 211f.

Significantly, Rudolf Burger writes: 'A patriot is a nationalist in peaceful times' in Burger, R., 'Patriotismus und Nation. Bemerkungen zu einem (nicht nur) österreichischen Problem', in Burger, R., Klein, H-D. and Schrader, W. H. (eds.), *Gesellschaft, Staat, Nation. Veröffentlichungen der Kommission für Philosophie und Pädagogik.* Heft 26 (Wien: Verlag der Österreichischen Akademie der Wissenschaften,1996) p. 46.

23 Vollrath, *op. cit.* (1993) 30f.

24 See Von Aretin, K. O. F., 'Reichspatriotismus', in *ibid.*, pp. 4–9; Stolleis, M., 'Reichspublizistik und Reichspatriotismus vom 16. zum 18. Jahrhundert', in: *ibid.*, pp. 21–8.

25 Quoted in 'Patriotismus', in Ritter. and Gründer (eds.), *op. cit.* (1989) p. 211.

26 See *ibid.*, pp. 209–12; Vierhaus, R., '"Patriotismus". Begriff und Realität einer moralisch-politischen Haltung', in *Deutschland im 18. Jahrhundert. Politische Verfassung, soziales Gefüge, geistige Bewegungen. Ausgewählte Aufsätze* (Göttingen, 1987). Representative examples of late eighteenth-century patriotism are included in: Batscha, Zwi and Garber, J. (eds.), *Von der ständischen zur bürgerlichen Gesellschaft. Politisch-soziale Theorien im Deutschland der zweiten Hälfte des 18. Jahrhunderts* (Frankfurt am Main: Suhrkamp, 1981) pp. 246–76.

27 Kantian passages and a profound analysis are offered in Maus, I., *Zur Aufklärung der Demokratietheorie. Rechts-und demokratietheoretische Überlegungen im Anschluß an Kant* (Frankfurt am Main: Suhrkamp, 1994) pp. 203–9; 'Staatssouveränität als Volkssouveränität. Überlegungen zum Friedensprojekt Immanuel Kants', in *Jahrbuch des Kulturwissenschaftlichen Instituts im Wissenschaftszentrum NRW 1996*, 187f. For Kantian constitutional theory, see Gregor, M. J., 'Kant's Approach to Constitutionalism', in Rosenbaum, A. S. (ed.), *Constitutionalism.* (New York: Greenwood Press, 1988) pp. 69–87; Joerden, J., 'From Anarchy to Republic: Kant's History of State Constitutions', in Robinson, H. (ed.), *Proceedings of the Eighth International Kant Congress*, Vol. I, No. 1 (Milwaukee: Marquette University Press, 1995) pp. 139–56; Clohesy, W. A 'Constitution for a Race of Devils', in Robinson (ed.), *op. cit.*, Vol. II, No. 2. (1995) pp. 733–41.

28 Until the eighteenth century, *natio, gens* and *populus* were often used as synonyms; See 'Nation, Nationalismus, Nationalität', in Ritter, J., *Historisches Wörterbuch der Philosophie*, Vol. 6 (Basel/Stuttgart, 1984), pp. 406–8.

29 See Nussbaum, M. C., 'Kant und stoisches Weltbürgertum', in Lutz-Bachmann, M. and Bohman, J. (eds.), *Frieden durch Recht. Kants Friedensidee und das Problem einer neuen Weltordnung* (Frankfurt am Main: Suhrkamp, 1996) p. 51. For Nussbaum's theory, see Nussbaum, Martha, C., *et al.*, *For Love of Country: Debating the Limits of Patriotism* (Boston: Beacon Press, 1996).

30 Klein, H-D., 'Nationalismus und partikularer Geist', in Burger, Klein and Schrader (eds.), *op. cit.* (1996) pp. 19–26, especially 19f.; Pelinka, A., 'Zur intellektuellen Widersprüchlichkeit des ethnischen Nationsbegriffes', in *ibid.*, pp. 27–33; Anderson, B., *Die Erfindung der Nation. Zur Karriere eines folgenreichen Konzepts* (Frankfurt am Main, 1988); Hobsbawm, E. J., *Nation and Nationalism since 1780. Programme, Myth, Reality* (Cambridge, 1990);

'Nation, Nationalismus, Nationalität', in Ritter, *op. cit.* (1984), pp. 406–14; Kluxen-Pyta, D., *Nation und Ethos. Die Moral des Patriotismus* (Freiburg: Karl Alber, 1991), especially pp. 45–56, pp. 120–30, 180ff.

31 See Kluxen-Pyta, *op. cit.* (1991) 122f.

32 See Coulmas, P., *Weltbürger. Geschichte einer Menschheitssehnsucht.* (Reinbek bei Hamburg: Rowohlt, 1990) pp. 333–86; Heater, D., *World Citizenship and Government. Cosmopolitan Ideas in the History of Western Political Thought* (Basingstoke: Macmillan, 1996) pp. 60–88; 'Kosmopolit, Kosmopolitismus', in Ritter, J. and Gründer, K. (eds.), *Historisches Wörterbuch der Philosophie*, Vol. 4 (Basel/Stuttgart: Schwabe & Co., 1976) pp. 1159–64.

33 See Vierweg, K., 'Jenseits von Nationalwahn und schwärmerischem Kosmopolitismus – zum Problem der Zustammenstimmung von Nationalem und Europäisch-Weltbürgerlichem', in Burger, Klein and Schrader (eds.), *op. cit.* (1996) p. 67. For him, Scheler, M., 'Über die Nationalideen der grossen Nationen', in *Nation und Weltanschauung* (Leipzig, 1923) is a good example.

34 See Drescher, S. (ed.), *Wer war Kant? Drei zeitgenössische Biographien von Ludwig Ernst Borowski, Reinhold Bernhard Jachmann und E. A. Chr. Wasianski* (Pfullingen, 1974) p. 161.

35 Important contributions of Kantian scholars are: Archibugi, D., 'Models of International Organization in Perpetual Peace Projects', *Review of International Studies*, No. 18 (1992) pp. 295–317; Brandt, R., 'Vom Weltbürgerrecht', in Höffe, O. (ed.), *Immanuel Kant. Zum ewigen Frieden. Klassiker Auslegen* (Berlin: Akademie Verlag, 1995) pp. 133–48; Marini, G., 'Il diritto cosmopolitico nel progetto Kantiano per la pace perpetua con particolare riferimento al secondo articolo definitivo', *Studi Kantiani*, Vol. 8 (1995) pp. 87–112; Marini, G., 'Kant e il diritto cosmopolitico', *Iride*, Vol. 17 (1996) pp. 126–40; Williams, H., 'Universal Hospitality: Kant's Critique of Colonialism and Slavery', in Koller, P. and Puhl, K. (eds.), *Current Issues in Political Philosophy. Justice in Society and World Order* (Wien: Hölder-Pichler-Tempsky, 1997); Bohman, J., 'The Public Spheres of the World Citizen', in Robinson (ed.), *op. cit.* (1995), Vol. I, No. 3 pp. 1065–80.

36 Ferencz, B. (with Keyes, K.), *Planethood: The Key to Your Survival and Prosperity* (Coos Bay, OR: Vision Books, 1988) p. 138, quoted in Heater, *op. cit.* (1996) p. 176. The slogan reminds me of Fichte's description of the true cosmopolitan: 'Vaterlandsliebe ist seine Tat, Weltbürgersinn ist sein Gedanke', Fichte, J. G., quoted in 'Kosmopolit, Kosmopolitismus', in Ritter and Gründer (eds.), *op. cit.* (1976) p. 1163.

37 De Tocqueville, A., *Über die Demokratie in Amerika.* (Stuttgart, 1985) 139ff.; Habermas, *op. cit.* (1992) p. 612; Reese-Schäfer, W., *Grenzgötter der Moral. Der neuere europäisch-amerikanische Diskurs zur politischen Ethik* (Frankfurt am Main: Suhrkamp, 1997) p. 166.

38 Current global trends are described and evaluated in Archibugi, D. and Held, D. (eds.), *Cosmopolitan Democracy. An Agenda for a New World Order* (Cambridge: Polity Press, 1995); Falk, R., *On Humane Governance: Toward a New Global Politics* (Oxford: Polity Press, 1995); Held, D., *Democracy and the Global Order: From the Modern State to Cosmopolitan Governance* (Cambridge: Polity Press 1995); Held, D., *Political theory and the modern state: essays on*

State, Power and Democracy (Cambridge: Polity Press, 1995); Mathews, J. T., 'Power Shift', *Foreign Affairs*, Vol. 76 (1997) pp. 50–66.

39 Kimminich, O., *Der internationale Rechtsstatus des Flüchtlings* (Köln, 1962), was one of the first international lawyers to address the problem of refugees in the modern world. Delbrück, J., *Die Konstitution des Friedens als Rechtsordnung. Zum Verständnis rechtlicher und politischer Bedingungen der Friedenssicherung im internationalen System der Gegenwart* (Berlin: Duncker und Humbolt, 1996) is a useful introduction into current trends and problems of international legal theory. Richter, E., *Der Zerfall der Welteinheit. Vernunft und Globalisierung in der Moderne* (Frankfurt/New York: Campus, 1992) analyses modern models of world unity.

40 A brief discussion can be found in my book *Pax Kantiana. Systematisch-historische Untersuchung des Entwurfs 'Zum ewigen Frieden' (1795) von Immanuel Kant* (Wien, Köln, Weimar: Böhlau, 1992) pp. 425–31, a more extended one in Rentsch, T., 'Aufhebung der Ethik', in Hastedt, H. and Martens, E. (eds.), *Ethik. Ein Grundkurs* (Reinbek bei Hamburg: Rowohlt, 1994) pp. 114–43. A recent and convincing defence of a universalist position is included in Klein, H-D., 'Nationalismus und partikularer Geist,' in Burger, Klein and Schrader (eds.), *op. cit.* (1996) pp. 20–5.

41 Hegel, G. W. F., 'Enzyklopädie der philosophischen Wissenschaften', in *Werke in zwanzig Bänden, Vol. 10.* (Frankfurt am Main: Suhrkamp, 1986) 57f., quoted in Vierweg, K., *Nationales*, p. 69.

10
Peaceful Integration in Germany

Ralf Rytlewski

A new type of revolution?

In 1989/90 within just six months the population of the German Democratic Republic staged a peaceful revolution and brought down the political system. The leading communists retreated from the pressure of demonstrators marching in the streets. They stepped down without bloodshed and violence between the demonstrators and security forces, police and military. In the safe haven of a Protestant church Erich Honecker, Chairman of the Party, found shelter from the wrath of the population. Previously, this church had opened its doors to political and social opposition groups.

In the summer of 1990 most people in East Germany were proud of having rid themselves of the dictatorship of the party by peaceful means. They hoped that this might give the political culture and democratic traditions of the whole Germany a new strong and positive impetus. As in the German Democratic Republic, political revolutions took place throughout Eastern Europe and Russia. These were peaceful revolutions, apart from bloodshed in Romania when the communist dictator was overthrown, and a shooting near the parliamentary building in Moscow. As a result, the communist national constitutions were abolished.

However, isn't it always the case that political revolutions take a non-peaceful course? How would it be possible otherwise within a few weeks or months to withdraw the governing elite of a party, government and military from their positions of power in order to abolish the national constitution? How would it be possible otherwise to appoint in short order a sufficient number of new political leaders to positions of power? The change of power and constitution in the GDR and in Eastern Europe took place without violence – can we therefore, still speak of revolutions?

In the opinion of the Russian revolutionary Trotsky, revolutions are 'the raging inspiration of history'. By that he meant that revolutions break out when those in power leave the political agenda unchanged even though the norms, interests and attitudes of the population have changed. The rulers are no longer capable of a creative response but only of 'pathological learning'. Revolutions are the 'eruption of these new attitudes', which form the basis of a new political order.

For the political sciences the revolutions in the German Democratic Republic, Poland, Czechoslovakia and Russia were a rare opportunity to research the conditions of peaceful revolutions. These researches may lead to a revision of our understanding of revolutions, or at least to an extension of the classification of revolutions.

Since the eighteenth century the term 'political revolution' has been restricted to the forcible overthrow of a national constitution, whereas the term 'social revolution' refers to social changes which occur as a result of industrialization, for example. On the basis of criteria of the social stratification the social revolution can be perceived as a 'bourgeois' and 'proletarian' revolution. In short: political as well as social revolutions are connected with the long-term socioeconomic developments. In modern times this is the industrial development known as the 'industrial' revolution, and at present it means the revolutionizing of the economy and society by new information media. We know that we can differentiate between three dimensions of the revolutionary destruction of the political, social and economic systems.

However, a revolution can also be primarily motivated by ideology and oriented towards ideology. The best example of such a case is the German or Protestant Reformation in the sixteenth century. The first one of the great European revolutions of modern times did not only renew the religious and the ecclesiastical organization of Christianity, but manifested itself also as a social uprising of farmers, knights and radicals. In the seventeenth century it was followed by the English revolution, in the eighteenth century by the American and French revolutions, and in the nineteenth century by the European revolutions of 1848 when the proletariat emerged for the first time in world history. Finally, with World War I (1914–18) the revolution began to take a global dimension. As a national or colonial revolution it reached Turkey, Persia and China, and after World War II the whole of Asia and Africa. At the same time the revolutions in the twentieth century become more powerful and radical. As the Russian Revolution shows it's no longer just breaking with the political and social order of a country, but the goal is the reformation of the whole population.

Did the character of revolution change again at the end of the 1980s? There are some reasons to believe that the peaceful revolutions in the German Democratic Republic and in Eastern Europe have announced an evolutionary progress as an expression of political and social renewal in a civilized world.

In the following section we will discuss a number of conditions under which the peaceful revolution in the GDR was undertaken. First, we will go through the historical prerequisites and then discuss the considerations which are symptomatic for peace.

The GDR – anchored in the East and in the West

The German Democratic Republic was the result of the division of Germany and Europe into two opposing power blocs. Similar to the foundation of the Federal Republic of Germany the foundation of the GDR in 1949 was part of the conflict between the USSR and the USA. As long as no greater shifts of power took place between the blocs, the existence of the German Democratic Republic as a state was not endangered. The GDR was a typical status quo power. As a result, in the 1980s the GDR got into political difficulties to the same extent that the Soviet Union as the leading power lost its leadership in domestic and foreign policies. In 1985 when the Soviet Union started to revise its claims to power in the field of domestic and foreign policies the loss of power of the Communist Party in the Soviet Union and of East Germany became apparent. This loss of power had occurred during the many years of stagnation of domestic policy under Secretary General Breshnev.

By means of a change of the political strategy and a move towards more transparency – glasnost – and towards a reform of power – perestroika – the new Secretary General Mikhail Gorbachev achieved a realistic self-awareness of the country (probably for the first time in Soviet history). The Secretary General not only stated that the economy had ended up in a blind alley but he also complained about the decline of public morality, the ideological emasculation of Marxism-Leninism, the stagnation of party activities and the inadequacy of scientific research. By means of glasnost and perestroika the overdue modernization of the political processes and institutions should now be tackled. At first it was merely a question of reforming Soviet-style bureaucratic socialism, but soon it involved replacing socialism by means of free enterprise and pluralistic-democratic relationships were put on the agenda.

The political leaders of the German Democratic Republic were suspicious of these changes in the Soviet Union and the 'national ways' towards reforming the system which the Poles and Czechs had chosen. Until 1989 they continued to rule the GDR as a bastion of the traditional Soviet-socialist way. When these leaders had to quit the political stage in the GDR the remaining conservative communist leaderships in Czechoslovakia, Bulgaria and Roumania could no longer last.

The defeat of the German Reich after World War II in 1945 made the Germans soon aware that for the time being there would be no return to the European policy of a balance of power between national states. Due to their concentration in blocs it was impossible for the time being to unite the national German state. Initially the German Democratic Republic claimed equal status with the German Reich. In 1967 only a GDR nationality was made into a legal norm.

As a matter of fact the postwar policy of the four victorious powers resulted in dividing the territory of the German Reich into three: the territory of the Federal Republic of Germany (including West Berlin) and that of the German Democratic Republic (including East Berlin) and the territories (Silesia, Pomerania, East Prussia) ceded to Poland and Russia.

For the GDR the division of Germany posed a difficult economic problem. Until 1945 its territory was a central region of the Reich where now an independent 'national' economy had to be established. Being a territory without raw materials but with a strong industrial base, the GDR had to rely on the import of raw materials and food. This could be financed only by the export of finished industrial products.

In 1950 the GDR joined the Council of Mutual Economic Aid (COMECON) and organized predominantly with the Soviet Union an exchange of raw materials for finished products. At the same time the GDR introduced the old 'national-economic' model developed by Stalin which provided for self-sufficiency of the economy to the greatest possible extent. In parallel it encouraged an extensive industrialization as promoted in all COMECON member countries.

For this reason, any possible effects of specialization upon cost and benefits could not be realized within the COMECON. It is claimed that the relatively small-scale economy of the GDR as the industrial 'department store' had produced at times up to 80 per cent of the range of industrial products in the world.

There are other reasons why a high international integration within the COMECON could not be achieved: lack of convertible currencies, of a reasonable accounting and price system and of free personal and capital movement.

On balance the intermediate conclusion can be drawn that the GDR had become part of the Eastern bloc through the Soviet social-ist economic order and policy and because it recognized the dominance of Moscow. This included the formation of a 'National People's Army' and its integration into the military alliance of the Warsaw Pact.

Until the mid-1980s the military alliance was an instrument for disciplining domestic policy. Furthermore, despite the homogeneity of the system of rule the GDR differed from the other member states of COMECON and the Warsaw Pact by a whole host of remarkable ties with the Federal Republic of Germany and other member states of the Western bloc.

Despite the fortifications along the Elbe river, the border between the two German states, there were no customs barriers. The open economic border brought about two advantages for the GDR. On the basis of the legal agreement among the allies, and within the frame-work of an agreement concluded with the Federal Republic in 1951, the GDR could barter without the use of foreign exchange. From 1960 onwards barter amounted to between 8 and 10 per cent of the over-seas trade of the GDR. On the other hand, the German Democratic Republic was in direct contact with the domestic market of the European Union. The European Economic Community and the European Nuclear Community (European Community) had not asked the Federal Republic of Germany to apply European Community laws to intra-German trade with the GDR. Therefore, the citizens of the GDR, nationals within the terms of the constitution of the Federal Republic, were at the same time 'market citizens' of the European Community. For the German Democratic Republic German–German trade and access to the European market afforded a favourable oppor-tunity to receive technological innovations by means of trade. The GDR maintained intensive trading relations with the OECD countries. Compared with the total overseas trade of the GDR, trade with these countries greatly increased during the 1960s. Only the very high inter-national indebtedness of the GDR in the early 1980s finally led to a steep decline in this trade.

There is a second field where the integration of the GDR in the

Western system of alliances was stronger than that of its East European neighbours. In 1969 the Brandt/Scheel administration undertook a course correction of intra-German and foreign policies. In 1970 this resulted in the Moscow Treaty by which both countries recognized the status quo in Europe and agreed to normalize their relationships.

Now the way was smoothed for contractual agreements with the German Democratic Republic. A number of bilateral agreements finally culminated, in 1973, in the admission to the UN of the two German states. Thanks to German–German treaties and the admission to the UN, therefore, the claim of the political leaders of the GDR to rule a socialist state on German territory had more validity in domestic and foreign policy. At the same time this meant that the political relationships of the GDR with the Federal Republic and the Western neighbouring countries became closer.

Taking into consideration all the abovementioned conditions, the GDR appeared to be a country which was anchored in the East as well as in the West. From the viewpoint of military and security policy the GDR was firmly integrated in the Warsaw Pact and, therefore, in the bipolar security system. This was overlapped, however, by an obligation on both German states to recognize the status quo, to encourage political détente and to respect the conditions of peaceful existence in Europe (the Helsinki Final Act). Though the national orientation of the economic policy to achieve far-reaching self-sufficiency had encouraged the national establishment of the GDR in a decisive way, the struggle for a separate state never did go so far as to break off trade relations with the Federal Republic which had existed since the postwar period.

Though militarily and politically the GDR was a firmly integrated Western link in the Soviet system of alliances, it nevertheless cultivated economic relations with the 'hostile' states to their mutual advantage. Furthermore, on the one hand, the GDR was keen to achieve national sovereignty, but on the other hand, the 'special relationships' with the Federal Republic of Germany were not infringed.

Peace and co-operation as prerequisites of unification and integration

Kenneth Boulding summarized our understanding of peace in the following positive and negative definitions: 'The concept of peace has both positive and negative aspects. On the positive side, peace signifies a condition of good management, orderly resolution of conflict, harmony associated with mature relationship, gentleness and love. On the negative side, it is conceived as the absence of something – the absence of turmoil, tension, conflict and war'.

From a moral and political viewpoint the revolution in the German Democratic Republic in 1989/90 was highly appreciated in Germany and abroad because bloodshed was avoided. This means that a negative peace was maintained, but this was only one side of the coin. The other side was positive, because the peaceful revolutionary process was 'well managed'. The physical well-being of the population and the different groups in the cities and the country was never endangered. There was no violence at the borders or at the Berlin Wall. The people's sense of justice was not homogeneous but expressed in different ways. Many people gave quite different accounts of the role of historical-political justice in Germany but these views were never so radically different that a shared future for these groups seemed impossible. The political-objective trend underlying the behaviour and attitudes of the protagonists of the revolution in the streets, churches, factories and offices facilitated the involvement of all those who wanted to participate in the political events. Only the cadres of the *Stasi*, the political and secret police, were denied a role on the political stage as before. The protagonists of the revolution and the population were ready and capable of understanding themselves by way of discussions. They found a compromise in complete solidarity and managed well a complicated process, in which political organizations and institutions, programmes and personnel were changing.

During the transition from October to November 1989 the general target of the revolutionary process changed again. During the first phase (the 'October revolution') the demonstrators shouted '*We* are the people', whereas during the second phase (the 'November revolution') they had changed the slogan to 'We are *one* people'. In the beginning the opposition called for the democratization of the existing GDR and demanded reform, but not the end of the political system. Even today writers and intellectuals who distinguish themselves by a continuous loyalty to the basic communist idea of the GDR – like Christa Wolff – maintain that as a consequence of 'Western manipulation' the opposition dropped the goal of reforming the GDR and supported instead the unification of the two German states 'without further reflection'.

A look at the historical sources shows that there is every reason to believe that the slogan was changed 'spontaneously and not at instigation of Helmut Kohl or any other West German politician'.

However, it was not only those groups who – speaking with Albert O. Hirschman – had decided in favour of 'voice' characterized features of the revolution in the GDR. Other large groups had decided in favour of 'exit' and crossed over to the Federal Republic, initially via Prague and Budapest. In 1989, 350,000 of the 16 million inhabitants left the GDR. This migration continued in 1990 and the pressure weighing upon the decision-makers of the governments in East Berlin, Bonn, Washington and Moscow increased enormously.

Where could the solutions be found in this critical situation? Different options were at hand:

a) complete final separation of the GDR from the FRG,
b) complete unification of the two German states,
c) confederation of both German states,
d) an interim solution on a contractual basis and the postponement of a final decision.

In 1990 during the first free parliamentary elections in the German Democratic Republic an overwhelming majority of the population voted in favour of the offer of the Christian Democratic Union and the Kohl administration to unify the two German states as quickly as possible. And a contract was concluded immediately between the two German states establishing a monetary, economic and social union with the Deutschemark as the common currency. Political unification was achieved later and after a period of international co-ordination.

Today many Germans think it would have been better to have agreed political integration first and then carried out economic and social integration afterwards. This would probably have required less financial transactions from West to East.

In accordance with the Constitution of the Federal Republic of Germany two possible forms of a relatively quick unification now existed:

a) following Article 23 of the Basic Law the accession of the territories of the GDR – as new federal states – to the Federal Republic,
b) following Article 146 of the Basic Law the joint elaboration of a new German constitution and its adoption by the German people in West and East.

For obvious reasons the Federal Republic preferred unification by means of an accession (a). Only this would guarantee that the constitutional order of West Germany need not be changed. From the viewpoint of the GDR there were good reasons also for unification by accession:

a) The widespread and long-term confidence in the superiority of the West German economic system of 'social market economy'. This confidence was based primarily on experience over many years with the success and efficiency of this economic model in German–German domestic trade. The social system linked therewith promised even greater benefits especially for old age pensions than the GDR variant of a social state.

   Furthermore, even the party leaders of the GDR had bowed to the attractive Deutschmark as the German currency of choice: for many years they had officially tolerated the Deutschmark as an unofficial second currency in the GDR. As a consequence, in 1989/90 we often heard the slogan 'Should the DM not come to us, we will go to the DM'.

   Finally, the official interest of the GDR government in the Deutschmark was well known: they asked payment for using the road and communication systems to West Berlin and money for the release of detainees who were permitted to cross the border to the Federal Republic against a transfer of DM.

b) The fact that the structures of consumption were quite similar in West and East – although the quality was often different – was also connected with this recognition and confidence. At the top of the hierarchy of consumption in both East and West we find the private car and private social contact and recreation in holiday resorts, on private or co-operative estates. The GDR population particularly liked their allotments and weekend cottages ('dachas') and were called, therefore, a 'niche society'. It is quite understandable, therefore, that in the 1980s the West German VW started producing cars for customers in the GDR.

c) Many GDR citizens were familiar with important political and social procedures in West Germany. Since the Ostpolitik of Willy Brandt (the West German foreign policy regarding the Eastern bloc, especially East Germany and East Berlin) diplomacy under Foreign Minister Genscher was able to spread a tightly linked network of political, economic, social, cultural and scientific contacts over the two German states, their European neighbour countries and the leading powers, USSR and USA. The GDR was part and parcel of this national and international exchange of ideas and of a network of mutual material support. This meant contacts between diplomats, staff members, governments and administrations, members of parliament and party leaders, businessmen and vacationing old age pensioners. It meant also relations and partnerships between communities, churches, sports clubs, media, scientific institutions and lawyer's offices.

Thanks to these experiences many people were able to evaluate the West German and European situation in society, policy and culture. They knew about the structures and trends in the other Germany even though they were ignorant of many of the details.

In the months after September 1989 the special structural position of the German Democratic Republic between East and West made it decisively easier for the GDR to find a peaceful way out of its integration in the Eastern bloc and to transform its economic and political system. In this connection it was advantageous that after a phase of stagnation in 1987 the European Community had put into force the Uniform European Act which provided for the establishment of the European Market at the end of 1992. The radical change in the GDR and the East European states coincided with a further push for West European integration.

A preliminary outcome

Seven years later a seemingly positive balance can be drawn up. Germany, united as one nation, emerged out of this 'improvised unification'. When comparing the integration process of Germany, e.g. with the moderate success of the political integration of Europe, it can be considered a great success. The institutions and procedures of the parliamentary system in West Germany and its administration were quickly accepted.

In the meantime these procedures are being applied in all parts of Germany virtually unchanged. This can be shown by empirical data, e.g. on the behaviour of members of parliament in the German states. It proved relatively easy to bring state institutions, administration and policies, such as economic, financial and judicial policies, in line with a new political system.

With hindsight, however, we can see that the peaceful integration of two states and two societies was a very complicated process. This does not only pertain to the 'exterior unity' of the common territory, the accepted frontiers, their military protection and a uniform nationality, but also to the social, mental, cultural and economic conditions of the 'interior unity'.

Paradoxically, the effect of the GDR revolution and of the following unification and integration process were in completely opposite directions. The revolution was successful because it came 'from below'. By means of a new rhetoric of mass demonstrations the population was made aware of the contradiction existing between the masses and those in power and recognized this inconsistency. A similar process had happened much earlier in the workers' uprising of 17 June 1953.

Later, however, unification and integration were no longer from below, but managed 'from above'. It was not the social groups but administration and policies as providers of political legitimation that were controlling the process of bringing the populations together in terms of lifestyle and income. Initially the majority of the population saw themselves in the role of political protagonists, whereas the majority of the West Germans couldn't do anything but play the part of sympathetic spectators.

After the peaceful revolution the political administrative elite of the federal state kept both populations from innovative revolutionary roles.

This is one of the important omissions of the West German elite and needs to be acknowledged. They did exploit the potential for social innovation. Spontaneous actions were even slowed down by the fact that the regulatory details of unification and integration were set up either by the state administration or by experts of interest groups and professional associations slowly moving eastward. At any rate, approximately 5,000 general regulations had been laid down in the contract the two German states had concluded in 1990.

We have to realize, therefore, that the historical event of the unification of Germany is completely anchored in the tradition of the German state. This means that the structuring of public life and the system of social and cultural performances – which soon penetrated the private sphere of the people – was to be decided and implemented from above.

Though not in line with this tradition, it would have been appropriate to call for the staging of meetings between the populations of East and West, or to mobilize national resources to promote the economic and social development of East Germany. As it is well known that Germans are generous donors this omission is even more surprising. It is also surprising when we consider the funds which will be required in the longer term – taxpayers' money – to be transfered to the new states. In my opinion, the constitutional conservatism which even after unification left the political system of West Germany more or less unchanged is deeply rooted in this tradition of the state. The deciding factors which determined the extent and structure of the results of integration achieved so far are to be found in the political traditions of Germany and their practical implementation not only by the Federal Republic of Germany but also by the German Democratic Republic:

a) The new states have adapted relatively quickly to the political, administrative, military and economic system of West Germany. No serious differences exist in the attitudes of the populations to the various institutions.

b) In the meantime the structure and level of consumption are largely identical, although regional consumption preferences persisted and the different waves of consumption were different in the cities and in the country: first buying cars and food, followed by foreign travel, buying means of communication, furniture, and so on.

The favourable rate of exchange of 1:1 between the two German currencies stipulated by the monetary union in 1990 was the material basis for the similarity of the Germans as consumers. The federal government in Bonn had stipulated this rate of exchange for political reasons, though economically it could hardly be justified.

c) Although income levels are not yet parallel, income per private household is converging. In 1995 31 per cent of the private households in both the East and West had an average income of between 3,000 and 5,000 Deutschmarks a month, though low-income groups dominated in the East and the high-income groups in the West. In the high-income groups in East Germany we find primarily civil servants; in West Germany, independent professionals.

In the same connection, it is interesting that statistical data show that by 1993 monetary assets per private household in the new states amounted to half the assets of West German households.

With regard to pensions (pension insurance is the most important type of social security insurance and was chosen by 44 million people) only minor differences in the average monthy pension exist. In 1994 a typical pension amounted to 1,253 DM in West German and to 1,214 DM in the East German states.

d) Although there is hardly any difference in the consumption patterns of the Germans and although their aesthetic preferences are very similar, profound differences in social behaviour and lifestyle still exist. In order to be able to understand the differences in lifestyle we should remember that policy and economy in the former GDR demanded special civic techniques from the population. Thousands of groups for the exchange of material commodities as well as family discussion groups were established. A certain oral philosophy emerged within these small groups which was different from the officially formulated philosophy of the political system. In West German society no counterpart to these still prevailing civic cultures can be found.

Furthermore, social and political attitudes and behaviours in the East are effectively characterized by an everyday philosophical orientation which derives from the postulate of equality inherent in European modernity, which leads to a relatively small difference in the practical lifestyle of individuals and groups. Poverty as well as wealth are reflected more overtly than in West Germany.

In the political field everyday orientation does not so much rest upon a modern understanding of the prestige values of various policies but relies primarily upon the early modern more direct interpretations of freedom, equality and solidarity of the European revolutions in 1848.

In the eyes of the political elite these differences between East and West we have just outlined contravene a main principle of German policy. To create and maintain the same living conditions for all Germans is considered a task beyond the power of political parties; rather it is a continuous political and constitutional task, independently on whether people live in the East or in the West, in towns or in the country, whether their lifestyle is traditional or postmodern. This principle was a decisive reason for the integration-political strategy of the government and opposition in Bonn: to achieve equal living conditions as quickly as possible even though it would be expensive.

We can draw at least three conclusions from the peaceful integration of Germany:

1. The Germans in East and West have very similar socio-political convictions that equality should be an indispensable prerequisite for peace. On the basis of this maxim the objective and, if possible, the subjective conditions for the prosperity and well-being of the population should be managed with the instruments of the social

and cultural state. This was their conviction before and after the revolution in the GDR in 1989/90 – a heritage of the social democratic century.

2. The unification and integration of Germany was principally stimulated and managed by the political strategy of Bonn, not to make national interest and everyday 'political realism' the political centre of attention. Instead, German interests and concepts were always strictly included in the European and American sphere of interest. With regard to the GDR the Federal Republic implemented an open door policy, with regard to all neighbouring countries, a policy of long-term continuous interrelations. This allowed the protagonists in 1989/90 to assess their mutual attitudes and behavioural expectations in a realistic way.

3. Favourable personal, normative and institutional conditions were created which permitted the successful management of the centennial event of a peaceful change of system. Only against this background can be understood what is reported by insiders: only 11 politicians and diplomats from the three capitals Bonn, Washingtbn and Moscow were necessary in order to begin this successful example of political leadership and statecraft and finally to achieve this goal.

References

Ash, Timothy Garton 1995: *Im Namen Europas. Deutschland und der geteilte Kontinent.* Frankfurt a, M.

Berg-Schlosser, Dirk and Ralf Rytlewski (eds.) 1993: *Political Culture in Germany,* Basingstoke and London.

Burkhardt, Armin and K. Peter Fritzsche (eds.), 1992: *Sprache im Umbruch. Politischer Sprachwandel im Zeichen von 'Wende' und Einigung',* Berlin/New York.

Beyme, Klaus v. and Claus Offe (eds.), 1995: *Politische Theorie in Ära der Transformation,* Opladen.

Ellwein, Thomas and Joachim Jens Hesse, 1997: *Der Überforderte Staat,* Frankfurt a.M.

Friedrich, Carl, J., 1970: *Politik als Prozess der Gemeinschaftsbildung,* Koln-Opladen.

Genscher, Hans Dietrich, 1995: *Erinnerungen,* Berlin.

Hertle, Hans and Hermann, 1996: *Der Fall der Mauer. Die unbeabsichtigte Selbstauflösung des SED-Staates.* Opladen.

Huntington, Samuel P., 1991: *The Third Wave. Democratization in the Late Twentieth Century,* Norman and London.

Lehmbruch, Gerhard (ed.), 1995: *Einigung und Zerfall. Deutschland und Europa nach dem Ende des Ost-West-Konflikts,* Opladen.

Offe, Claus, 1994: *Der Tunnel am Ende des Lichts. Erkundungen der politischen Transformation im Neuen Osten*, Frankfurt a.M.

Schonbohm, Jorg, 1992: *Zwei Armeen und ein Vaterland. Das Ende der Nationalen Volksarmee*, Berlin.

Senghaas, Dieter (Ed.), 1995: *Den Frieden denken. Si vis pacem, para pacem.* Frankfurt a.M.

Statistisches Bundesamt (ed.), 1997: *Datenreport 1997*, Bonn.

Zelikow, Philip and Condoleezza Rice, 1995: Germany Unified and *Europe Transformed.* A Study in *Statecraft*, Cambridge, Mass. and London.

11
Preparing for the Political: German Intellectuals Confront the 'Berlin Republic'

Jan Mueller

The German word *Begründung* has two meanings. It signifies not only foundation, but also giving reasons, providing a rationale. We are now approaching the *Begründung* of what has been variously called the new Federal Republic, the Third Republic, or, most commonly, the Berlin Republic. Of course, one could argue that the real historical break occurred eight years ago, with the unification of the two Germanies in October 1990 as its official completion. But while 3 October 1990 might have been a formal foundation, there was arguably insufficient time for the other dimension of *Begründung* in the 'rush to unity'.[1] More importantly, there is a real sense in which the move of the Federal Government to Berlin, scheduled for 1999, is a highly symbolic, almost constitutional *Begründung* of the Berlin Republic in a way that the anti-climactic unification in 1990 never was.[2] Moreover, 1999 is the official starting date for European Economic and Monetary Union, a fact which is rapidly coming to the consciousness of most Germans. Consequently, we can speak of a double foundation that looms ever larger and poses the challenge of laying down some normative foundations and creating some public meaning.

In this essay, I want to analyse the public interventions of German intellectuals who have attempted to give a *Begründung* for the Berlin Republic in the sense of laying down normative foundations for the future polity. Because of the relatively drawn-out period between German unification and the final move of the Federal Parliament to Berlin, intellectuals have had ample opportunity to formulate normative frameworks for the new republic and to provide what German political scientists like to call a legitimation narrative. Unlike, then, in the case of Bonn or Weimar, and unlike the situation of the 'rush to unification', German intellectuals have been afforded the opportunity to draw lessons from 1989 and its aftermath and project them onto 1999 and beyond.

Recent years have seen a growing literature which deals explicitly with the Berlin Republic. This foundational literature, however, has had a whole other dimension, namely a discourse about what is to constitute the foundation of politics, or rather, 'the political', as such. This curious linguistic construction of 'the political', i.e. the transformation of the adjective 'political' into the noun 'the political', was made famous – or rather, notorious – by Carl Schmitt's 1927 book *The Concept of the Political*.[3] Before Schmitt, the concept of 'the political' was in use – but in the German tradition of general constitutional law doctrines (*Allgemeine Staatsrechtslehre*) it was equivalent to the state.[4] Georg Jellinek could still write that 'in the concept of the political one has already thought the concept of the state', a view shared by Max Weber.[5] Schmitt was the first to point out the circular reasoning from the state to the political and back. He detached the political from the state, and opened his most famous work with the dictum that 'the concept of the state presupposes the concept of the political'.[6] Schmitt went on to argue that 'the political is the most intense and extreme antagonism, and every concrete antagonism becomes that much more political the closer it approaches the most extreme point, that of the friend-enemy grouping.'[7] Just as much as Schmitt exercised a subterranean influence on conservative constitutional thought in West Germany, this 'concept of the political,' defined as a friend–enemy relationship, came to haunt West German political science, which explicitly understood itself as a science of democratic re-education.[8] Dolf Sternberger in particular, doyen of this democratic *Wissenschaft*, tried to wrest the concept from the right and redefine the political as the 'area of all endeavour to seek and secure peace'.[9] But Schmitt's agonistic definition remained a provocation (and an ideological weapon) in a country which had the largest peace movement in the Western world, and which remained largely sheltered from actual international conflict.

Recently, there has been an inflationary use of the expression 'the political', and the number of books dealing with its nature has grown exponentially. Just to provide a flavour of this literature, there is *Die Erfindung des Politischen, Maßverhältnisse des Politischen, Metamorphosen des Politischen, Die Transformation des Politischen, Theoretische Dimensionen des Politischen* and, finally, *Die Zukunft des Politischen*.[10] This preoccupation with the political, however, is not just a response to the Berlin Republic: most obviously, it is also a reaction to what has now become one of the great *idées reçus* post-1989, namely the often ill-defined notion of a 'return of the political' after the fall of the Wall, which is also subject to much debate in the United States and Western Europe.[11] German intellectuals also respond to what in the early and mid-1990s was perceived as widespread dissatisfaction with politics, the phenomenon which came to be known in an untranslatable phrase as *Politikverdrossenheit*, literally 'being fed up with politics'. This sense was aptly summarized in the title of a 1993 edited Suhrkamp collection, 'Politik ohne Projekt?' (Politics without a Project?).[12] Then and now large sections of the German population viewed the political class as unresponsive and as lacking vision. On a more subtle level, one could argue that intellectuals, and in particular left-wing intellectuals, have engaged with the 'political' because they felt the need to rebut the conservative charge of 'failure' and being 'apolitical' before and during unification.

Finally, there is the impact of globalization on Germany: two Scottish names increasingly come to haunt the lives of ordinary Germans, namely McDonald's, as shorthand for a low-wage service economy which Germans see prefigured in the United States; and McKinsey, as shorthand for a thoroughly rationalized state and economy which jettisons welfare benefits and dissolves the consensus underlying the social market economy. The 'McKinsey state' has become a synonym for a streamlined administration, which satisfies the ressentiment which most Germans feel towards bureaucrats, but also puts an end to any paternalist notion of the state, still best expressed in Thomas Mann's reverence for the *General Dr. von Staat*.[13] Thus, the process of globalization and the exposure of Germany to world politics and the world economy have been an additional motive force in engaging with 'the political', since globalization, far from being merely a matter of objective necessities (*Sachzwänge*), is also perceived as a political project.

This essay categorizes these various double or even triple foundational exercises. It analyses the ideological strategies which have been prominent in the emerging discourse on the future Berlin Republic, and the attempt to fix the meaning of the political. I shall start with what one might call the Old Right, i.e. the liberal-conservative opinion-makers of the old Federal Republic. Subsequently, I shall move on to the three main responses by the Left, and argue that explicitly, or implicitly, all these approaches situate themselves with reference to what are usually seen as the two German classics of 'thinking the political', namely Carl Schmitt and Hannah Arendt. This is not to say that either a Schmittian or an Arendtian conception of the political exhausts this concept. While Schmitt is often called 'the first philosopher of the political', the case of Arendt is much less clear-cut.[14] John Ely has recently argued that theorists who marshall Arendt in their definition of the political have fundamentally misconstrued her thought in a typically German étatist manner.[15] Ely points out that the very attempt to make Arendt into a political existentialist and a 'philosopher of the political' attests to the weakness of civic republican traditions and modes of thought in Germany. In any case, I shall pay careful attention to the particular conception of the political being proposed: is it posited as a kind of system, or subsystem, in line with Luhmann and, arguably, Weber? A conception of the political as a separate sphere (though not as a system) was also Carl Schmitt's first version of *Concept of the Political*, before Leo Strauss pointed out that such a differentiation of the political from other domains remained within the logic of liberalism.[16] Or is the political conceived as a kind of attribute, which makes another thing political, or as a peculiar relation, or as something substantive, or even as a sort of energy, a form of raw material, as Oskar Negt and Alexander Kluge have argued?[17] Schmitt himself, under Strauss's influence, shifted to the concept of the political as a degree of intensity: 'political' now denoted any antagonism which became so intense as to pose an existential threat. Hannah Arendt, however, did not seek one definition of 'the political'.[18] She made a great number of claims about 'politics,' and was adamant that politics was primarily action, and the meaning of politics freedom and disclosure.[19] But can an Arendtian conception of politics nevertheless be recast as 'the political' and then be played off against *die Politik* as official politics, i.e. the political sub-system? As we shall see, many observers make this seemingly paradoxical move by claiming that the political has disappeared, or is at least being drained, from politics.[20] Finally, this investigation has to confront Agnes Heller's claim that 'the concept of the political yields radical political philosophies', and that 'the malaise which, as a rule, accompanies the concept of the political' is the 'obsession with exclusion'.[21] While exclusion is in fact inherent in any concept or definition, the suspicion remains that a deinstitutionalized 'political' dispenses with the liberal, i.e. moderating rules of the political game and becomes freely available to politicize other domains of human life. Moreover, in the wake of the pre-1989 resurgence of civil society in Eastern Europe, might Western intellectuals not be led to confuse anti-politics with the political?[22] In short, then, the question remains whether the very concept of 'the political' works its own logic, even against explicitly liberal or republican intentions.

However, before I start, two caveats: the obvious omission in my story about left and right is the so-called 'New Right', over which much ink has been spilt recently. The reason is simply this: I do not believe that the New Right, despite having adopted both Schmitt and Gramsci as their guiding spirits, has had much success in its self-conscious attempt to establish a cultural hegemony in Germany. Just reading the rebuttals of Jacob Heilbrunn's scare story about the New Right in the recent issue of *Foreign Affairs*, one senses a consensus among both German intellectuals and foreign observers that the danger posed by the New Right has been effectively banished.[23] Moreover, apart from the idea of replicating 1968 from the right, their politics was 'without a project' just as much as the conservative or liberal mainstream. While we might live in a time when taboo-breaking can pass for theorizing, the fact that the two are not the same is made painfully obvious when it comes to filling policy with substance. In that regard, the New Right could offer only slogans which remained negatively fixated on the generation of 1968, or propose policies which, by and large, the Kohl government was already pursuing.

Secondly, a more general remark on terminology, namely the use of a distinction between left and right. A post-1989 *idée reçu* which easily beats the return of the political in its popularity, is the argument that 'left' and 'right' have lost their meaning. Now, curiously, hardly anyone on what used to be called – and still calls itself – the right actually says this. It is a confused left that blurs the distinction between left and right, thereby unwittingly enabling the right to co-opt leftist ideas and formerly left-leaning intellectuals who can present themselves as original, taboo-shattering thinkers. The right, whether old or new, know exactly who they are, though they do not always know what they want apart from discursive hegemony.[24] There is at least some reason, then, to believe that we are experiencing a 'Sternhellish moment' in which concepts, arguments and intellectual figures migrate from a left, mired in crisis and confusion, to the right.[25]

Old right, newly political

Henning Ritter, in a recent article in the *Frankfurter Allgemeine*, asserted that 'the expectation directed towards the future Germany can be formulated as follows: that the Berlin Republic will be more 'political' than the Bonn Republic'.[26] According to Ritter, this is not only due to the fact that Germany has regained its sovereignty. The Berlin Republic is also particularly political in contrast with its predecessor, the first postwar Republic with its apolitical basic features. The Bonn Republic was one of the few instances in which Walther Rathenau's dictum that the economy is fate (*Die Wirtschaft ist das Schicksal*) actually turned out to be true. Ritter also argued that Bonn had developed a certain utopian tendency in its post-national idealization of its own status of occupation, which was projected as the future of nation-states in general. In retrospect, Ritter argued, the Bonn Republic would be praised as a paradise, although no one noticed its utopian qualities at the time of its existence.

Many conservative intellectuals have adopted this contrast and the notion of a future that is somehow more 'political'. What does the political refer to in this context? It signifies above all regained national sovereignty, but, even more importantly, an increased potential for conflicts, with regard to both a new role for Germany on the world stage and conflict within Germany. Normality is regained, but 'normality, i.e. Berlin Republic instead of Bonn Republic, means most of all the normality of instability'.[27] This prediction of normality as instability was made by Johannes Gross in his 1995 book *Begründung der Berliner Republik*, which remains so far the most comprehensive conservative statement on the Berlin Republic. Gross, publicist, political pundit, TV personality and friend of the old Carl Schmitt, has followed the development of the old Federal Republic with many books commenting the state of the Germans, and can be taken as a generally reliable guide to centre-right sentiments. Internally, the normality of instability predicted by Gross results from the disappearance of the corporatist consensus underlying the old Federal Republic, as the parties, the unions and the Churches, and the whole system of *Proporz* and patronage, are weakened. With this weakening, the legitimacy of the political system is increasingly not a matter of legality, but of security: only the state that functions in the sense of providing its citizens with security will be accepted.[28] Gross repudiates Rathenau's dictum and reaffirms Napoleon's that in fact *Die Politik ist das Schicksal*. For Gross, following the jurist Ernst Forsthoff and Forsthoff's teacher, Carl Schmitt, the old Federal Republic was apolitical, because the state became merely an instrument for the satisfaction of social needs. The state, increasingly indistinguishable from society, was all-pervasive in its interventions, and yet weak in its unwillingness to exercise authority.[29] According to Gross, redistribution, which knows neither friends nor enemies, but only ever more recipients, is apolitical, while decision-making, and the realization of different political options is political. As much as West German politicians might reject the friend–enemy thinking of Carl Schmitt, in their support of an indiscriminate welfare state they actually preserve a National Socialist legacy: the idea of the *Volksgemeinschaft* (national community).[30] Surprisingly, Chancellor Kohl represents a truly political figure, because he pursues interests and engages in an unrestrained friend–enemy thinking, while publicly denouncing it.[31]

Externally, Gross sounds a wake-up call for Germany to face the reality of power politics and finally to define its national interests, which is of course another way of saying that the country should think more clearly about who its friends and enemies are. On the other hand, thanks to the EU, Germany is said to experience a loss of political substance in the form of decision-making capacity, which can be somewhat compensated for by increased national representation. In other words, while the substance of the political as decision-making capacity in the face of conflict is drained away by Brussels, the aestheticization of state power in the new capital could at least preserve the façade of politics. Not by chance, the cover of Gross's slim volume shows the fake Berlin *Stadtschloß*, i.e. the make-believe palace façade which Berliners could contemplate for a while to see whether they might enjoy having the real copy around. However, while Europe limits the scope of the political in foreign policy, Berlin will retain a 'reservation of the political' (*Reservat des Politischen*) in domestic policy. Finally, in Gross's prediction, Berlin will be both the German Washington and New York, a metropolis which finally unites the elites of business, media and politics, and which could satisfy Gross' nostalgia for a more *großbürgerliche* [tasteful upper-class] age. Hostesses will keep open houses, the political class is supposed to open itself up to the democratic public sphere, and the so far often enough merely moralizing media representatives might finally find a little more respect for political realities.

On the other hand, and somewhat surprisingly, Gross predicts that the Berlin Republic will be more political because it will contain more plebiscitary elements. This is advocated to counter the juridification of German politics through the Constitutional Court, and actually to increase stability by channelling political energies which the old parties and organizations can no longer attract.[32]

Gross's analysis has a mildly Schmittian subtext, but, more importantly, follows a pattern of thought set by the *enfant terrible* of the

German intellectual establishment, Karl Heinz Bohrer. In the early 1980s, Bohrer had combined a cultural critique of the old Federal Republic as provincial and apolitical, with an affirmation of the autonomy of the political from moral considerations.[33] Bohrer had also called for a new political class capable of sovereign decision-making, which would be similar to the metropolitan, *großbürgerliche* elites of London and Paris. On this reading, the state needs a new form of representation and aestheticization, but also a new *Selbstbewußtsein* (self-assurance). Thus, for conservatives, the political remains, above all, a synonym for conflict. They insist that the political remains the monopoly of the state, as authoritative decision-making remains the answer to the challenge of increased external and internal conflict. Plebiscitary elements might bolster the legitimacy of the state, but its capacity to provide security in an increasingly uncertain world remains its prime source of support. All of this, however, remains well within the mainstream of conservative thought of the old Federal Republic, and could be found in any book by Hans-Peter Schwarz, Hermann Lübbe or Odo Marquard. Thus, conservative responses to the Berlin Republic remain surprisingly conventional.

Habermas: the Berlin Republic between normality and postnationality

Jürgen Habermas best represents those West German intellectuals who have argued for an extension of the political principles underlying the old Federal Republic, combined with a further transfer of sovereignty to European institutions. For Habermas, the legacy of the hasty unification and the absence of a republican re-foundation is that a comprehensive political discursive agreement (*Selbstverständigung*) has yet to take place about what the 'normality' of the approaching Berlin Republic should look like.[34] The irony is that Habermas, while being the intellectual most in favour of continuity with the political culture of the old Federal Republic, was also the intellectual most vocally in favour of a grandiose act of foundation.[35] However, the foundation of the new German republic was always intended as strictly a re-foundation, precisely so as to ensure the strengthening of the emerging German republican consciousness. For Habermas, 1990 remains a lost opportunity to reaffirm the Western values of the old Federal Republic and to begin the life of the larger Germany with a democratic self-reassurance (*Selbstvergewisserung*).

As always in Germany, and with Habermas in particular, the question of discursive self-understanding (*Selbstverständigung*) is bound up with German historiography. Habermas sees two revisionary readings emerging which undermine the old Federal Republic as a Western success story: one is the return to a national history, in which continuities with the Second Empire are affirmed and the Federal Republic necessarily appears as the real *Sonderweg*; the other is the narrative of a global civil war, inspired by Carl Schmitt and, more recently, Ernst Nolte, which places the Nazis on the side of the occidental bourgeoisie in its fight against Bolshevism. Of course, Habermas wants to affirm the radical break of 1945, but also seeks to relativize the regaining of national sovereignty in 1990: '1989 will only remain a happy date, as long as we respect 1945 as the one that really taught us lessons.'[36] For Habermas, the nation-state has outlived its usefulness in dealing with problems which respect no national boundaries. In the face of globalization, new forms of social cohesion are necessary to preserve both democracy and the rule of law: this new social cohesion is of course to be a post-national, republican one, parts of which Habermas sees prefigured in the US.[37] To cope with global challenges, new supranational, more 'abstract' public spheres and new forms of social solidarity have to be created at the European level. Thus, the Berlin Republic can only be thought with Strassbourg and Brussels in mind.

Where does this leave the political? Habermas hardly needs a theoretical discourse of the political post-1989, because his conception of communicative action already contains an implicit engagement with Arendt and Schmitt. Whether or not the view of Arendt's major disciple in Germany, Ernst Vollrath, is correct that Habermas has misread and continues to misread Arendt by forcing her conception of a plurality of opinions into a consensualist and voluntarist straitjacket, the fact remains that Habermas was one of the few thinkers on the left who engaged creatively with Arendt's notion of *praxis*.[38] In his recent turn to legal and political theory, Habermas has again affirmed his commitment to a procedural and deliberative democracy, rejecting a republicanism which he sees as 'ethically overburdened'.[39] Taking elements from both classic liberalism and republicanism (in the sense of communitarianism), Habermas proposes an understanding of democracy as both deliberative and proceduralist. He rejects an Arendtian republicanism, which he equates with the (incidentally, Schmittian) category of a 'political self-organization of society', as an 'understanding of politics which is polemically directed against the state apparatus'.[40] Habermas rejects what he sees as Arendt's tendency to fuse state and society, and her neglect of the importance of institutionalizing procedures for public reasoning, as she relies solely on communicatively generated power.[41] Against such an account of both popular sovereignty and public ethical life (*Sittlichkeit*), Habermas wants practical reason to retreat from the concrete *Sittlichkeit* of a community, and be institutionalized in the procedures which ensure the communicative presuppositions of democracy.[42] Habermas's vision is thus not very far removed from American-style liberalism and, arguably, the status quo of the old Federal Republic. It certainly remains closer to that status quo than to any grand republican renewal *à la* Arendt.

Beck invents the political

Second, there has been what I would call an implicitly Arendtian approach to the post-1989 constellation. This is particularly clear in the case of a self-styled iconoclast like the sociologist Ulrich Beck. Beck has arguably become something like a sociological prophet in the public sphere since his successful 'risk society thesis'. The initial book *Risk Society: Towards a New Modernity* was fortuitously timed: it came out just after Chernobyl and crystallized the environmental anxieties of the 1980s, but at the same time painted an optimistic picture of what Beck called a 'different modernity'.[43] This different modernity in many ways resembled Habermas's incomplete project of modernity: it was to be a radicalized modernity that transcended industrial society, and was brought about by the silent revolution of a 'reflexive modernization', i.e. by 'simple modernization's' unintended, externalized and invisible consequences, which would add up to a structural rupture. This idea of what Peter Osborne has aptly characterized as a 'persisting but transformed modernity' has arguably satisfied a longing among the post-socialist left for engaging with 'the totalizing heritage of the philosophical discourse of modernity', and for holding on to the project of modernization, while also radically criticizing it.[44] On another level, *Risk Society* offered to 'break the stranglehold on conceptual innovation imposed by the fruitless postmodernity debate'.[45] It also nonchalantly repudiated the dreariness and paralysis of systems theory and Marxism, which could not conceive of a modernization of modernity without political revolution or large-scale social disruptions. Beck's emphasis on new spaces opening up for political action, on subterranean changes which would suddenly erupt, and on the delegitimation of experts chimed well with 1989 and with the desire to break out of what German citizens perceived as an immobile, corporatist society. Another, not entirely irrelevant factor was that sociology *à la* Beck could simply be fun to read. While his fellow sociologists have continued to sneer at Beck's popularizing flair, he certainly did provide the old Federal Republic with a self-image in which it could and did recognize itself.

In the 1990s, Beck has called for nothing less than the 'invention of the political', arguing that 'our fate is that we have to invent the political anew'.[46] The question is, of course, what Beck understands by the political. He defines it, in a manner both limited and optimistic, as the capacity to shape social reality, conspicuously leaving out questions about the legitimation of domination, power and interests.[47] He then makes the very theoretical move that is at the heart of Carl Schmitt's *Concept of the Political*: he detaches 'the political' from the notion of the state and what he calls official politics, and then plays the political off against the state. As Ernst Vollrath has pointed out, Schmitt made this move in response to a crisis in the peculiar German tradition of constitutional law doctrines (*Staatsrechtslehre*), in particular its formalistic positivism, without truly transcending its categories and its perception of the political.[48] Schmitt had deinstitutionalized the political only to think state and the political together again, by means of defining (and by a circular reasoning) the state as the political unity capable of authoritative friend–enemy distinctions. At the same time, however, he had made the concept of the political freely available to movements like the National Socialists.

Beck wants to avoid Schmitt's *étatist* approach, and any constraining of the political in an either/or logic. In fact, he identifies such a move with the functional differentiation of subsystems typical of systems theory, thereby implicitly associating Luhmann with Schmitt.[49] Beck instead relocates 'the political' in what he calls 'sub-politics', and what Schmitt would have called the 'self-organization of society': 'sub-politics' refers to the arena where the political, defined by Beck as large-scale social change, actually takes place: economic-technological development, the natural sciences, but also private life. Latent, invisible side-effects of economic-technological development, rather than rational will-formation in parliaments, are the source of the transformative power of a radical modernity.[50] While this critique of parliament is, of course, also a classic trope of Schmittian thought, Beck suggests that with increased civil and participation rights, citizens could become capable of exerting power over subpolitical processes.[51] Subpolitics can thus be both a Benjamin Barber-type 'strong democracy', and a direct, de-institutionalized, non-legal politics, which crucially depends on mediatized symbols. Democracy, like modernity itself, can now come into its own in a more participatory manner. This claim about the political parallels Beck's overall claim about the nature of reflexive modernization: it constitutes a profound transformation of society, without any outward revolutionary change: Beck leaves the system intact, but behind its façade, the *Entkernung* (hollowing out) of the political silently proceeds. Thus, rather like Gross, Beck's Berlin Republic would represent the state as make-believe: behind the façade, the political has escaped into society, since 'subpolitics' means shaping society from below. Thus, the differentiation process of modernization gives way to one of de-differentiation, in which, ideally, politics becomes decentralized and open for widespread decision-making: but while making room for decisions, Beck wants to avoid decisionism, by claiming that decisions are open to democratic negotiations and that subpolitics should become an arena in which a new political subjectivity can constitute itself.[52] The political, as it turns out, can be reinvented without a revolution.

What is needed, however, is what Beck calls a 'politics of politics', i.e. a politics that changes the very rules of politics and at the same time controls the shape of the political. This 'politics of politics', or, one might say, reflexive politics, is at least partially equivalent to Hannah Arendt's conception of politics. While Beck does not make any civic republican or even civic humanistic claims, he does describe politics as a realm of action and freedom, and predicts 'the return of individuals into society'.[53] Like Arendt, he rejects a Marxist or functionalist framework and emphasizes the scope of action for individuals. Their capacity for crossing the iron borders erected by systems theory, but also the imperative for them to cobble together their own biographies, is the second major aspect of Beck's overall thesis of 'reflexive modernization'. As the prophet of individuation, Beck has hit yet another raw cultural nerve, this time the dissolution of a corporatist Germany, in which individual flexibility acquires a premium and more than a few solid German traditions melt into air. Beck's emphasis on action, the individual and the art of the impossible fits into a larger paradigm shift, in which the social sciences, and history, place greater value on individual action, rather than structure, and on culture, rather than economics. Arguably, this reorientation is a result of both the social sciences' failure to predict 1989, as well as the cultural impact of 1989, and the desire of disenchanted younger scholars to assert themselves against *Gesellschaftsgeschichte* (social history) and systems theory.[54]

Beck has, of course, incurred his share of criticism: his flippant *Feuilleton* style, his tendency never to resist the temptation of a bad pun and his overall optimism make him look like a proponent of 'sociology lite'. Stefan Breuer has noted that Beck's theory, with its emphasis on 'politics as art', is suffused with aestheticism, calling it a 'Marlboro philosophy', in which liberated individuals ride on horseback into the sunset of simple modernization.[55] More importantly, one might ask whether the whole theory of reflexive modernization appears to be an extrapolation of the experiences of the old Federal Republic of the 1980s: Beck's risk society is also a rich society, which can afford the kinds of anxieties that he posits in order to explain the loss of faith in industrial society, in expert opinion and a traditional political class. And it is very much the experience of the Greens and citizens' movements which informs the notion of sub-politics. The question arises, then, whether this is merely another instance of German apocalyptical anti-modernism, often typical of the Greens and, of course, older, romantic social theorists? Is it a sociology of *Angst*, so to speak?

The answer is a resounding yes and no, because Beck, in a sense, has it both ways: there is a critique of instrumental rationality in bleak, apocalyptical tones reminiscent of Horkheimer and Adorno, even of Walter Benjamin, for instance when Beck writes that 'the risk society is not a revolutionary society, but more than that: it is a society of catastrophes: in it, the state of emergency threatens to be the normal state of affairs.'[56] But Beck combines this apocalyptical language with the hope of fulfilling the promises of modernity *à la* Habermas precisely through the very negativism of ecological dangers:[57] Horkheimer and Adorno's normative aim of enlightening Enlightenment about itself is sociologically generalized and, one would hope, empirically grounded: modernization is becoming modernized, half-modernity, half-democracy are becoming fulfilled. In one sense, this is simply dialectical: the systems of modern industrial society produce their own dangers, i.e. their own negation. In the sublation of this contradiction, humanism and individual agency are miraculously resurrected.[58] But one might ask whether Beck does not underestimate the resourcefulness of 'simple modernity', and whether his theory is not driven by the same search for a 'third way' that once animated the theorists of a legitimation crisis in late capitalism: Beck seems to have simply substituted the ecological crisis for the contradictions of capitalism, and reassured disillusioned Marxists that, even with the façades of official politics and industrial society intact, revolutionary change is under way.[59]

Beck's entire notion of the invention of the political is also questionable. It would seem that Beck's definition and relocation of the political are altogether too optimistic, emphasizing the creative elements of politics at the expense of the coercive ones. To overlook the ineradicable presence of violence in politics qualifies him for Max Weber's charge that whoever denies this presence is politically infantile.[60] Moreover, while Beck does make a lot of ill-defined notions such as 'a new art of politics', and other playful linguistic inventions, the emergence of the risk society, as predicted by Beck, implies a new kind of moral seriousness. This challenge of moral seriousness might of course provoke an empty gesture of resoluteness – precisely the decisionism which Beck wants to avoid. But to that end, Beck would have to indicate some normative guidelines for how individuals are to face the decision-making process. Moreover, as much as Beck wants to provide a sociological argument for a more participatory politics, he has little to say about the constitution of various public spheres in the realm of sub-politics. And as much as the whole notion of subpolitics is obviously a reflection of the experience of the Greens and the citizens' movements of the West Germany of the 1980s, there is little in Beck's theory which would point to the concrete constitution of political agency in a world where 'the political' seems to be crushed by neoliberal economic imperatives. This is the instance in which an Arendtian notion of politics and a heavy dose of empirical sociology might help to rescue the theory from an empty voluntarism and from illusions about the capacity of individuals to overcome obstacles to decide democratically on the assessment of new risks. Consequently, Beck can hardly claim to have reinvented the political, or even to have produced a political theory at all. Still, he has made an interesting start in reconceptualizing the autonomy of the political which is not authoritarian or amoral in the way that the autonomy of the political advocated by conservatives is. Moreover, Beck attempts a theory which does not necessarily privilege society over and above the political in a way that sociologists would be expected to do.[61] But it is still ironic that the return of rehashed Arendtian elements should be embedded in a sociological theory, given Arendt's attempt to separate the social from the political.

A more republican Germany?

Finally, some intellectuals have argued for a 'Berlin spirit' that draws on the constitutional achievements of the Federal Republic as well as the memory of the revolutionary action of East Germans in 1989. Here, the GDR revolutionaries are portrayed as acting spontaneously and as experiencing their capacity to act politically, thereby opening up new republican perspectives.[62] For intellectuals following this interpretation, the belated nation can finally arrive on the basis of the common experience of republican freedom and an act of mutual recognition: West Germans have to acknowledge the 'great achievement' of the East German revolution, while East Germans have to recognize the free institutions of the old Federal Republic.[63] On the basis of such a self-recognition, the Berlin Republic will be capable of coping with the challenges of the political. In other words, where the conservatives demand *Selbstbewußtsein* (self-confidence) for the state, the republicans ask for a *Selbstanerkennung* (self-recogntion) of the republic. For advocates of a new Berlin republicanism, intellectuals like Habermas and Gross remain thoroughly caught up in the experience of the old Federal Republic.[64] Rather than projecting the features of the old Federal Republic onto Berlin, as Gross and Habermas do, a recognition of the genuinely new and a broad public discourse are required. In this project, Arendt is singled out as a guiding spirit and as providing a possible answer for the meaning of politics.[65] In recent years, Arendt has been the subject of a remarkable renaissance in Germany. Although her thought remains still more popular in the US, there is now a growing literature and recognition of her possible importance for the Berlin Republic. The City and the University of Bremen established a Hannah Arendt prize for political thought in 1993, which has so far been awarded to Agnes Heller and François Furet.[66] Some of the intellectuals associated with the prize have tried to influence Green policies, shifting *Basisdemokratie* in a more republican direction. Moreover, there is now a Hannah Arendt Institute in Dresden, which mainly sponsors research on totalitarianism.

Arendt's political theory is taken up for two reasons in particular: first, 1989 is interpreted through Arendt's theories, both as an historical moment in which non-violent revolutionaries spontaneously brought about something entirely new, experiencing what Arendt called 'natality'.[67] The GDR revolutionaries experienced the power they could constitute by acting together, their capacity for responsible political judgment and action, and the feeling of public happiness which goes along with it, and finally, they realized what it meant to constitute a public space and to move in this public space. In an Arendtian view of unification, this experience of politics was crowded out by the social, just as the French Revolution was distorted and ultimately destroyed by people's 'real wants'.[68] While in Germany, there was no effort to 'solve the social questions by political means', and therefore no terror, it still remains true that no constitutional discussion, either at the national level or in German townhall meetings took place.[69] Given these deficits, some Arendtians can only hope that narrating 1989 over time will keep this experience of politics alive, and that spaces for political action as freedom can be strengthened within the institutional framework of the Berlin Republic.

On another level, Arendt's claim that totalitarianism meant a radical break in historical continuity and the Western philosophical tradition is applied to 1989 in reverse. In other words, Arendt, as the theorist of natality, is viewed as offering a way out of the historical categories of process and progress inherited from the nineteenth century and the Enlightenment. Arendt's categories are mobilized against those intellectuals who respond to the radically new, the great caesura of 1989, with the familiar categories and strategies of nationalism and geopolitics on the right, and antifascism on the left.[70]

Finally, Arendtian thought is mobilized against a neoliberal politics which entirely occupies itself with economic constraints and 'the social'. But at a time, when more and more people are involuntarily freed from the burdens of labour, Arendt is reproached for not having realized that in modern democracies, the social form of a job constitutes the underpinnings for democratic citizenship. Thus, the answer to the present predicament has to be sought in the realm of 'the social' first. Traditional criticisms of Arendt as an elitist 'aristocratic liberal', who ignored both social equality and the institutionalization of freedom, are rearticulated, overlooking, however, that the question of how to deal with 'the social' is itself again a political question and that Arendt did pay attention to the importance of political institutions as manifestations of power.[71] On a more fundamental level, Arendt is yet again reproached with nostalgia for the Greeks and for ignoring the 'differentiation gains' of modernity.[72]

But could the post-1989 constellation be a genuinely new departure for the left? After the left had shunned her for being a Cold Warrior, an elitist and a philosophical anthropologist, does a rediscovery of Arendt now provide republican resources for a renewal of an emancipatory project?[73] The answer can hardly be affirmative. As in the work of Habermas and Beck, Arendt's republicanism is shorn of its more radical elements, and not much more remains than a classical Habermasian call for more political participation. Her emphasis on a human plurality of opinions, on the formation of political judgment and on the power of narrative are alluded to, but hardly explored in their meaning for a more republican Germany. On the other hand, the danger that a republicanism of virtue might pose is hardly discussed at all. Thus, the relationship between Arendt and the left remains largely a history of *rendezvous manquées*.

Moreover, the right's reaction to Beck, the Bremen group and the contributors to Baule's book has been somewhat predictable. In a recent issue of *Merkur*, Jan Ross has appealed to Ernst Forsthoff's critique of the old Federal Republic to reassert the authority of the state, and defended the state as protecting traditions and individuality against the Beckian individuation which only leaves fungible, atomized individuals.[74] As the Berlin Republic approaches, then, tame initiatives from the left are answered by conservative claims from the old Federal Republic.

The anthropological turn: neither left nor right?

Hans Magnus Enzensberger, Peter Sloterdijk and Botho Strauß remain some of the more nonconformist thinkers in an intellectual milieu still very much suffused with *Lagerdenken*, i.e. friend/enemy thinking. However, in the very name of politics, these intellectuals have asserted anthropological and therefore, in Arendtian terms, apolitical claims against the notion of 'normal' politics. In the face of violent conflict, whether in Yugoslavia or on the streets of Rostock, they have done nothing less than reduce the political to the anthropological. Strauß, in his infamous piece 'Anschwellender Bocksgesang', sounded the clarion call for the New Right by mixing Girardian anthropology with a cultural critique of the Federal Republic.[75] Enzensberger, always a whisker ahead of the *Zeitgeist*, went right back to the unstable anthropological constitution of homo sapiens, and predicted a global civil war.[76] Sloterdijk, finally, in his slim volume *Im selben Boot: Versuch über die Hyperpolitik*, tells a psychopolitical story of mankind, in which he distinguishes between paleopolitics, classical politics and the coming hyperpolitics.[77] Paleopolitics is simply the miracle of human self-reproduction in a plurality of primal hordes which act like extended families. In classical politics, the *polis* and then the nation-state pretend to act like a horde writ large, like a giant social uterus. But while these larger entities allow for all sorts of refinement founded upon domination, the reproduction of mankind is ensured by the remnants of the hordes culture. Now, with a move towards even larger entities which require more sophisticated and demanding forms of social cohesion, new kinds of socialization and 'political training' are needed, to make up for man's 'anthropological insufficiencies'.[78]

Sloterdijk predicts a revenge of the individual and the local against the global, and a new wave of 'conservative revolutions' in the wake of 'post-political panics'.[79] To survive in the age of hyperpolitics, fully insular, last men have to find new ways to reconfigure the relationship between the small communities that allow for both regeneration and reproduction, and the global. If they want to avoid being literally last men, human beings have to recreate a social uterus and a horde which allows them to reproduce themselves. Thus, hyperpolitics needs to be the continuation of paleopolitics with other means.

The anthropological turn by Strauß, Enzensberger and Sloterdijk are of course not without precedent in German history. The peculiar tradition of philosophical anthropology flourished in the 1920s, when it was associated mainly with Helmuth Plessner and Max Scheler. The argument about anthropological insufficiency was most prominently reiterated by Arnold Gehlen.[80] But what the recent commentators mostly agree on is that homo sapiens is a dangerous and yet vulnerable being. Once again, Schmitt said it first: In the *Concept of the Political*, Schmitt gave the 'disquieting diagnosis that all genuine political theories presuppose man to be evil, i.e., by no means an unproblematic but a dangerous and dynamic being'.[81] The anthropological turn remains the least visionary, in a sense the least political of all the approaches surveyed here. It offers at best a reminder and a warning to utopian pacifists and *Gesinnungsethiker* (intellectuals clinging to an ethics of conviction) of the old Federal Republic – but their number has in any case substantially decreased after the Gulf War and after Bosnia.

Between Schmitt and Arendt: taming the political

We have seen, then, that as the Berlin Republic approaches, German intellectuals do not only engage in a discourse that aims to be foundational for the Berlin Republic (and Europe), but also contest the meaning of what is to count as the foundation of 'the political' *per se*. Not surprisingly, most intellectuals who confront the Berlin Republic *and* the political, situate themselves vis-à-vis the classic thinkers of 'the political', Carl Schmitt and Hannah Arendt. In the case of left-wing intellectuals, Carl Schmitt is usually cast in the role of *bête noire*. This is particularly the case with Habermas who remains, one might say, negatively fixated on Schmitt. In his recent turn to legal and political theory, just as much as in his early writings, Schmitt is usually set up as the one opponent most worthy of a lengthy refuta-tion.[82] On the other hand, there remain a number of self-declared leftist Schmittians, who adopt his decisionism and his theory of the state.[83] Moreover, the political anthropology proposed by Strauß, Enzensberger and, to a lesser extent, Sloterdijk, reverts to a Schmittian view of man, which, of course, leaves no political space in an Arendtian sense. In conservative contributions, Schmitt is present in major arguments concerning the critique of the self-organizing society usurping the state, a foreign policy which fails to take account of ineradicable conflict, and any attitude which denies that politics is fundamentally about friends and enemies. Mostly, Schmitt is only acknowledged at the margins. It is likely that with a further retrench-ment of the welfare state, and a reassertion of the state as provider of security, the arguments of Schmitt and his pupil Forsthoff will be heard over and over again. Moreover, interest in Schmitt is part of a larger wave of interest in the constitutional thought during the Weimar Republic. Some political scientists argue that the country is facing a situation, which, in terms of sheer political openness, has not existed since the 1920s. Weimar is perceived as a laboratory of the political, and particularly of different conceptions of political unity *Einheit*.[84] Integration is perceived as the most pressing problem of the present day. This is obviously a consequence of unification and the internal *Einheit* yet to be realized. But it is also a response to the rifts and conflicts opening up in West Germany itself with the retrench-ment of the welfare state, generational change and globalization. The 1920s are taken up as a period, during which, at least in thought, a great number of conceptions of political unity were played out.[85]

On the other hand, a number of left-wing intellectuals have tried to recover Hannah Arendt's republicanism for the new polity, building partly on the literature on civil society, partly on what is perceived as the already Arendtian foundations of Habermas's theory of commu-nicative action. Arendt's republicanism is seen as a possible antidote to the new wave of nationalism and to the general 'erosion of the political', but also as a new perspective in the wake of the exhaustion of utopian energies.[86]

This polarization between Schmitt and Arendt has clearly some-thing to do with the fact that 1989 can be given a Schmittian or an Arendtian reading: translated into the terms of Schmitt's political theology, 1989 was a miracle, and constituted a 'challenge of the exception'.[87] In Schmittian constitutional thought, 1989 meant that sovereignty in Eastern European states was reconstituted by a *pouvoir constituant* reasserting itself.[88] But it can also be read as the beginning of ethno-nationalist enmity, of a friend/enemy logic and an ultimate shrinking of political space in the Arendtian sense: Schmitt, in other words, as the prophet of ethnic cleansing, and post-communism as the period in which man, that 'dynamic and dangerous being', is no longer held in check by an authoritarian state.[89] On an Arendtian note, the peaceful revolutions of 1989 were a symbol of ordinary people acting in concert, generating power and engaging in an act of founding and constitution-making no less momentous than the American one Arendt described in *On Revolution. Pace* the Schmittian interpretation of a homogeneous will of the people asserting itself, 'the people' were a plurality of citizens' groups gathered at the round table.[90] This substitution of plural and self-reflexive for unitary popular sovereignty enabled the revolutionaries to avoid what Arendt described as 'the problem of the absolute', and ultimately, the logic of friend/enemy thinking, political justice and the unleashing of violence in revolutinary civil war.[91] Moreover, 1989 was a spontaneous moment when individuals reasserted the power to set a new beginning. It also confirmed Arendt's advice 'to be prepared for and to expect "miracles" in the political realm'.[92]

It is no accident, then, that the current debate coincides with a major renaissance of scholarship on both Schmitt and Arendt, and that these two theorists, sometimes lumped together as 'political existentialists', are consciously or unconsciously instrumentalized for the new foundational discourse. The question, however, is whether any of the intellectuals engaging with Schmittian and Arendtian thought actually take the two theorists up on their more radical claims. Schmitt's followers emphasize the *étatist*, agonal and broadly Hobbesian elements in his thought – but not in a way which deviates significantly from postwar West German conservatism. Were it not so difficult to translate Oakeshott, one could think that conservatives might just as well have taken up the foremost British follower of Hobbes in the twentieth century. In so far as Schmitt's theories of *Großräume* (great geopolitical spaces) are revived, it is also reduced to a 'realist' reading which could as easily be found in Kissinger or Huntington.[93] Apart from marginal right-wing figures, nobody is willing to resuscitate Schmitt's political theology, the radical vitalist and authoritarian elements of his constitutional thought, or his emphasis on substantial homogeneity, let alone his idiosyncratic Roman Catholicism with his peculiar faith in the biblical figure of the *Katechon*.[94]

In a way, the same holds true for Arendt. Her followers want a Berlin Republic which is actually more republican, but hardly make any claims for civic humanism, a radical political decentralization in councils, or an institutionalization of continuous political action. The element that both the consensus-oriented Habermas and the republican-minded Arendt disciples overlook, it seems, is her emphasis on plurality. Thus, arguably both Schmitt and Arendt followers, while remaining in a broadly liberal-democratic framework, fail to see the potential for making the Berlin Republic above all a more liberal and tolerant polity. They tame whatever is radical about the political in Schmitt or Arendt, but do not engage with what often strikes foreign observers as the most obvious question about German political culture: could there be a more heterogeneous, civic, liberal in the sense of tolerant, Germany?[95]

Finally, it is important not to overestimate the impact of even an attenuated Arendtianism or Schmittianism on 'politics' understood in traditional terms as the old party system. There can be no one-to-one mapping of these ideologies onto the political cleavages of present-day Germany, and neither can any lasting political force be attributed to them, as long as no significant party adopts them. Returning to the failure of the New Right, one might say that it was precisely their inability to capture a party-political vehicle, in this case the FDP, which doomed their effort to establish a right-wing cultural hegemony and exercise influence on policy.

German intellectuals have laid out two future visions of the polity: an *étatist* one, indebted to Schmitt, which takes the regaining of sovereignty in 1990 as foundational and envisages the Berlin Republic as more political in the sense of a sovereign pursuit of national interests outside and a state confronting a more active civil society within; the other a republican one, in which the memories of 1989 are kept alive, civil society valorized and foreign policy is increasingly dealt with in European federated structures (which Arendt also favoured). In a sense, both visions presume that new spaces for action are opening. Consequently, both visions can be seen as countering a current public discourse which primarily consists of economic and technocratic necessities, neoliberal pieties and the need to adapt to globalization. In that sense, they set the power of politics against what Musil called *Herrschaft der Sachzusammenhänge* (the domination of objective relations). On a more pessimistic reading, the Arendtian moment is a fleeting one, and Beck and the Arendtians merely project the developments leading up to 1989 onto 1999, when in fact the future belongs to overt and covert Schmittians. A third possibility remains, of course, namely that Germany neither embarks on an Arendtian adventure, nor follows a more sinister Schmittian course, but simply continues to be as generally stable, consensus-oriented, and, plainly speaking, boring, as it has in fact been since 1989. Thus, it might well be true that *Die Politik ist das Schicksal*, but the fate of the political in its friend/enemy, or republican version might well be sealed by the fact that most Germans, still clinging to a 'culture of restraint and reticence', desire neither a more authoritarian state nor a public *Sinngebung* (provision of meaning) through political action.[96] It might be unexciting, but maybe politics can and should do without the political.

Notes

1 Jarausch, K., *The Rush to German Unity* (New York: Oxford University Press, 1994).

2 See also Dieckmann, F., 'Fünfhundert Kilometer Ostnordost: Was bedeutet die Verlagerung der deutschen Bundeshauptstadt?', *Merkur*, Vol. 51, No. 4 (1997) pp. 308–18.

3 Schmitt, C., *The Concept of the Political*, trans. Schwab, G. (Chicago: Chicago University Press, 1996). See also Meier, C., 'Zu Carl Schmitt's Begriffsbildung – das Politische und der Nomos', in Quaritsch, H. (ed.), *Complexio Oppositorum: Über Carl Schmitt* (Berlin: Duncker & Humbolt, 1988) pp. 537–56.

4 See Palonen, K., *Politik als Handlungsbegriff: Horizontwandel des Politikbegriff in Deutschland 1890–1933* (Helsinki: The Finnish Society of Sciences and Letters, 1985).

5 Anter, A., *Max Webers Theorie des modernen Staates: Herkunft, Struktur und Bedeutung* (Berlin: Duncker & Humbolt, 1995) p. 51.

6 Schmitt, *op. cit.*, p. 19.

7 *Ibid.*, p. 29.

8 On Schmitt's influence through the conservative circles (*Gesprächskreise*) around him, see Van Laak, D., *Gespräche in der Sicherheit des Schweigens: Carl Schmitt in der Geistesgeschichte der frühen Bundesrepublik* (Berlin: Akademie Verlag, 1993).

9 Sternberger, D., *Die Politik und der Friede* (Frankfurt am Main: Suhrkamp, 1986) p. 76.

10 Beck, U., *Die Erfindung des Politischen: Zu einer Theorie reflexiver Modernisierung* (Frankfurt am Main: Suhrkamp, 1993); Negt, O. and Kluge, A., *Maßverhältnisse des Politischen: 15 Vorschläge zum Unterscheidungsvermögen* (Frankfurt am Main: S. Fischer, 1992); Göbel, A., Van Laak, D. and Villinger, I. (eds.), *Metamorphosen des Politischen: Grundfragen politischer Einheitsbildung seit den 20er Jahren.* (Berlin: Akademie Verlag, 1995); Meyer, T., *Die Transformation des Politischen.* (Frankfurt am Main: Suhrkamp, 1994); Pfetsch, F. R., *Handlung und Reflexion: Theoretische Dimensionen des*

Politischen. (Darmstadt: Wissenschaftliche Buchgesellschaft, 1995); Kemper, P. (ed.), *Die Zukunft des Politischen: Theoretische Ausblicke auf Hannah Arendt* (Frankfurt am Main: Fischer, 1993).

11 Most famously, Mouffe, C., *The Return of the Political* (London: Verso, 1993).

12 Unseld, S. (ed.), *Politik ohne Projekt? Nachdenken über Deutschland* (Frankfurt am Main: Suhrkamp, 1993).

13 Mann, T., *Betrachtungen eines Unpolitischen* (Frankfurt am Main: S. Fischer, 1956) p. 239.

14 Bielefeldt, H., *Kampf und Entscheidung: Politscher Existentialismus bei Carl Schmitt, Helmuth Plessner und Karl Jaspers* (Würzburg: Königshausen und Neumann, 1994) p. 19.

15 Ely, J., 'Political, Civic and Territorial Views of Association', *Thesis Eleven*, No. 46 (1996) pp. 33–65.

16 See Meier, H., *Carl Schmitt & Leo Strauss: The Hidden Dialogue.*, trans. Lomax, J.H. (Chicago: Chicago University Press, 1995).

17 Negt and Kluge, *op. cit.* (1992).

18 But Arendt at one point claimed that the Greeks 'discovered the essence and the realm of the political'. Not by coincidence, she went on to make a remark, which, in all of her work, might put her closest to Schmitt, when she wrote that 'only foreign affairs, because the relationships between nations still harbour hostilities and sympathies which cannot be reduced to economic factors, seem to be left as a purely political domain.' See Arendt, H., *Between Past and Future: Eight Exercises in Political Thought.* (New York: Penguin, 1993) pp. 154–5.

19 On the importance of the disclosive nature of politics in Arendt, see the excellent discussion in Villa, D. R., *Arendt and Heidegger: The Fate of the Political* (Princeton: Princeton University Press, 1996).

20 In particular, Meyer, *op. cit.* (1994).

21 Heller, A., 'The Concept of the Political Revisited', in Held, D. (ed.), *Political Theory Today* (Cambridge: Polity Press, 1991), pp. 330–43, here pp. 332 and 336.

22 For two very effective critiques of the enthusiasm for civil society, both in its Tocquevillian and Eastern European version, see Berman, S., 'Civil Society and the Collapse of the Weimar Republic', *World Politics*, Vol. 49, No. 3 (1997) pp. 401–29, and Mastnak, T., 'Fascists, Liberals, and Anti-Nationalism', in Caplan, R. and Feffer, J. (eds.), *Europe's New Nationalism: States and Minorities in Conflict* (New York: Oxford University Press, 1996) pp. 59–74.

23 Heilbrunn, J., 'Germany's New Right', *Foreign Affairs*, Vol. 75, No. 6 (1996) pp. 80–98, and the letters to the editor by Joffe, J. *et al.*, 'Mr Heilbrunn's Planet', *Foreign Affairs*, Vol. 76, No. 2 (1997) pp. 152–161.

24 On movements across the ideological spectrum and some of the central beliefs of the New Right, see Lohmann, H-M. (ed.), *Extremismus der Mitte: Vom rechten Verständnis deutscher Nation* (Frankfurt am Main: Fischer, 1994), and, for a nicely polemical treatment of the subject, Herzinger, R. and Stein, H., *Endzeit-Propheten oder Die Offensive der Antiwestler: Fundamentalismus, Antiamerikanismus und Neue Rechte* (Reinbek: Rowohlt, 1995).

25 Sternhell, Z., with Sznajder, M. and Asheri, M., *The Birth of Fascist Ideology: From Cultural Rebellion to Political Revolution* (Princeton: Princeton University Press, 1994). See also Ely, *op. cit.* (1996) p. 52.

26 Ritter, H., 'Translatio rei publicae: Der Umzug von Regierung und Parlament als Gründungsakt der Berliner Republik', *Frankfurter Allgemeine Zeitung*, 18 December 1996.

27 Gross, J., *Begründung der Berliner Republik: Deutschland am Ende des 20. Jahrhundert* (Stuttgart: Deutsche Verlags-Anstalt, 1995) p. 42.

28 *Ibid.*, p. 53.

29 *Ibid.*, p. 61.

30 *Ibid.*, p. 62.

31 *Ibid.*, pp. 71–72.

32 *Ibid.*, pp. 110–17.

33 For instance Bohrer, K. H., 'Die Ästhetik des Staates', *Merkur*, Vol. 38, No. 1 (1984) pp. 1–15.

34 Habermas, J., *Die Normalität einer Berliner Republik: Kleine Politische Schriften VIII* (Frankfurt am Main: Suhrkamp, 1995) p. 171.

35 Habermas, J., 'Yet again: German Identity', in *New German Critique*, No. 52 (1991) pp. 84–101.

36 Habermas, *op. cit.* (1995) p. 187.

37 *Ibid.*, p. 181.

38 Vollrath, E., 'Hannah Arendt bei den Linken', in Grunenberg, A. and Probst, L. (eds.), *Einschnitte: Hannah Arendts politisches Denken heute* (Bremen: Edition Temmen, 1995) pp. 9–22.

39 Habermas, J., *Die Einbeziehung des Anderen: Studien zur politischen Theorie* (Frankfurt am Main: Suhrkamp, 1996) p. 277.

40 *Ibid.*, p. 286. See Schmitt, C., *Positionen und Begriffe im Kampf mit Weimar – Genf-Versailles* (Berlin: Duncker & Humbolt, 1988) p. 151.

41 See also Habermas, J., *Faktizität und Geltung: Beiträge zur Diskurstheorie des Rechts und des demokratischen Rechtsstaats* (Frankfurt am Main: Suhrkamp, 1992) pp. 182–7.

42 Habermas, *op. cit.* (1996), p. 286.

43 Beck, U., *Risikogesellschaft: Auf dem Weg in eine andere Moderne* (Frankfurt am Main: Suhrkamp, 1986). Beck, U., *Risk Society: Towards a New Modernity*, trans. Ritter, M. (London: Sage, 1992).

44 Osborne, P., 'Times (Modern), Modernity (Conservative)? Notes on the Persistence of a Temporal Motif', *New Formations*, No. 28 (1996) pp. 132–41, here p. 132.

45 Beck, U., Giddens, A. and Lash, S., *Reflexive Modernization: Politics, Tradition and Aesthetics in the Modern Social Order* (Cambridge: Polity Press, 1994) p. vi.

46 Beck, U., 'World Risk Society as Cosmopolitan Society? Ecological Questions in a Framework of Manufactured Uncertainties', *Theory, Culture & Society*, No. 4 (1996) pp. 1–32, here p. 11. See also Beck, U., *Die Erfindung des Politischen*; the English version appeared in 1996: Beck, U., *The Reinvention of the Political* (Cambridge: Polity, 1996).

47 Beck, U., *op.cit.* (1986) p. 311.

48 Vollrath, E., 'Wie ist Carl Schmitt an seinen Begriff des Politischen gekommen?', *Zeitschrift für Politik*, Vol. 36, No. 2 (1989) pp. 151–68.

49 It is noticeable, however, that Beck incorporates Schmittian thought patterns without acknowledging them: he repeats Schmitt's conception of modernity as a quest for neutralizations and depoliticizations, but adds a scepticism à la Montaigne. See *ibid.*, pp. 263–268, and Schmitt, C., 'Das Zeitalter der Neutralisierungen und Entpolitisierungen', in: Schmitt, C., *op. cit* (1988) pp. 120–132.

50 Beck, U., *op. cit.* (1986) pp. 304–307.

51 Schmittt, C., *The Crisis of Parliamentary Democracy*, trans. Kennedy, E. (Cambridge, Mass.: MIT Press, 1985)

52 Beck, U., *op. cit.* (1993) p. 157.

53 *Ibid.*, p. 149.

54 See also Wehler, H-U., 'Von der Herrschaft zum Habitus', *Die Zeit*, 25 October 1996.

55 Breuer, S., quoted by Narr, W-D. 'Begriffslose Politik und politikarme Begriffe: Zusätzliche Notizen zu Becks "Erfindung des Politischen"', *Leviathan*, Vol. 23, No. 3 (1995) pp. 437–44; here p. 437.

56 Beck, *op. cit.* (1986) p. 105.

57 See also Blanke, T., 'Zur Aktualität des Risikobegriffs: Über die Konstruktion der Welt und die Wissenschaft von ihr', *Leviathan*, Vol. 18, No. 1 (1990).

58 See also Breuer, S., 'Das Ende der Sicherheit: Ulrich Becks "Gegengifte"', *Merkur*, Vol. 43, No. 8 (1989) pp. 710–15.

59 Beck admits as much in a footnote. See Beck, U., 'Vom Veralten sozialwissenschaftlicher Begriffe: Grundzüge einer Theorie reflexiver Modernisierung', in Görg, C. (ed.), *Gesellschaft im Übergang: Perspektiven kritischer Soziologie* (Darmstadt: Wissenschaftliche Buchgesellschaft, 1994) pp. 21–43, here p. 41.

60 Weber, M., 'The Profession and Vocation of Politics', in Lassman, P. and Speirs, R. (eds.), *Weber: Political Writings* (Cambridge: Cambridge University Press, 1994) pp. 309–69.

61 See also Palonen, K., 'Die jüngste Erfindung des Politischen: Ulrich Beck's 'Neues Wörterbuch des Politischen' als Beitrag zur Begriffsgeschichte', *Leviathan*, Vol. 23, No. 3 (1995) pp. 417–36.

62 Baule, B., 'Freiheit und Revolution: Die Bedeutung von 1989 für die Berliner Republik' in Baule, B. (ed.), *Hannah Arendt und die Berliner Republik: Fragen an das vereinigte Deutschland* (Berlin: Aufbau, 1996) pp. 82–106, here p. 86.

63 Baule, B., 'Einleitung', in Baule, B. (ed.), *ibid.*, pp. 7–13, here p. 8.

64 *Ibid.*, p. 10.

65 For similar concerns in Austria, see Kubes-Hofmann, U. (ed.), *Sagen, was ist: Zur Aktualität Hannah Arendts* (Vienna: Verlag für Gesellschaftskritik, 1994).

66 For infomation on the Hannah Arendt Association for Political Thought, see http://zfn.alf.uni-bremen.de/~blaha/verein.html.

67 Arendt, H., *The Human Condition* (Chicago: Chicago University Press, 1989) pp. 176–8.

68 Arendt, H., *On Revolution* (New York: Penguin, 1990) p. 109.

69 *Ibid.*, p. 112.

70 Grunenberg, A., '"Macht kommt von möglich …"', in Grunenberg and Probst (eds.), *op. cit.* (1995) pp. 83–95, here p. 83.

71 Engler, W., 'Berliner Republik in Bedrängnis oder Die neoliberale Herausforderung des politischen Liberalismus', in Baule (ed.), *op. cit.* (1996) pp. 180–195, here pp. 184–7; Kallscheuer, O., 'Mit Arendt über Arendt hinausdenken: Offene Fragen an das neue Deutschland und die europäische Zukunft', in *ibid.*, pp. 196–213, here p. 205, and Greven, M. T., 'Hannah Arendt – Pluralität und Gründung der Freiheit'; Kemper (ed.), in *op. cit.* (1993) pp. 69–96, here pp. 82–3.

72 See in particular Brunkhorst, H., *Demokratie und Differenz: Vom klassischen zum modernen Begriff des Politischen* (Frankfurt am Main: Fischer, 1994).

73 See Vollrath, *op. cit.* (1995) pp. 9–10, and Greven, *op. cit.* (1993), pp. 88–9.

74 Ross, J., 'Staatsfeindschaft: Anmerkungen zum neuen Vulgärliberalismus', *Merkur*, Vol. 51, No. 2 (1997) pp. 93–194.

75 Strauß, B., 'Anschwellender Bocksgesang', in Schwilk, H. and Schacht, U. (eds.), *Die Selbstbewußte Nation: "Anschwellender Bocksgesang" und weitere Beiträge zu einer deutschen Debatte* (Frankfurt am Main: Ullstein, 1994) pp. 19–40.

76 Enzensberger, H. M., *Civil Wars: From LA to Bosnia* (New York: The New Press, 1994).

77 Sloterdijk, P., *Im selben Boot: Versuch über die Hyperpolitik.* (Frankfurt am Main: Suhrkamp, 1993).

78 *Ibid.*, p. 54.

79 *Ibid.*, pp. 57–8.

80 Gehlen, A., *Man: His Nature and Place in the World*, trans. McMillan, C. and Pillemer, K. (New York: Columbia University Press, 1988).

81 Schmitt, *op. cit.* (1996), p. 61.

82 For instance Habermas, *op. cit.* (1996) pp. 226–36 and pp. 160–71.

83 On the issue of leftist Schmittianism, see Lübbe, H., 'Carl Schmitt liberal rezipiert', in Quaritsch (ed.), *op. cit.* (1988) pp. 427–40; Lauermann, M., 'Begriffsmagie. "Positionen und Begriffe" als Kontinuitätsbehauptung – Bemerkungen anläßlich der Neuauflage 1988', in Flickinger, H-G. (ed.), *Die Autonomie des Politischen: Carl Schmitts Kampf um einen beschädigten Begriff* (Berlin: Acta humaniora, 1990) pp. 97–127; and, still relevant, Neumann, V., 'Carl Schmitt und die Linke', *Die Zeit*, 8 July 1983. Finally, revisit the debate between Kennedy, E., Preuß. U. K., Jay, M. and Söllner, A. *Telos*, No. 71 (Spring 1987); and, more recently, on the relationship between Schmitt and the legal theorists of the Frankfurt School, Kirchheimer, O. and Neumann, F. see Scheuerman, W. E., *Between the Norm and the Exception: The Frankfurt School and the Rule of Law* (Cambridge, Mass.: MIT Press, 1994).

84 Van Laak, D., 'Einleitende Bemerkungen', in: Göbel, A., Van Laak, D. and Villinger, I. (eds.), *Metamorphosen des Politischen: Grundfragen politischer Einheitsbildung seit den 20er Jahren* (Berlin: Akademie Verlag, 1995) pp. 7–21; here p. 10.

85 *Ibid.*, p. 13.

86 Kemper, P., 'Vorwort', in Kemper (ed.), *op. cit.* (1993) pp. 7–12.

87 Schmitt, C., *Political Theology: Four Chapters on the Concept of Sovereignty* trans. Schwab, G. (Cambridge, Mass.: MIT Press, 1985).

88 Schmitt, C., *Verfassungslehre* (Berlin: Duncker & Humbolt, 1970), p. 51.

89 Beck, *op. cit.* (1993), p. 227.

90 See Preuß, U. K., *Revolution, Fortschritt und Verfassung: Zu einem neuen Vefassungsverständnis* (Frankfurt am Main: Fischer, 1994) pp. 84–8.

91 Arendt, *op. cit.* (1990) pp. 158–159 and pp. 202–14.

92 Arendt, *op. cit.* (1993) p. 170.

93 Vad, E., *Strategie und Sicherheitspolitik: Perspektiven im Werk von Carl Schmitt* (Opladen: Westdeutscher Verlag, 1996).

94 On Schmitt's private political theology of the *Katechon*, see Meuter, G., *Der Katechon: Zu Carl Schmitts fundamentalistischer Kritik der Zeit.* (Berlin: Duncker & Humbolt, 1994) and Meier, H., *Die Lehre Carl Schmitts: Vier Kapitel zur Unterscheidung Politischer Theologie und Politischer Philosophie* (Stuttgart: J.B. Metzler, 1994).

95 See for instance Maier, C. S., *Dissolution: The Crisis of Communism and the End of East Germany* (Princeton: Prrinceton University Press, 1997) p. 334.

96 Markovits, A. S. and Reich, S., *The German Predicament: Memory and Power in the New Europe* (Ithaca: Cornell University Press, 1997) p. xiii.

Index